Real IMPACT

Daily Inspiration

Dennis J. Henson

Vanguard Marketing & Investments Inc.

COPYRIGHT @ 2024 Vanguard Marketing and Investments, Inc.
Printed in Canada, First Edition 2024
ISBN 978-1-7362772-9-4
Stock Images: Canva, Shuttershock, Pexels, Vecteezy
Editor: Kristine Skiff, Gift an Author Publishing, LLC.
Proofreader: Kathy
Formatting and Design: Worth Media
Cover Artist: Daniel Dye

Find these books, an updated list, and where to purchase at
dennisjhenson.com.

"Of all things, I liked books best."
~ Nikola Tesla

TABLE OF CONTENTS

DEDICATION

This book is dedicated to my Mentors, without whose guidance and encouragement I could not have survived in the world of business. These kind and generous individuals have had a Real IMPACT on my life and on the lives of everyone they touched.

J. Burney Bishop, High School Band Director, Centre, Alabama.

D. D. Black, Instructor at the University of Alabama Music Camp.

Dr. David L. Walters, Director of Bands, Jacksonville State University, Alabama

Jack McConnico and Tom Hendrix, Executives at Henco, Inc. Selmer, Tennessee

Charles G. Bowden, President B&B Beverage, Athens, Georgia

And the many great authors who poured their very souls into the books referenced in these pages. Especially Napoleon Hill, Og Mandino, Zig Ziglar and Jim Rohn

TESTIMONIALS

Publisher's Note:
The following testimonials are not typical book reviews because this is not a conventional book. "Real IMPACT" was produced to be a device that will, when used as intended, provide the reader the knowledge to attain anything they desire. The reviews below are of the author, who has been instrumental in helping enumerable novices and seasoned professionals become successful.

Dennis was a key influence early in my career. He was kind enough to let me be his helper organizing his events, and I soaked up a wealth of knowledge by being around him. Since then, I've bought over $25,000,000.00 in commercial real estate across seven states. Dennis has a pleasing personality, strong ethics, and is always willing to help. I will forever be grateful for the role he played in my life.

— Shishir Kaushik

Dennis J. Henson is pure genius. His story is stimulating, thought-provoking and touching. He teaches techniques, even some of the seasoned professionals I work with didn't know. He passes on wisdom and guidance that will help in any area of life. I truly believe that what he has to say changes lives. His wisdom is continuously helping me in real estate as well as my personal life.

— John de Souza, Real Estate Investor

In a few short years, I have transitioned from a novice investor to a highly successful business owner. Yet I did not do it alone. My mentor educated and encouraged me, and it changed my life. Listening to Dennis made all the difference. A great mentor not only trains but also guides, counsels and coaches you. Dennis' teachings transformed me from a high school shop teacher to a multi-millionaire business owner in less than 90 days. I could never have done it without Dennis' guidance. His teachings have made a tremendous difference in me, and they can do the same for you.

— Greg Gray, Investor and Business owner

Dennis J. Henson is an insightful, motivating mentor whose advice is well worth listening to. Not only does he offer wisdom gained over his decades of real estate investing and business experience. But he provides step-by-step strategies that will lead you straight to success in any area of life.

—Shereyar (Jordan) Jawaid, Real Estate Investor & Business Owner

When I arrived in the U.S., I researched statistics and learned that 80% of the wealth here started with Real Estate. I only had three months to come up with a workable business plan, because of my visa! So, I started looking for markets with affordable pricing for single-family homes and robust activity in the market. Although I searched many markets in Mississippi, Tennessee, Kansas and Okl homa, I decided to invest in Dallas, Texas.

In spite of my very limited English, I started talking to realtors, contractors, and brokers. Their questions were, "What are your experiences in this market? How many properties have you already

*bought? What is your farm area? Where will you get the money?!"
I was insecure but my dream screamed louder than my insecurity. I
had no idea what a farm area was. I didn't even have a social security
number or a credit score. My heavy Portuguese accent made it hard
for anyone to understand me. My answers shocked them, for I was
thinking outside the box!*

*They all told me how difficult it would be for me to buy houses in the
U.S. They said, "It will be impossible!" One by one, they tried to shut
me down. They didn't know my passion for reaching my dream; they
didn't know about my burning desire to achieve my goals.*

*I was absolutely determined to pursue my dream, and nothing or no
one was going to change my mind or convince me I couldn't. The small
town where I am from in Brazil was quite poor, and so was my family.
We grew up without toys, money, and not much food. My parents
struggled a lot, and I thought, "If I don't work hard, I'll have the same
life." So, I put money away from my childhood jobs and even thought
about becoming a pirate.*

*Instead, I moved away at age 14 to work my way through college.
Every minute I wasn't studying, I was working. My passion was to
change the world!!! Go ahead! "Tell me to quit 999 times, and I'll start
again 1,000 times!!!" I studied Spanish, which led to a job traveling
for my employer. It was the first step into a different world. I lived in
Argentina, France, Italy, England, India, and Thailand before coming
to the United States.
In Dallas, I went to all the meetings: REIA (Real Estate Investors
Association), workshops, and seminars. I did all the free educational
stuff available. I said to myself, "I don't need to pay for these classes.
I'm smart enough to figure it out on my own." Yet, I was still
lacking the right knowledge.*

*Many contractors turned me down, until I finally met a contractor
willing to listen to me. He became my partner, and we worked together
on a few deals. I made a little money, but he made three or four times
more, because he was charging me twice the market price for the*

repairs. I quickly realized that wasn't the partnership I had anticipated. I needed more knowledge, and it was time to be humble and get it from the right sources. I sought a mentor to give me the best education possible. Yes, I was willing to be taught, to be humble, and to be the mentee. "If you think education is expensive, try ignorance."
Derek Bok

I found a wonderful mentor, Dennis J. Henson, and decided to take his full-year program, one that would teach me the rules of the American Real Estate Market and eventually change my life. He was such an amazing teacher and coach, that I was later able to extend my visa.

Dennis's training was going to cost me every penny I had! That's right, literally everything! I agonized over how much I could do with that money. But I also thought of how much I could make if I had the right knowledge and the benefit of his guidance. Finally, I decided I was going to purchase his training and I'm so glad I did. That was the day my life was changed.

Within just one year, I had earned more than ten times the money I paid. "I became successful because I followed Dennis's advice, and you can too!"

Linda Pisani Elder, Real Estate Investor and Best Selling Author.

"There is more treasure in books than in all the pirates loot on Treasure Island and at the bottom of the Spanish Main – and best of all, you can enjoy these riches every day of your life."

~ Walt Disney

INTRODUCTION

Are you happy with everything in your life? Is there anything you would like to change? Would you like more money, a nicer car, a bigger home? Do you want to travel to exciting locations throughout the world? What about having better relationships? Is there something you would love to accomplish? Who or what would you like to become?

This book can be the key to unlocking the potential to realize those desires.

Dear Reader:
Reflecting on my career, I savor the sweet tastes of victory yet bear the scars of numerous defeats. Now that life's winter has overtaken me, I feel it is important to share with you some of what I've learned. And, because my time is limited, I will reveal to you the one thing I believe will most impact your life.

That one thing is to… *"Form the habit of reading every day!"*

Although this might not sound like earth-shaking advice. It can be your *"Open Sesame"* to the *"Wisdom of the Ages"*, access to the *"Greatest Words Ever Spoken"*, and a connection to the collective knowledge of brilliant thinkers from Socrates to Einstein!

If you choose to take this advice, I assure you, it will have a massive effect on the things you will be able to accomplish.

More than fifty years of getting up after being knocked down
have taught me that this simple habit can change people.
Forming it will strengthen your response to failure and allow you to
succeed despite the setbacks you will surely experience! It will provide
the wisdom to take on and succeed at monumental challenges. Then,
most importantly, it will permit you to attract influential people who
can propel you to heights you never imagined.

*"No matter how busy you may think you are, you must find
time for reading, or surrender yourself to self-chosen
ignorance."*
~ Confucius

One of my greatest joys has been witnessing the impressive
achievements of my students. The seeds planted in their minds by
their daily reading have grown, and now they're reaping harvests of
success.

What really excites me is that you can do the same! Anyone can!
It's a *"Law of Nature"*, a seed planted in fertile ground and tended
will sprout, grow and produce a plant containing many new seeds.
If you plant good seeds in your mind, seeds of health, success, and
prosperity, you will harvest those very things. And, as with the plants,
what you will receive will be significantly multiplied.

Practicing what I preach over the decades, I have read many outstanding
books, stories, poems, and quotes. Years ago, I developed the habit of
listing the finest of them, and those listed items are contained in these
pages. I value this collection more than most earthly treasures.

Let me challenge you to take this opportunity to produce a harvest
of positive changes. Use this book to unlock the mysteries of better
health, business success, higher knowledge,
powerful relationships, and manifest your fondest dreams.

But remember, only planting seeds doesn't guarantee a bountiful harvest. You must plant good seeds, and your crop must be continuously nourished and cared for to have a chance to bear fruit.

"All your dreams are possible as a byproduct of the habits you form today."

Use this book as a catalyst for forming the vital daily reading habit. As you strive to develop this habit, remember: "It is not the quantity of reading that is important, but rather the quality of the information you read!" I sincerely wish you abundant success and happiness.

— Dennis J. Henson

"Not all readers are leaders, but all leaders are readers."
~ Harry S. Truman, 33rd President of the United States

HOW TO READ THIS BOOK

When a new student comes to me for instruction and guidance, the first thing on their mind is, "What can you do to help me succeed quickly?"

Understanding this early in their training, I teach them: "Changing your habits will have a Real IMPACT on your future!" I then lay out a plan for them to start doing the right things repeatedly until they become routine parts of their lives.

Of course, some habits are more significant than others.

Once, during an interview, I was asked, "if you had to name the one thing that's had the greatest impact on your students, what would it be?" I thought for a second and said, "Form the habit of reading the right things every day!"

The next question was, "What do you mean by the right things?" "Well, that depends; let me explain. Suppose you want to become a medical doctor. In that case, you should read things about the practice of medicine, but if you want to become a real estate investor, read real estate-related materials. It's also important to read about other areas of life; education, health, relationships, religion, success, money, etc."

After that interview, I wondered, "What would I suggest should be read first? Wouldn't it be great if there was a book ..." And, like a bolt out of the blue, it hit me. "That's it! I'll write a book to help people start the habit of reading daily. I already have a list of great books that can easily be placed in priority order."

Then, I remembered my collection of quotes and motivational stories. As more things came to mind, I got excited and made the book a project. After that, things seemed to fall into place until, one day, Real IMPACT became a reality.

Before giving you the formula to form the reading habit, let me explain three things…

IMPORTANT, PLEASE READ

First, this book was not intended to be read from cover to cover, but rather a little at a time. It should be sipped like fine wine and consumed in combination with other good books (for reading in more extended time slots).

Second, the quantity of the reading is not as important as the quality. So the 80-20 Principle should be used to help focus on reading the things offering the most significant benefit. In other words, focus on getting 20% of the things on your list completed that are most important first. Then, accomplish the other 80%. Make sure reading falls in the top 20%.

Third, anyone's life will change for the better by merely forming the habit of reading the right things daily! Keep in mind that developing a new habit requires a strong commitment.

Here is the "Magic Formula"

1. Immediately start a new reading habit. Each day, read about subjects that will help you attain your goals and achieve your dreams.

2. Schedule and set aside a time for daily reading.

3. Once you start, never let a day go by without putting something positive into your mind.

4. Go to the chapter on "Life Changing Books" (page 417). Acquire the top book on that list and keep it next to this book. Read from it when you have larger blocks of time.

5. Put the two books in a conspicuous location where you can't miss seeing them, and be sure to pack them when you travel.

6. Should you begin to slide, find a support person to hold you accountable.

7. Go back to the "Life Changing Books" list and order or purchase the next book. Always order one or two books ahead to avoid interruptions.

Do not be fooled by the simplicity of this formula. Used properly, it's like rubbing "Aladdin's Lamp", and can be the "Open Sesame" to your fondest dreams.

You may be thinking, "I am already so busy! I don't have the time to read every day for the rest of my life." Well, you're not alone; everybody is busy. Some days it will be challenging to find time to read. That is the beauty of Real IMPACT! It was written for active people.

The first chapters are short stories that can be read in several minutes, followed by poems and quotes that will only take minutes or even seconds to read. As I said before, what matters is not the quantity but the quality of the reading.

Anyone can fit in a quote or two each day, and these quotes aren't only powerful, they're also thought-provoking. If you want a happier, more successful life, don't miss this opportunity to change your trajectory.

*"Focus on your dream and never quit.
It is always too soon to quit."*

Rudy Ruettiger

A ROCKY START

Summarized from a speech by Sylvester Stallone

 In the early 1970s, Sylvester "*Sly*" Stallone was an unknown actor trying to make it in New York City. He'd achieved minor success in the movie The Lords of Flatbush, but then Sly moved to California since roles were scarce in The Big Apple.

Having spent most of his money on a plane ticket, he found himself among thousands of actors seeking parts, so his prospects were not good. Months passed without work, and Sly ended up homeless and sleeping in a bus station. He was so broke he couldn't afford to feed Butkus, his dog, best friend, and constant companion. So rather than letting him starve, he chose to sell Butkus to someone who could provide for him. Although he desperately needed the $25.00, Sly left crying.

A few days later, Stallone witnessed a boxing match featuring the greatest boxer of all time, Muhammad Ali, versus The Bayonne Bleeder. Sylvester couldn't believe an unknown fighter that no one thought would last one round lasted fifteen. The Bleeder was even able to land an incredible punch, putting Ali on the mat. Inspired by what he witnessed, Sylvester wrote an entire movie script. It was a story about an average guy who, against all odds, faced a superior foe. A man willing to get knocked down and get up again, as many times as it took to go the distance. For three straight days, Sly wrote, ending up with fewer than one hundred pages, but the essence of the story was complete.

The young actor attended a casting call the following week, but the part wasn't a fit. As he headed for the door, it hit him, and he turned and approached the producers. *"Guys, I forgot to mention that I have written a new screenplay."* Half listening, they said, *"Bring it by, and we will take a look."* To their surprise, the following morning, Sylvester arrived with the script in hand. The producers liked what they read but balked when they learned that Stallone insisted on playing the main character. They wanted the lead for this movie to be a star, like Ryan O'Neil or Burt Reynolds. So, instead, they offered $350,000.00 for his script, but without other conditions.

Sylvester was homeless, living in a bus station, didn't own a car, and he'd just sold his dog to keep him from starving. However, Sly had become accustomed to that lifestyle, and he knew that if his movie were to become a hit without him as the protagonist, it would kill him. So, Stallone rolled the dice and turned down their offer. The producers eventually relented and agreed to pay him $35,000.00 and a percentage of the movie's profit (if any).

The movie's budget was set at one million dollars, and Sylvester Stallone was cast to play Rocky Balboa. Keep in mind that in the mid-'70s, one million dollars was a shoestring budget for movie production. Nevertheless, the project came in below budget by casting family and friends as actors, limiting most scenes to one take, and filming with handheld cameras.

Stallone's film received good reviews when shown around Hollywood. However, the real test came at the Director's Guild screening. Hundreds of Hollywood elites showed up, and the theater was filled to capacity. Sylvester was extremely nervous.

Sly watched the executives closely as the film played. They sat quietly throughout the movie. No one laughed at the jokes or gasped at the fight scenes. As the audience silently filed out of the theater, Stallone stayed seated, his breath caught in his throat. *"The movie bombed,"* he thought as he sat humiliated and disappointed, with tears rolling down his cheeks.

Eventually, he mustered the strength to stand and slowly descend the long staircase. He then realized that something unusual was taking place. Everyone was gathered in the lobby. Once he appeared, a few began to clap; and as others saw him, they joined in the applause. The ovation was loud and long, its echoes reverberating off the theater walls.

Shocked, Stallone stood speechless. He couldn't believe his eyes. *"Hollywood"* loved his movie, and they loved him for making it. Sylvester Stallone's days of living in a bus station had come to an end. He later stated, "I'll never experience a moment like that again." Rocky went on to gross over 200 million dollars, won Oscars for Best Picture, Best Directing, and Best Film Editing, and received six other nominations. The picture was even inducted into the American National Film Registry as one of the greatest movies ever made!

Since that time, the Rocky movie franchise has earned more than 1.4 billion dollars, making it one of the most successful movies of all time. The same Sylvester Stallone who slept in a bus station and was forced to sell his dog became one of Hollywood's most famous stars! One other thing, Sylvester spent $15,000 of his initial $35,000 to buy back Butkus, who also appeared in the movie!

"I believe any success in life is made by going into an area
with a blind and furious optimism."
- Sylvester Stallone

"YOU CAN DO IT!"

Mary Kathlyn Wagner was born in Hot Wells, Texas, in the early twentieth century. She was a spirited, adventurous, and delightful girl whose favorite color was pink. Mary was an exceptional student in elementary school, though her childhood wasn't what most people would consider normal.

When she was seven, Mary's father became bedridden. This forced her mother to get a job to provide the family's income. So, she was left to cook, clean, wash dishes, do laundry, care for her father, and even do some shopping.

Mrs. Wagner didn't relish leaving a child with so much responsibility. However, her job demands left her no other option. So Mary bravely accepted the duties usually expected of a grown woman.

Being away from home so often, her Mom strove to instill in Mary the confidence to complete her onerous duties. When faced with a problem, the little girl telephoned her mother for guidance. Mrs. Wagner always found time to talk and would encourage Mary by repeating.

"Don't worry honey, you can do it! You can do it!"

Mary received many honors in high school, including graduating at the top of her class. However, after graduation, when most of her friends were headed for college, her family couldn't afford the tuition.

Consequently, Mary stayed in Houston, married, and started a family. The young mother loved and wanted the best for her kids. So, Mary's heart was broken when a door-to-door saleslady offered to sell her a set of children's books. She truly wanted those books but couldn't afford them.

The saleslady saw that Mary wanted those books.
"What if I could get them for you for free?"
Mary was all ears! *"How?"*
"Well, if you will help me sell ten sets, say to your friends, I will give you a set!"
"You will do that?!"
"Yes, I'll leave these here, and we can start on Monday."

But the good mother didn't wait until Monday. That weekend she sold all ten sets. The following week, when the lady learned what Mary had done, she exclaimed, *"With your kind of talent, you should be in direct sales!"* Then she offered Mary a commission for any additional books sold.

Nine months and $25,000.00 of book sales later, Mary couldn't believe the amount of money she'd earned or how much she'd enjoyed earning it. However, books didn't lend themselves to repeat sales, so she made it her mission to find something that did.

A short time later, Mary discovered Stanley Home Products. She realized she needed sales training when her first attempts with the new products failed. Borrowing twelve dollars from a friend, Mary took a train to Dallas to attend Stanley's National Convention.

At that meeting, the company's top saleslady received special recognition and a grand prize. Mary resolved, "Next time, I will be the one receiving the glory and getting that prize!"

Introducing herself to the reigning queen, she convinced her to demonstrate a Stanley Party. Mary took nineteen pages of notes at that party. On the train ride back to Houston, she memorized every word. Her ingenuity paid off. The following year, Mary was crowned Stanley's Queen of Sales.

Having found something enjoyable that paid well, she relished her freedom to spend time with her children. Stanley paid her commissions for both selling and recruiting. Mary was consistently a top producer and successfully recruited more than 150 salespeople.

However, Mary resigned when Stanley insisted she move to Dallas and refused to continue her Houston commissions. Yet, with her track record, securing a similar position with the World Gift Company was no problem.

There, her sales and recruiting success continued, and she quickly earned the position of National Training Director. For the next eleven years, Mary poured her heart and soul into World Gifts and successfully opened an additional forty- three states for them. Many of her recruits became the company's top producers.

With all the new business and her ability to hire and train, World Gifts placed Mary on their board of directors. Yet, to her dismay, her suggestions and ideas were met with skepticism and negativity. Other board members would often say, "Mary, you're thinking like a woman."

And though her team members were the company's top performers, Mary received little praise. But rather than being moved to a better place or getting more pay, she watched as the recruits she had trained were promoted. Those men received salaries twice that of hers. The final straw came when a position she'd earned was given to someone less qualified. Mary knew the reason she was passed over was that she was female. Then, when her expression of concern was met with apathy, she resigned.

Depressed and out of work, Mary started writing a book about her experiences. A composition to help women avoid the obstacles she'd faced. Becoming an author was challenging. Not sure how to proceed, Mary wrote down every good thing her employers had provided. Then she listed the problems she'd encountered and those things that might have been done better.

Once she'd finished and re-read her notes, it became apparent that her creation was more of a marketing plan than a book. It was something that women could use to accomplish anything if they were simply willing to pay the price! "That's it! I'll create a company to provide women with the opportunity to be the best that they can be!"

Mary Kathlyn was inspired. In her dream, she saw hundreds of women breaking the bonds of a society where the rules and norms were stacked against them. She imagined them being rewarded for their successes and encouraged to do better and to have more.

Mary's mind was spinning. Her company needed great products that women could use, believe in, and recommend to others. For days, she anguished over what would work. Then, it came to her, beauty products that women could use, believe in, and recommend to others. For days, she anguished over what would work. Then, it came to her,

"Every woman, by the age of twenty, already believes she is a cosmetics expert!" And, cosmetics are repeatable, affordable, glamorous, and there is already a big market for them."

So Mary knew she'd found the perfect product!!

Her next step was to find the right products. While searching for suppliers, she remembered a lotion she'd used for years. It was a cream that softened her skin and made her face feel wonderful. Best of all, it was made exclusively by a local friend, so Mary purchased the rights to that formula.

Her new business was taking shape. It had a great marketing plan and an incredible product. All that remained was for her to take action. So, she and her ---husband, George, went to work producing the product and putting together the company's structure.

George would manage the business and financials, and Mary would handle the sales. They located a nice office in Dallas and signed a lease. But tragically, one month before the company was to open, George suffered a heart attack and died.

Distraught, Mary wondered, "How can I go on?" Yet, everything she owned was tied up in the new business, so a decision had to be made. Mary pondered, "If I go this alone, who can assume George's responsibilities?"

While still dealing with the grief, her attorney and accountant strongly recommended that she "Forget the opening, liquidate the inventory and find something else." They predicted failure and bankruptcy, not only for the business but for her as well. All her friends and even some family urged her to give up and move on.

No one would have blamed her for walking away. It seemed to be the right thing to do. However, Mary's children did not share the professionals' feelings and encouraged her, insisting, "Mom, you can do it! You can do it!"

Ben, her oldest son, handed her his bank book, which contained his life savings ($4,500.00), stating, "I can't think of anyone I would rather invest in--than you!" Subsequently, all of her children agreed to pitch in and help with the business.

Hearing her mother's words again, words she'd said to her children numerous times, plus their willingness to pitch in, were just what

Mary needed. From the depths of despair and with every odd stacked against her, Mary Kay Cosmetics took shape on September 13, 1963, marking the beginning of one of the most remarkable and inspiring business successes of the twentieth century!

The Dallas location was a small 500-square-foot office that housed nine employees. Her son Richard took over the financials and business management. Mary Kay developed products, made sales, and recruited, trained, and motivated the Beauty Consultants.

That first year, the lights in the Dallas office could be seen burning late into the night and were back on before sunrise.

Everyone took massive action, and to the skeptic's amazement, with sales of over $198,000.00, Mary Kay Cosmetics showed a profit in its first year. The following year, sales approached a million dollars, and they were off.

Mary Kay did everything and was everywhere! She sold, recruited, trained, motivated, acknowledged, and rewarded her sales force. She created promotional materials and even published a newsletter for the new recruits.

The company grew daily, relying on its philosophy of encompassing the strengths familiar to women. Mutual support and teamwork were its foundation, and their "Beauty Consultants" were encouraged to attain and help others attain their goals. No matter how small or large, every accomplishment was recognized and rewarded.

"The company's goal was to become the largest and the best in the country."

~Mary Kay Ash

The company's product lines featured skincare creams and cosmetics that women could sample at home and order from their personal consultant. Its growth plan was to organize successful sales units that could be duplicated.

Although her business was doing well, she knew it would be impossible to grow if she continued doing everything herself. So, a "National Director" system was created to clone the new "Mary Kays."

The world's best motivational and business speakers were featured at the annual Director's meetings (the seminars). Mary Kay taught her staff and consultants "The Golden Rule" to see the invisible sign. The sign, worn by everyone, said, "Make Me Feel Important!" The focus was always on service rather than sales!
Consultants were told,

> *"You're not really selling cosmetics. You're offering youth, beauty, hope, and self-esteem!"*

As years passed, Mary remarried, and the company began to have a *Real IMPACT* in the marketplace. Mary Kay never stopped searching for better and more exciting awards for her most successful consultants.

The first company award was a Golden Goblet. The cup initially worked, although Mary Kay realized her repeat winners needed something different. So Golden Trays and similar prizes were added. Yet Mary Kay dreamed of something better. Then the Star Consultant Program was introduced. It featured an attractive ladder lapel pin. When a consultant reached her quarterly goal, a jeweled star was placed on the next rung of their pin.

The Star program also created some excitement. However, one day, Mary Kay read an article stating,

"An aerodynamics' study had proved the bumblebee's body was too large and its wings too small for it to fly."

Turning to her husband, she exclaimed, *"That's just like women!"*

A few days later, a package addressed to her arrived at her home. Inside she found a diamond bumblebee pin. Once she saw that pin, a brand-new awards program came into being. Her Queen-level consultants would receive a diamond bee pin. And though the Bee Pin was popular and other rewards were added, Mary Kay was never quite satisfied. She still imagined something spectacular!

The company's massive success gave her the freedom to spend money as she pleased. However, Mary Kay didn't have time to spend money on herself. Yet one morning, she pulled into the Dallas Lincoln Dealership on a whim. And, before she could even explain what she wanted, the salesman stopped her. And, in so many words, said,

> *"Little lady, go home, get your husband, and when you come back, we'll get you into a Lincoln."*

Big mistake!

Mary Kay simply took her business to the Cadillac dealership, where her welcome was much better. Yet, when she opened her compact and said, "I want a car this color," the shocked salesman exclaimed, "That's PINK! You want a pink car?!! Do you realize how much it will cost to have one car painted PINK?! And you won't be able to return it if you're not happy!"

Mary never flinched and ordered a car the color of her compact's "Mountain Laurel" tone. A few weeks later, when her PINK car arrived, she picked it up and drove to her company's parking lot. Five of her National Directors were working at the office that day. When those women saw what she was driving, they were speechless! All five directors had to have one! Then the light came on in Mary Kay's head. This eye-catching automobile would become the company's ultimate award. Not only would it provide a powerful sales incentive, but it would become a potent new company symbol. So, for the first time in 1969, Mary Kay awarded her top five producers a two-year lease on a brand-new blush- colored (pink) "Cadillac Coupe de Ville."

And did that ever work?! The Pink Cadillac became the most coveted award in the company's history and a symbol that the world would identify with Mary Kay Cosmetics. To an outsider, spotting one of those pink cars was as exciting as coming across a Rolls Royce, a DeLorean, or the infamous "Oscar Mayer Wienermobile."

GM's "Pink Mary Kay Fleet" would eventually be valued at over one hundred and thirty million dollars. For over 50 years, those "Pink Cadillacs" have remained a coveted symbol of success throughout the civilized world.

Now you might think this would be enough sales motivation. But not for Mary Kay. She never stopped searching. The next ultimate achievement award was to become a "Queen for a Day." Those winners were honored by sending them down a runway in front of thousands of screaming "Mary Kay Consultants" to be crowned with a jeweled tiara, wrapped in fur, given a gorgeous diamond ring, and presented with a massive bouquet of pink roses.

The Mary Kay annual events rivaled "Broadway," "Hollywood," and "The Miss America Pageant" in their dazzle and elegance. But the spirit of camaraderie and motivation they produced was worth the effort.

Mary Kay knew these ladies would never have a chance for that kind of experience anywhere else. So she provided them with one. She loved and respected her consultants! And they not only loved her, but they also appreciated the unmatched opportunity she offered them. Ash once said,

> *"The success of Mary Kay Inc. is much, much deeper than just dollars and cents and buildings and assets. The real success of our company is measured to me in the lives that have been touched and given hope."*

The company's spirit and the underlying philosophy continued to propel "Mary Kay Cosmetics" to success after success! Her Mother and children were right, "She could do it!" And she did it!! Mary Kay was able to help women throughout the world. At her death in 2001, her company had over 800,000 consultants in 37 countries with annual sales of more than 2 billion dollars.

Loved by all who knew her, Mary Kay left a legacy that will live on in the many people she touched. She certainly left her mark on the business world, and it was PINK!

In 2000, Lifetime Television named Mary Kay Ash the most outstanding woman in business in the 20th century.

"I envisioned a company in which any woman could become just as successful as she wanted to be. The doors would be wide open to opportunity for women who were willing to pay the price and had the courage to dream."
~ Mary Kay Ash

THE LEGEND OF RUDY

It wasn't the top-rated movie in 1993; it came in 69th. It wasn't even the highest-ranked college football film that year. Yet, Rudy has become a film classic that has motivated thousands with its touching story of a boy's struggles to make his dream a reality.

Daniel Ruettiger was born in Joliet, Illinois, in 1948, the third of 14 children. Rudy, as he was called, lived in a small home outside Chicago. His father was a miner who barely earned enough to feed his large family. Still, as bad as things were, he loved to watch Notre Dame Football on Saturdays in the fall. Rudy also loved Notre Dame and dreamed of someday playing for the Fighting Irish.

So the first day he was eligible, he signed up for Joliet Catholic Academy's varsity football team.

Rudy practiced hard, earned a starting position, and led the team in tackles in his final two seasons. Unfortunately, he wasn't built like a football player. He was only 5' 6" and weighed just 165 pounds. But Ruettiger strove to compensate for his slight build by giving every play 100% of what he had.

He didn't just play hard--he also talked tough. And it was no secret that he planned to become a member of Notre Dame's Fighting Irish! Of course, when his classmates heard that, they got a good laugh. "Rudy, you're nuts! That's impossible!" And almost everyone at Joliet believed Rudy had no chance of suiting up for the Irish.

After all, Notre Dame could recruit the best players from anywhere in the nation. Why in a million years would they ever consider anyone like Rudy?! "That's simply impossible!"

However, one person didn't laugh at Rudy and even encouraged him to go for his dream. That was his father's best friend, Pete. Pete listened to Rudy and offered him advice. But, one day, Pete was killed in an accident at his job. Young Ruettiger, though grief-stricken, vowed to take Pete's recommendations and pursue his dream.

So after graduating high school, he moved to South Bend, Indiana, where he hoped to become a student at his beloved college. Unfortunately, he didn't qualify to enroll. Noticing his disappointment, a helpful priest suggested he apply to Holy Cross Junior College as a stepping-stone to entering Notre Dame.

The bar at Holy Cross was lower, and Rudy was accepted. Although Rudy was dedicated and worked hard to earn high marks, he had dyslexia, which made reading and studying slow and challenging. His disability made achieving good grades arduous.

Rudy turned in applications each of the subsequent five semesters, just to be rejected again and again. Yet, his desire to play for the Irish was stronger than ever. So, he spent as much time walking the university's grounds as he could. On one campus visit, Rudy spotted a flyer touting a groundskeeper position and jumped at the chance.

While working on campus, he had access to and explored the tunnels of historic Notre Dame Stadium. From the front of the Hesburgh Library, he admired the 68 ft. mural of The Word of Life, also known as Touchdown Jesus. But when the mid-day sun reflected from the golden dome of Notre Dame's main building, he closed his eyes and saw himself dawning the golden helmet of the Irish.

If Rudy had been motivated before, he was now on fire!! So, he renewed his vow that somehow, someway, he was going to dress in the blue and gold and take the field with the Fighting Irish.

Although he doubled down on his studies, he knew his time was running out. And he realized his dream would be dead if he was rejected once more. You see, Notre Dame didn't accept senior transfers. So, Rudy prayed and submitted his application for the final time. When the verdict was announced, it was good news!

Rudy's dream was still alive! But being accepted as a football player would be a much higher hurdle. Most college teams allow walk-ons, and Notre Dame was no different. His problem was that only two walk-on positions were available, and Rudy would compete against fifteen top-quality players. Nevertheless, Ruettiger approached the tryouts as if his life depended on it. When the whistle blew, you wouldn't have wanted to be standing in front of him!

He poured every ounce of courage and fight he had into those tryouts! And to everyone's amazement, Rudy Ruettiger was selected as one of the chosen two. Overjoyed, he knew he had come a long way, but his real dream was to suit up in the blue and gold and play in a real game! And though making the team was a giant step, the next step would require the heart of a champion.

Scout teams consisted of players who, at practice, played against the first string. They were the guys who took all the blows and got little, if any, glory. But that didn't bother Rudy. He was determined to do his part to help the Fighting Irish win regardless of his position. So day after day, the pint-sized defender battled those enormous five-star players. His effort displayed the meaning of heart, passion, and devotion.

Rudy played bruised, he played hurt, and he put all he had into every play! Even facing pushback from some of his teammates, he never gave an inch. Fortunately, his efforts didn't go unnoticed by the elite players he faced every day. They came to love and respect him for his selfless actions.

As his final season of eligibility approached, some of the team's leaders encouraged him to tell Coach Parseghian about his dream. So, Ruettiger gathered his nerve and knocked on the coach's door.

Ara Parseghian realized how hard Rudy had worked and promised to play him in at least one game next season. Rudy was thrilled and believed his dream was about to become a reality! He could see himself donning a golden helmet and running onto the field of the most historic stadium in college football! He couldn't wait for his family and the many doubters to see it.

However, Parseghian stepped down as coach at the end of the season and was replaced by Dan Devine. Devine wasn't aware of Ara's promise or Rudy's hard work. And he was much too busy to discuss anything with a player on the scout team. So, when fall brought about the new season, Rudy continued to do his best at every practice. Once again, he slammed those big guys with all his might and strove to keep everyone's enthusiasm high on the practice field.

As the games came and went, the Irish were having a good year. Boston College was a win, Purdue a win, and Northwestern was also a win. However, the next game was a loss to Michigan State. And with that, Coach Devine became even more focused on righting the ship and certainly had no time for an individual player's dream.

Wins against North Carolina and Air Force followed. But with a loss to Southern California, Rudy could feel his hopes evaporating. The Irish did come back to defeat the Navy. But Georgia Tech was the last game on their schedule, and everyone knew that the Yellow Jackets would not be pushovers. Rudy's teammates were aware of Coach

Parseghian's promise. Yet, none of them dared try to influence coach Devine, especially this year. So no one said a word.

In the Georgia Tech game, Notre Dame built a healthy lead. And as the game's conclusion approached, the Irish could have won by simply running out the clock.

But Rudy's teammates knew there would probably never be another chance for him to play if the game ended. So the team leaders persuaded their quarterback to try to score rather than running out the clock.

If Notre Dame could score, the defense would have to re-enter the field, giving Rudy one more chance to play. Their plan worked, and they scored. Coach Devine was dumbfounded! He couldn't believe his eyes! "What in the HE-- is going on here?!"

At that point, some Irish players started chanting "Rudy, Rudy," and soon others joined in. As the chant began to get louder ("Rudy, Rudy!"), the cheerleaders and some of the home crowd took up the mantra. Then his family and friends joined in, and even some coaches followed suit.

The sound of "Rudy, Rudy, Rudy!" rang out in Notre Dame Stadium. Then finally, Coach Divine caught on and, with a scowl, motioned for the defensive coach to send in Ruettiger.

While it may seem like no big deal, Rudy's lifelong dream was realized. And for the next two plays, Ruettiger dawned his "Golden Helmet" and proudly wore the "Blue and Gold" for his Fighting Irish.

On his first play, he was stopped and couldn't reach the runner. But on the second, he broke through an elite Yellow Jacket line manned by 300-pound players. Then, little Rudy Ruettiger tackled Georgia Tech's quarterback for a loss on the game's final play.

A mighty roar rose from the fans as the Irish Band played their famous Notre Dame fight song, The Victory March. There were smiles and high-fives from Rudy's family. Once the final seconds ticked off the clock, Rudy's teammates lifted him to their shoulders and carried him off the field. This was the only time in Notre Dame history a player was carried off by his teammates.

So "The Legend of Rudy" began and lives on, even today. Although Ruettiger played only two plays, he not only realized his dream but also accomplished the impossible and provided encouragement to nameless thousands!

"Focus on your dream and never quit.
It is always too soon to quit."
~ Rudy Ruettiger

SHE TURNED A DIME INTO MILLIONS

Martha McChesney Berry grew up on a large cotton plantation in the foothills of the Blue Ridge mountains near Rome, Georgia. Her father managed their estate and several other businesses. After completing high school, she also received a degree from Edgeworth Finishing School.

However, the young Miss Berry was aware that, sadly, the mountain children around her would never have the opportunity to participate in any school. After a chance meeting with a few children on a Sunday afternoon, she resolved to afford those little ones the prospect of an education. So in the late 1890s, Martha Berry constructed a one-room whitewashed building on a corner of her father's estate.

Once completed, The Berry School began offering classes to the children in the North Georgia hills. Students wanting to attend were allowed to barter for their tuition. And there was a good reason for that option; the children's families had little or no money!

The families were excited at the prospect of their kids having an opportunity to attend school. So, for the youngsters' tuition, they contributed whatever they had.

Some brought eggs, others a jar of jam, a quilt, or a chicken. One family even brought their milk cow.

To receive room and board, the students worked in the garden, kept up the grounds, chopped wood, cleaned the classroom, gathered eggs, cooked meals, and scrubbed the floors. They grew what they ate.

As word spread of a free education, attendance mushroomed, and more food and larger buildings were needed. Martha's heart was big, but her bank account was small. The little school faced crisis after crisis, and the cause was always the same, money. Yet, Miss Berry was devoted to her students and dreamed of finding a way to keep the school open. Still, the prospects weren't good!

Then one day, a little boy ran up to Martha, holding a newspaper clipping.

"Miss Berry, Miss Berry!" "What is it, Johnny?"
"Oh, Miss Berry, you need to talk with Henry Ford!"
"Why on earth should I do that?!"
"It says in this paper that he's got a lot of money, and he gives it to people who need it!"
Then Johnny said, his hands trembling, "I think we need it, Miss Berry!"

A short time later, the young educator did write to Ford to explain her dream of educating the poor children of the Blue Ridge Mountains. After mailing the envelope, Martha prayed that the wealthy philanthropist would understand the situation and provide some financial assistance to her school.

Unfortunately, the crusty old industrialist had been contacted by so many asking for his money; he'd become cynical and believed that every person and organization in the country was looking to him for a free handout. So Ford had little sympathy for Martha's situation. However, he did send her something. He sent her a dime. One thin dime, worth ten cents and nothing more. Martha Berry could have taken that dime and told herself, "I tried, and it just didn't work out." But the young teacher wasn't quite ready to give up.

Taking a pen and paper, she jotted down a plan encompassing all the resources in her control. Her list included: her knowledge of farming (having been raised on a plantation), the strength and loyalty of her students, the availability of her father's land, the tools and resources on his plantation, nature's ability to multiply, and of course that dime from Henry Ford.

Once her plan was complete, Martha took the coin to a feed store in Rome and bought ten cents worth of peanuts. When she returned, she gathered her students and presented them with a new project. They were told their part would be difficult, it would take hard work, and they would still be expected to do their classwork and other chores. Then, emphasizing its importance, she asked the children if they would see the project through.

All the students accepted the challenge. So Martha took four stakes and marked off a small section of land near the schoolhouse. Then she set up teams and appointed a leader for each one. The older boys were to clear the small trees and bushes from the field. Meanwhile, the younger children placed each peanut seed in a small container, added fertilizer, and watered it daily.

The other groups gathered rakes, hoes, buckets, and other items needed to tend a crop. Once the field was cleared, the older boys plowed the ground and prepared it for planting. All the students diligently prepared each furrow. When the sprouts were ready, they carefully placed the tiny buds in the furrows.

Each day, in the hot Georgia sun, while one team worked to pull the weeds from among the young plants, others carried buckets of water into the field.
No peanut crop had ever received such copious attention.

As their harvest grew, Martha again asked the older boys to start clearing, only this time, the new field was not small. She laid out a section of more than an acre. And, of course, it took the boys longer to prepare the larger area for planting. The children never complained and worked diligently to ensure the projects succeeded.

That first peanut crop responded well to all the attention and the nice Georgia weather. Their harvest was bountiful, and those little ones had never seen so many peanuts. Yet, their project was only beginning. The peanuts from the first crop were again prepared to be planted in the larger field.

With both fields seeded, Martha staked out what must have seemed like a hundred acres (88 acres). Nevertheless, the children remained loyal; clearing, plowing, planting, and tending were again completed. The crop not only responded, it out produced the first one. This harvest was so massive that it took several wagons to deliver the produce to the feed company.

When little Berry School's peanut harvest was weighed, it brought the astonishing sum of fifteen hundred dollars. Her students had masterfully accomplished their part of Martha's plan. But the young teacher's strategy was not yet complete.

After placing the fifteen hundred dollars in her bank account, she wrote a check to Henry Ford for the entire amount. Then signing the check, she put it in an envelope along with the following letter and mailed it to Henry Ford.

"Dear Mr. Ford:
Here is your fifteen-hundred-dollar dividend for the ten-cent investment you made in Berry School."
Faithfully Yours,
Martha Berry

When the old business magnate read that letter and saw the check, he was so moved that he took the next train to Rome to meet this Miss Martha Berry. While in Rome, Ford visited the little schoolhouse and saw the poor children working their hearts out. He watched them study and saw their devotion to Martha and to learning. And before he departed, the great car maker wrote Berry School a substantial check. That money was only the first of a long string of donations.

Henry and his wife, Clara, formed a lifelong friendship with Martha. His total donations to the "Berry Schools" were estimated to be over three million dollars.

*"Failure will never overtake me if my
determination to succeed is strong enough."*

Og Mandino

PROVIDENCE

Abraham Lincoln is remembered as one of America's greatest Presidents. So much so that until recently, his birthday was a national holiday. He is known for his log cabin birthplace, honesty, and stovepipe hat. However, he also significantly impacted the direction of our nation through watershed moments, including the *Lincoln Douglas Debates*, becoming the first Republican President, and *The Gettysburg Address*.

But what most people don't know is the improbable series of events that allowed him to become the 16th President of the United States.

What changed this barefoot boy, who was so poor that his pants were always too short, into one of the most successful attorneys in Illinois? What transformed the son of illiterate parents from the backwoods of Kentucky into one of the world's greatest orators? And, how did that poor farm boy with little to no schooling become the President of the United States?

Abraham Lincoln had less than the equivalent of a first- grade education. Yet, his speeches have been renowned as some of the most eloquent in the history of the world. How did that happen, and what circumstances prove his rise to power was providence?

A Humble Beginning

The boy's early life was a struggle. He was born in a tiny, dirt-floor log cabin deep in the Kentucky backwoods. His father, Thomas, a cabinet maker, had recently spent his life savings purchasing their farm. Yet, a title dispute cost him all his land and most of his money. Consequently, young Abe's family was forced to move several times, finally squatting in a thick, dangerous Indiana forest on government land.

Seven-year-old Abe once again found himself in a tiny cabin surrounded by dense woods filled with wild animals. The little boy's father gave him an ax and put him to work cutting trees, notching logs, chopping firewood, and fetching water from a stream two miles away.

Abe's mother, Nancy Hanks Lincoln, a talented seamstress, tried hard to make her family comfortable. She cooked, cleaned, made clothes, and recited poems and scriptures from the Bible. Little Abe loved to listen and had the unique ability to hear something and repeat it almost verbatim.

Neither Nancy nor Thomas had a formal education. The only books in their home were the Bible, a catechism, and a spelling book. Even though little Abe couldn't read, he enjoyed looking at the pages and longed to understand their meaning.

In the following two years, their little farm began to take shape. But then, Nancy fell ill from milk sickness. With no doctors or medicine nearby, the disease took her life in a short time. Abraham was only nine when his precious mother passed away. The young boy was devastated.

Abe remained despondent even though his sister Sarah did her best to be a mother to him. He had no way of knowing that this would be the first of a series of events that would ultimately lead him to greatness.

A New Mother

The next providential event occurred when Thomas, knowing he needed help, left little Abe and Sarah alone and headed back to Kentucky.

Upon his arrival in Elizabethtown, he learned that a previous acquaintance, Sarah Bush Johnston, had recently become a widow. So Thomas visited her and made this proposal...

> *"I have no wife and you no husband. I came a-purpose to marry you. I knowed you from a gal, and you knowed me from a boy. I've no time to lose: and if you're willin', let it be done straight off."*

The following day, Sarah and Thomas were married in a log house on Elizabethtown's Main Street.

When the two, along with Sarah's three children, returned to the Indiana cabin. Little Abe and Sister Sarah were excited to have a mom again and relished their new playmates. They also appreciated their help in the fields. The merged family quickly bonded, and Abe's new stepmother loved him as much or more than her own children. And, when Mother Sarah saw the makings of a great man in him, another remarkable event took place.

After learning of a school opening several miles from their farm, Sarah enrolled young Abe. She saw that he attended the classes each day. Abraham loved school and appreciated learning. He even created his own *Book of Sums* to help him with math problems.

Nancy Hanks Lincoln's cousin, Dennis Hanks, joined them at the farm for an extended stay during this period. While there, he taught young Abe his ABCs and helped him with reading.

Because Abe's father cared little about his education and needed his help, Abe was forced to drop out of school. Yet, with his new mother's encouragement, he never stopped studying.

Sarah kept him at his lessons and gifted him her books. Soon young Abraham was spending his free time reading books such as *The Life of Washington, Aesop's Fables, Pilgrim's Progress, and The King James Bible.* He even took his books to the field to read while plowing and resting his horse.

The Boy's Habit

Young Lincoln became a virtual vacuum, eagerly consuming every book, newspaper, pamphlet, article, or anything else he could find to read. For years, he read by firelight deep into the night and resumed at the first sign of the sun. Although he completed his chores, he had a marked preference for reading, writing, and ciphering.

Once he had read and reread the books in his home, Abraham walked to the nearest trail. He befriended any hunter, trader, peddler, or politician who chanced by. If a traveler had a book, Lincoln was sure to have a look. He even borrowed from his neighbors and once boasted, *"I've read every book within 50 miles of my home."*

He read texts such as Nicholas Pike's *New and Complete System of Arithmetic* and Thomas Dilworth's *New Guide to the English Tongue.* And classics like *Robinson Crusoe*, Benjamin Franklin's autobiography, and anything else he could find.

Although he became more knowledgeable through reading, the teenager realized that his grammar was inferior. And though he was surrounded by illiterate parents and neighbors, he knew where to find help and was quoted as saying...

> *"The things I want to know are in books; my best friend is the man who'll get me a book I ain't read."*

Abraham continued to work in the fields throughout his teens, swinging his ax and reading. In those days, it was the custom for families to rent out their children until they turned twenty-one, and Thomas made prime use of that custom.

So, in addition to his chores, Abraham was obligated to chop trees, split fence rails, and do other work for his neighbors. With all that physical labor and reading, he eventually became a knowledgeable and muscular young man.

Young Lincoln always carried a book, and it was common to see him with an ax in one hand and a book in the other. But, as time passed, he grew weary of his labor and began to resent his father.

When he was twenty-two, his family moved again, settling in central Illinois. After that move, Abraham left his family to seek his fortune and took whatever honest work he could find. Yet, he especially liked sailing cargo down the Mississippi River on flatboats. The main reason was the boat's owner brought a stack of newspapers and a copy of *A History of the United States*. So, on these trips, Abe had more to read than ever before.

Marooned

The following year Abraham continued to do odd jobs and ferry cargo. Fate stepped in on his last voyage when his flatboat became stranded on a sandbar near New Salem, Illinois. As the crew struggled to free the vessel, a large crowd formed. The town's citizens watched as a tall, lanky fellow took charge. Under his direction, the crew members unloaded the cargo from one side, causing the boat to shift.

Then the impressed observers witnessed the boy go ashore, locate a copper shop, and borrow an auger. He then drilled a hole in the boat's bow, which allowed the water to drain out and the boat to ease over the dam.

The flatboat's owner, Denton Offutt, was impressed with Abraham's handling of this incident. He liked what he'd seen of New Salem. So, he pledged to return to open a general store and asked Abe to join him in that venture. When the young ferryman agreed, he unknowingly took his next step toward his ultimate destiny.

Imagine that, with more than 800 miles of shoreline, Abraham Lincoln's flatboat marooned precisely on the shores of New Salem, Illinois. A town, most likely the only one along that voyage, which contained a debating society.

New Salem 1831

Once the flatboat crew returned from New Orleans, Offutt fulfilled his pledge and opened the New Salem General Store. Lincoln was hired as the store's clerk and allowed to sleep in a back room. The town's residents were soon being entertained with yarns and funny jokes. In a short time, Abe was a town favorite as the word spread of his humor, knowledge, and honesty.

"Honest Abe," as he was called, enjoyed the freedom his new job gave him to read and study English grammar. During this time, he engaged the local schoolteacher to help him with his writing and speaking skills. At his teacher's urging, Lincoln joined the New Salem Debating Society. There, he gave his first public speech and met many influential people. Impressed with what they heard, the townspeople convinced Lincoln to enter the Illinois General Assembly race.

Although Abe was staying busy, the general store was losing money. And panic spread when Chief Black Hawk of the Sauk tribe and several hundred braves crossed the Mississippi into Illinois without warning. So, the State's Governor decreed that males between eighteen and forty-five were obligated to enlist in the militia. When the call came, with the store failing, Offutt allowed Lincoln to enlist.

The Army assigned Abraham to a battalion containing a number of his friends from New Salem. So, when his Company chose a captain, they picked Lincoln by a large majority. Although he saw no action, he demonstrated bravery and was highly respected.

After his military discharge, he returned home and resumed his race for the General Assembly. Though his run was unsuccessful, he met many citizens throughout Illinois, some of whom would later help elect him to the Legislature. Despite losing his first election, his enthusiasm for politics grew after he received 277 of New Salem's 300 votes.

1833

With the election over and out of work, Lincoln searched for new opportunities. But when many things he attempted failed, the people of New Salem appointed him their Postmaster. And, when the Post Office was moved to another town, he was tapped to be Deputy to the County Surveyor.

Lincoln had a strong desire to be successful at something; he just wasn't sure what it was. And though he loved politics, he hesitated to enter for his lack of education and contacts. At that point, he described himself as "*a piece of floating driftwood.*"

While strongly considering opening a blacksmith shop, an acquaintance offered to sell him a fully furnished general store on credit. The deal sounded too good to pass up, so Lincoln accepted the offer. Running his new store gave him ample time to do his favorite thing, reading.

The Old Barrel

Many days were spent sitting under a tree near the store's entrance, studying English grammar and reading anything he could borrow from his customers. He consumed newspapers, textbooks, and classics like the works of Shakespeare and the poems of Robert Burns. Although he enjoyed this time, poor sales were pulling him into debt. In fact, except for the fifty cents in his pocket, he was broke.

One morning, while sitting under that tree, his eyes were drawn to an approaching covered wagon. The driver pulled up in front of him and steadied his horses. Jumping down, he walked toward Lincoln and exclaimed, *"This pioneer life is not for me, and I'm taking my family back East. My wagon is overloaded. Will you take a look inside to see if there is anything you might want?"*

Since Abe had no money, he was hesitant and told the man he wasn't interested. But the driver was insistent, *"What about this barrel? You can use it to store things. I'll let you have it for only four bits (50 cents). Could you take it off my hands?"*

Now Lincoln didn't need another barrel. Most of his store's supplies arrived in barrels. Yet, he reached in his pocket and handed the man his last penny. Bidding the traveler farewell, he placed the old relic in a back corner and forgot about it.

After several months, he found a use for the barrel. And, once he removed the top, he noticed it wasn't empty. Dumping the contents on the floor, Abraham was surprised when something heavy fell out. As he looked more closely, there on the floor, partially covered by debris, lay a complete set of *Blackstone's Commentaries*. These were Sir William Blackstone's 18th-century essays on the common law of England.

Lincoln wasted no time putting those books to use and spent the remainder of the summer consuming their pages. The more he read, the more interested he became. Saying, *"Never in my whole life was my mind so thoroughly absorbed. I read until I devoured them."*

Even before completing the essays, he started visiting courthouses and observing trials. Once he'd had a glimpse of those hearings,

Abraham Lincoln realized his search for a profession had ended. And, for the first time, he envisioned himself as an attorney. Lincoln then committed he'd do whatever it took to accomplish that goal.

Who knows if the story of the barrel is true? A much older Lincoln often told it using the third person. I merely wrote what his listeners must have surmised.

Yet, some historians think it has merit. I know Lincoln had access to Blackstone's Commentaries. It is irrelevant whether he got them from a farmer or his mentor and future business partner, John T. Stuart. But that he used them as the first step toward a highly successful legal career is an acknowledged fact.

The Law

The same year Lincoln decided to become an attorney (1834), he was elected to the Illinois General Assembly. A short time later, Springfield attorney, John T. Stuart, befriended him and offered him the use of his law library.

At age 23, Lincoln was still living in New Salem and managing his general store. What free time he had, he spent preparing to take the multiple steps required to pass the Illinois bar. Purchasing a book of legal forms, he drew up mortgages, deeds, and other documents for his friends at no charge.

He even argued a few minor cases with Stuart's advice and encouragement. He often traveled twenty miles to his friend's office to retrieve and return law books. In 1836, his diligence paid off, and he was granted a license to practice law. The following year the Illinois Supreme Court awarded him admission to the State Bar. Then, Mr. Lincoln started a career that he would pursue for the remainder of his life; he was no longer "*a floating piece of driftwood.*"

Once the Illinois Legislature adjourned, Lincoln saw little future in

New Salem for his legal work or political ambitions. Yet, Springfield offered both; he was well known for his successful efforts to make that city the new state capital. So, on a borrowed horse and with everything he owned in two saddlebags, Abraham Lincoln departed the city that gave him his political start.

He boarded with friends for the next four years or stayed in country inns and farmhouses. Lincoln was 28 when he opened a law office with Stuart and became a circuit judge. His responsibilities required him to travel throughout Illinois, visiting numerous cities and courts. For months, he would journey with his clothes and toiletries in his saddlebags. And he always carried a few books for entertainment on those long rides.

In addition to his law career, Lincoln continued in politics and used his travels to broaden his base. Within a few years, he was earning between $1,200.00 and $1,500.00 a year when the state's governor was only receiving $1,200.00. In 1841, Stuart and Lincoln dissolved a partnership that had handled more than seven hundred cases.

But another door opened when the top lawyer in Illinois, Stephen Logan, offered him a partnership. Upon accepting this position, his status as an attorney was significantly elevated. During those two years, Abraham Lincoln was introduced to and represented the most influential leaders in Illinois and the surrounding states.

The Rail road Wind fall

In 1857, Lincoln took another step toward destiny when he served as a lobbyist for the Illinois Central Railroad. After assisting them in getting a charter from the state, he was retained as their regular attorney. Upon successfully defending the "ICR" against the county in a tax matter, he received the largest fee of his legal career, $5,000.00 ($166,000.00 in today's money). And by the time Abe became a prominent national politician, he was one of Illinois' most distinguished and successful attorneys.

The Douglas Debates

Lincoln's windfall from the railroad gave him the money and time to pursue his higher ambition; politics. Consequently, in 1858, he ran for the Illinois Senate. While Lincoln was inexperienced and awkward, his opponent, the incumbent Senator Stephen A. Douglas, was rich, powerful, and charismatic.

Fighting an uphill battle against a better-financed and more organized opponent, Lincoln planned to follow Douglas and speak in the same cities. Suddenly the idea of battling him face-to-face came to mind. So, he wrote Douglas and challenged him to share a debate platform.

Douglas certainly had no desire to elevate Lincoln to his level. But, the fear of being called a coward prompted him to take on this lightweight. So Douglas, planning to put him in his place once and for all, accepted his challenge.

Many thousands came to hear, and hundreds of newspapers reported their contests. Still, it wasn't until the 1860 publication of those deliberations that the Lincoln-Douglas Debates legend began. And though Lincoln lost that Senate race, his published words introduced him to the nation.

Chicago

In 1860, Lincoln had just entered the race for the standard- bearer of the newly formed Republican Party when providence again appeared. This time it came from the City of Chicago. Chicago's businessmen, citizens, and politicians transformed Abraham Lincoln from an unknown backwoods lawyer into the Republican Party's candidate. Without her help, Lincoln would not have become the nominee.

What was his appeal to the Windy City? He'd rarely visited there and had spent most of his time serving southern Illinois. Even though Chicago was a growing metropolis and was striving to be a "refined" city, its working people (the voters) loved Abe's "western man" image. They saw his tall, muscular, rough-looking, and disheveled appearance as their kind of candidate.

Once he began to speak, Chicagoans were captivated by his earnest and powerful delivery. His image of a poor man's Caesar was enough to convince thousands to support this "rail-splitter." Even though her masses got behind him, he still needed the support of the city's middle and upper classes. When Lincoln spoke to her working men, he also drew the attention of her wealthy. The influential Eastern Illinois businessmen believed him to be their businesses' best protector once they examined his policies. While Lincoln touted his humble origins to her masses, he proclaimed conservative fiscal policy, protective tariffs, and railroad expansion to her upper crust.

The city's elites not only offered Abe moral support; they also poured thousands of dollars into his campaign. Although, as great as it was to have her unanimous support, that would be irrelevant if the Windy City wasn't chosen to host the Republican National Convention. And the prospects of that were extremely low.

A Site for the Convention

Representatives of the Northern Republican segments gathered in 1859 to discuss the site of their convention. Each delegation argued it should be in its own locality. Cities like Buffalo, St. Louis, Cleveland, Cincinnati, and Indianapolis seemed to have the upper hand on Chicago.

However, the Illinois delegation lauded her as the only neutral site where everyone would have an even chance. Despite their allegiance to Lincoln, they never mentioned his name. After many votes, the choice came down to St. Louis and Chicago.

Not to be outdone, the Illinois group pledged free food and a splendid reception for all the convention's members. As a kicker, they offered a grand convention hall at no cost. So, with a promise of a cheap convention, the meeting site was snatched away from St. Louis by one vote. *A single vote!*

The Competition

Lincoln not only had the city's support but was Illinois' "Favorite Son." However, he would face a formidable list of more experienced and better-known opponents.

William H. Seward was the most likely nominee. An experienced politician, he had been the Governor of New York, a previous state, and the current United States, Senator. He had also amassed a powerful group of backers, a large amount of money, and the New York delegation's muscle. Seward brought many followers and a brass band, all in uniforms. The only thing he didn't have going for him was Chicago!

Lincoln also faced two other formidable opponents. The well- known Republican Senator and Ohio Governor, Salmon P. Chase and the influential Virginia politician Edward Bates. Each of these men held high political offices at the national level. And both had powerful friends who could easily put them in the White House.

In contrast, Lincoln had only served in the Illinois General Assembly and as an Illinois Congressman. With the limited knowledge of a small-time politician, he couldn't possibly match his competitors' experience. So, going into the convention, all signs pointed to an effortless defeat of "The Rail-splitter."

The Chicagoan's Plot

Understandably, Lincoln himself was skeptical about receiving the nomination. Yet, he'd underestimated the power of his backers. His Chicago supporters were not only well organized, but they'd also put together a flawless plan.

Immediately following the site conference, their team sprang into action. Norman Judd, a prominent lawyer, persuaded the railroads to provide cheap fares from all parts of Illinois, so Lincoln's enthusiasts could flood the convention without worrying about the cost.

Then came their marketing campaign. Newspapers were the only media of the day. So, the considerably influential Chicago Press began publishing articles promoting Lincoln as the nominee. That meant the first thing convention delegates would see in their morning papers was a strong endorsement of "Honest Abe."

Lincoln's devotees marched in the streets daily, touting "The Rail-splitter." However, it would be on the convention floor where they would turn the tide. Prominent Chicagoans Norman Judd and Joseph Medill were conveniently appointed to handle the seating arrangements for both the audience and the delegates.

Somehow Lincoln's enthusiasts found tickets easy to procure, while the other candidate's supporters found gaining entrance difficult. Inside the convention hall were wall-to- wall Lincoln fans. While outside, the attractively uniformed Seward protagonists had no way to influence the delegates.

Therefore, the nation's representatives only saw a hall full of passionate Lincoln devotees touting their favorite son's auspices. Next, the Chicagoans carefully isolated the New Yorkers from the other state delegations who weren't in Lincoln's camp. They then secured a simple majority rule. And after accomplishing that, the plot's final and most crucial phase was put into action; behind-the-scenes politicking.

It was common knowledge the battleground states of Indiana, Ohio, Illinois, New Jersey, and Pennsylvania thought Lincoln's competitors too radical on the issues to be electable. So the Chicago team took charge and, backed by a committee of their politicians, held closed-door meetings. They visited each delegation to convince them Lincoln was the only man who could glean the nation's support.

Despite ethics, Lincoln's team stopped at nothing. They spread a rumor that five state governors had threatened to resign if Seward should be nominated. Then, without the authority to do so, they offered key delegates high-level positions in the Lincoln administration.

Each man was assigned a specific state. Their goal was to cut off support for Seward and win them over to the "Rail- splitter." Indiana was the first to be turned by promises of a prominent position in Lincoln's cabinet.

Then deals were struck with New Jersey and Pennsylvania, both fervent followers of Seward. Those delegates agreed to make Lincoln their choice should Seward show weakness on the first ballot. The team worked tirelessly until the last vote was cast. Three of four battleground states were now in Lincoln's camp. It would be up to the Chicago delegates and their crowds to fan the flames. With negotiations closed and deals secured, all of Chicago watched as the convention played out.

The Republican Convention

When the meeting was called to order, the New Yorkers rose first and exclaimed support for their Favorite Son, Seward. His few devotees inside the hall applauded so loudly that it annoyed the other delegates.

Nonetheless, the work of the Chicago team started paying dividends when Lincoln's name was first mentioned. One reporter recalled…

> *"Five thousand people jumped to their feet at once! The audience erupted, like a wild colt with a bit between his teeth!" It rose above all cries for 'order. 'Again and again, their irrepressible cheers broke forth and bounced off the walls. Their outcries were repeated to the dismay of the other delegates."*

Seward took the lead on the first ballot but failed to take the majority. Simultaneously, behind closed doors, the Chicagoans again put their plot into action. The second ballot showed a remarkable improvement for Lincoln. The tight race now stood between only two: Lincoln and Seward. The tension in the hall was palatable. When the voting continued, Lincoln received gains from Pennsylvania and Massachusetts, bringing him within an eyelash of victory.

The packed hall was about to burst out at the seams with tension at a fever pitch. Seconds passed like hours as the vote came down to Ohio. Ten thousand eyes were fixed on the delegation from the Buckeye State. After what seemed like an eternity, Ohio announced that four of her delegates had switched their votes to Abraham Lincoln…

> One reporter wrote, "There was a brief moment of silence, then there rose a noise like a rush of a terrible storm."

Outside the hall, cannons fired, and people danced in the streets. All of Chicago rejoiced, for their favorite son, "The Rail-splitter," was the Republican nominee for President of the United States.

From the celebration, you'd think Lincoln had already won the Presidency. And though "Honest Abe" walked away with the prize, he realized that he wouldn't be the nominee had the convention been held elsewhere. And he knew his chances of actually becoming the President were abysmal. In fact, his prospects were so poor that it would probably take an act of God for him to triumph.

So, despite the cannon fire, street dancing, and hoopla, the Democrats were still sure to win the election. And though Lincoln had his party's nomination, his ascent to the Presidency was improbable, if not impossible.

The Election of 1860

Here are a few of the myriad obstacles between Abraham Lincoln and the Presidency. After the convention's shenanigans, many Republicans were upset with the outcome, meaning a split in the party wasn't only possible but quite likely.

Lincoln's views were polarizing, and the voters either loved or hated him. The country was extremely divided on the issues, and the vast majority didn't believe Lincoln had the answer.

Most newspapers did not support him and allowed his opponents to paint him as inexperienced. Since he wasn't photogenic, their cartoonist had a field day with his looks. Abe's likely competition, the Honorable Stephen Douglas, had soundly defeated him in the Illinois Senate race only two years earlier.

Adding to those concerns, a third party emerged, The Constitutional Union Party. Their views were similar to the Republicans and would most certainly peel away crucial votes. Yet by far, Abe's worst problem was that 10 out of the 34 states wouldn't even allow his name on their ballots. So, Lincoln's chances were not only slim; they were so bad it would take a miracle for him to emerge with a victory.

Yet, Lincoln and his party had no way of knowing that the Democrat Party was in shambles. They should have been the party of unity. However, they were deeply divided.

The Southern Democrats walked out at their first convention, and the convention ended without a nominee. With such confusion among the ranks, it was unclear if the Democrats would even have a candidate for the 1860 election.

Two months later, they made another attempt, but the Southerners again left in disgust. The delegates who remained named Douglas as their candidate. When the South learned of this, they formed another party, the Southern Democrat party. That new party voted to have John Breckinridge as their candidate. So, with the Democrats split in two, four parties offered their nominees to the electorate.

- The Republicans
- The Constructional Union Party
- The Southern Democrats
- And the Democrat Party

These changes resulted in Lincoln's miracle. When the Americans voted for President of the United States, Abraham Lincoln won in a landslide. Douglas only received 12 electoral votes, not nearly enough to offer Lincoln a serious challenge. The Southern ballots were split between Breckenridge with 72 and Bell with 39. So, with 180 electoral votes, Abraham Lincoln became the 16th President of the United States.

Which Brings Us Back to the Story's Original Questions;

What transformed the son of illiterate parents from the backwoods of Kentucky into one of the world's greatest orators? And how did that poor farm boy with almost no schooling become the President of the United States?

How is it that Lincoln's speeches have been renowned as some of the most eloquent in the history of the world, considering he had less than the equivalent of a first-grade education? What circumstances prove his rise to power was providence?

Answers

- As for answers to those questions, Lincoln, the teenager, said it best; "The things I want to know are in books..."

Was it providence, or was Lincoln just lucky?

- I'll let you decide, but looking at his life in its entirety, few would consider him "lucky."

What are the Chances?

What are the chances that…

- A young boy's illiterate mother would take ill and die, leaving the door open for a stepmother who would see he received an education?
- A woman would accept a pitiful proposal from a man she had not seen in several years?
- A young boy with less than one year of school would learn to read and make reading a habit?
- On an eight-hundred-mile voyage, a flatboat would become stranded precisely on the shore of a town with a debate club?
- A friend would offer him a fully stocked general store, entirely on credit?
- A farmer would sell him an old barrel containing a complete set of the Blackstone Commentaries?
- A prominent attorney would make a complete law library available to him?
- The top Law Firm in Illinois would offer a partnership to an inexperienced rookie?
- A railroad would pay an astronomical sum for winning a single case?
- A sitting United States Senator would agree to debate a no-name lightweight?
- The City of Chicago would embrace a simple rail- splitter?
- The first Republican Convention would be held in his home state?
- The powers in Chicago would rig the convention to ensure "Honest Abe's" nomination?
- And the Democrats would split in two, leaving a path for a virtually unknown to walk away with the presidency?

Luck or Providence? What do you think?

Lincoln's Reading List

Title...Author

Life of Washington..Mason Locke Weems
Aesop's Fables..Aesop
The Arabian Nights...............Compiled by Sir Richard Francis Burton
Slavery, Discussed in Original Essays............................Leonard Bacon
History of the U.S. ....George Bancroft
Editorials...Henry Ward Beecher
The Bible..Compiled by King James
Commentaries on the Law.......................William Blackstone
The Pilgrim's Progress..John Bunyan
Poems...Robert Burns
Poems.. Lord Byron
Don Juan...Lord Byron
New and Complete System of Arithmetic.......................Nicholas Pike
Elements of Character.....................................Mary Chandler
Speeches...Henry Clay
Robinson Crusoe...Daniel Defoe
A New Guide to the English Tongue.......................Thomas Dilworth
Journals and Debates of the Federal Constitution........Jonathan Elliot
Geometry...Euclid
Sociology for the South...................................George Fitzhugh
History of Illinois..Thomas Ford
Autobiography of Benjamin Franklin.....................Benjamin Franklin
Decline and Fall of the Roman Empire ....Edward Gibbon
The Theory and Practice of Surveying ....Robert Gibson
Fanny, With Other Poems................................Fitz Greene Halleck
Poems ....Oliver Wendell Holmes
Poems..Thomas Hood
Mormonism..John Hyde
Joe Miller's Book of Jests...Joe Miller
Commentaries on American Law................................James Kent
Poem...William Knox
Poems...Henry Wadsworth Longfellow
Complete Works...Edgar Allen Poe

"When you reach the end of your rope,
tie a knot and hang on."
~ **Abraham Lincoln**

THE GREATEST SALESMAN

Summarized from a speech by Og Mandino

Augustine Mandino, who was affectionately known as Og, is one of America's most beloved authors. His book, "The Greatest Salesman in the World," has sold millions of copies worldwide and continues to sell more than 100,000 copies monthly! Yet his story had a shaky, almost fatal, beginning.

Og's loving mother had a big dream for her little boy. *"Someday,"* she told him, *"You are going to become a writer. Not just any writer, but a great writer!"* Little Og would smile and agree.

To help lay the foundation for her son's future, Mrs. Mandino would take Og to visit the public library. He enjoyed those visits and relished picking out the books his mother would read him. Even before he started elementary school, Og was exposed to information on an assortment of advanced subjects, including becoming an author.

While attending school, he wrote short stories to show his mom for her approval. And when he was a high school senior, he served as his school's newspaper editor.

Mandino's mother planned for him to attend the "University of Missouri" because it had one of America's best journalism schools. But those plans were tragically thwarted when his precious mother suddenly died weeks after his high school graduation.

Og, struggling to deal with his mother's death, took a job in a paper factory rather than attending college. A few months later, the United States entered World War II, and Og joined the Army Air Corps. Military life suited him well, and he quickly moved up the ranks. He became an officer and earned his silver wings. As a bombardier, Mandino flew thirty missions over Germany.

After the war, he returned to the States and started looking for employment. But there were few jobs for bombardiers with only a high school diploma. After many months of endless searching, he found himself selling life insurance.

His sales income gave him the courage to propose to an old girlfriend, and he attempted to settle into family life. But the next ten years didn't go well for him or his family. Even though he worked long hours trying to make sales, his expenses were more than his commissions, causing his debts to mount.

Discouraged, he started stopping at bars to drown his problems. With time his drinking escalated and became so bad his wife took his daughter and left. Og's heart was broken. Lonely, broke, and addicted to alcohol, Og lived in a daze. He did odd jobs to earn enough for his next drink. His downward spiral eventually led to homelessness and a sidewalk for a bed.

Having hit rock-bottom; one cold winter morning, he happened by a pawn shop. Glancing in the window, he spotted a small handgun. The price on the handle read $29.00. He pulled out three ten-dollar bills from his pocket, all he had left in the world.

> *"There's the answer to all my problems. I'll buy that gun, put it to my head, and pull the trigger! Then I'll never have to face that miserable failure in the mirror again."*

Luckily, he decided not to buy the gun and continued to walk in the snow. After a while, his eyes were drawn to a sign, "Public Library." Suddenly, his mind was flooded with memories of how his mother would take him to the library when he was a young boy. And he remembered how she read to him and told him, "Someday, you will become a great author."

Mandino turned and entered the building. Inside, the warmth was comforting, and as he walked through the stacks, the surroundings felt familiar. Wandering around, looking at the books, he felt drawn to a particular area. When he looked up, he'd stopped in front of the self-help section. Picking out a few volumes, he took them to a table and began to read.

He searched for answers to,

> *"Where have I gone wrong? Can someone find success with only a high school education? Is there still hope for me? What about my drinking? Is it too late?"*

His library visit was the first of many as he searched for meaning in his life.

Soon, reading became an everyday habit. He read hundreds of books about success, self-motivation, and people who struggled but came back to impact the world. He also read about becoming an author. Before long, his drinking started to subside. During one library visit, he discovered *Success Through a Positive Mental Attitude* by W. Clement Stone. Reading that book was the turning point in his life!

Mandino was so impressed with Stone's philosophy of success that he decided to go to work for him. Carefully examining the pages, he found Stone's company address and mailed a letter seeking a position. Days later, he received an application for an opening. After returning it, Og was hired.

At his new job, he strove to make a positive impression. Within a year, he received a promotion and was assigned a territory. So, Og went to work hiring young potato farmers and teaching them to sell insurance, applying Stone's philosophy. In no time, his team was breaking company records.

Thinking ahead, Og rented a typewriter and produced a sales manual, *How to Sell Insurance in Rural Areas*. Then he sent the manual to Combined Insurance's home office and prayed someone there would read it and recognize his talent. Someone did!

Mandino was summoned to the company's headquarters and assigned to the sales promotion department. His job was writing bulletins. At last, he was writing!

Mr. Stone was the publisher of a small publication called *Success Unlimited*, which he circulated to his employees and shareholders. After Og spent several months in the home office, the editor of Success Unlimited retired. Although he knew nothing about magazine editing, Og applied for the job.

Not only did he get the position, but Stone also gave him a new mission. He asked Og to convert the paper from an in- house instrument into a national magazine. He was given an unlimited budget and the option to take whatever steps he needed to accomplish that goal.

Under Mandino's direction, the magazine's readership grew along with his staff. On the day he took over, only a handful of readers and two employees were there. By his tenth year, paid circulation grew to over a quarter million, and his staff to sixty-two!

Shortly after becoming editor, the magazine needed an additional article. So Og worked all night and wrote a piece about Ben Hogan. A short time later, fate took over, and he received a letter from a New York publisher. The letter said that the article was excellent and believed Og had talent. It also stated that should Og write a book, their publishing company would like to review it.

Eighteen months later, *The Greatest Salesman in the World* was published. Since no one had heard of Og Mandino, the first printing was only 5,000 copies. Then, another miracle happened.

In a speech to the Amway Corporation's National Convention, their President, Rich DeVos, recommended reading this new book. He told them that it would help them and motivate their entire sales organization!

This triggered an unbelievable number of sales and spurred numerous reprints. In only two years, the book's sales reached 350,000. Then Bantam Books made Og an offer he couldn't refuse. They purchased the paperback rights, and Mandino received a check for, in his words, *"More money than I knew existed."*

The Greatest Salesman in the World became a classic. Even now, many years after its publication, it continues to sell more than 100,000 copies a month.

Og's mother had a dream and instilled in her son the desire to become a great writer. That desire guided him to succeed despite the obstacles life placed in his pathway.

"Failure will never overtake me if my
determination to succeed is strong enough."
~ Og Mandino

"YOU DON'T HAVE WHAT IT TAKES TO BE A COACH!"

Louis (Lou) Holtz was born in the late 1930s, raised a Roman Catholic, and attended East Liverpool High School in Ohio. Lou was a gifted high school football player, and after graduation, he dreamed of attending his favorite college, Notre Dame.

Most boys who played football in a Catholic school or worshiped in the Catholic Church wanted to play for The Fighting Irish. Lou was no exception, but he was too small to be considered for a team of their caliber. So, Holtz attended Kent State University.

While at KSU, he decided he wanted to become a football coach. And in 1960, he started his coaching career as a graduate assistant. Lou always set his goals high, made a strong commitment, and took the necessary steps to achieve them. Although Holtz planned to become a great coach, his true passion was to someday become the Head Coach at, you guessed it, Notre Dame! Though, no one other than him believed he could fulfill that lofty dream.

In college football, there are only a handful of genuinely elite programs. Programs with rich histories and great traditions. Teams like the Alabama Crimson Tide, Ohio State Buckeyes, Oklahoma Sooners, and Notre Dame Fighting Irish.

Some of the greatest college coaches in history had roamed the sidelines of Notre Dame Stadium. Knute Rockne (with 105 Irish wins), Frank Leahy, and Ara Parseghian were among them. So setting a goal of becoming Notre Dame's coach was comparable to dreaming of becoming the Pope! And, his chances were about the same.

As with the Pope, a coach had to have something special to be considered for an Irish coaching position. Yet Lou dreamed his dream and never took the odds into account. He just started to move toward his goal and did his best every day.

In 1960, Holtz started coaching as a graduate assistant at Iowa State, followed by staff positions at William & Mary and Connecticut. Then in 1966, he landed an assistant coaching position for the South Carolina Gamecocks.

Lou was on his way, but at the end of his first year as a real coach, not only was he fired, the Gamecock's head coach told him,

"You better get out of coaching because you just don't have what it takes to be a coach!"

Lou held to his dream despite the setback and did what all successful people do. He got up, dusted off his britches, and moved forward.

Note: Elite college football programs offer their coaches many benefits that other colleges cannot; a huge salary, a large staff, the best facilities and equipment, and the cream of the recruiting crop.

Holtz put out the word that he was available to several prominent schools, and miraculously (one of those elite programs), Ohio State hired him as an assistant. That fall, with the help of Lou, The Buckeyes won college football's *National Championship!*

With a championship on his resume, Lou's stock was on the rise, and he was soon hired to be the Head Coach for the Tribe at William & Mary. While there, he led his new team to the *Southern Conference* title and a trip to the *Tangerine Bowl*, prompting more offers.

In 1972, a larger school, North Carolina State, came knocking. Lou's coaching success continued with the Wolfpack, and he stacked up a winning record during his four seasons there.

The Wolfpack earned Top 20 rankings for the next three seasons, including one Top 10 finish in 1974. NC State was invited to four bowl games and was the *ACC Champion* in 1973. Lou's win-loss record there was the best in Wolfpack history.

In 1976 Holtz became a head coach in the National Football League with The New York Jets. But he wasn't happy coaching professional football. Lou missed working with and helping build the character of young college students. So the following year, he accepted an offer to coach for the Arkansas Razorbacks.

Lou was back in his element and happy to be molding the Razorbacks into a quality team. His coaching philosophy instilled honesty, character, integrity, and teamwork in his players. By the end of the '77 regular season, the Razorbacks boasted a 10-win, 1-loss record, earning them an invitation to the *Orange Bowl Classic*, a major bowl.

Lou's Razorbacks were scheduled to face the nation's #2 team, The Oklahoma Sooners (one of those elite programs). Holtz was excited, for a good showing against a highly ranked team would be an opportunity for him to be noticed by Notre Dame. However, he understood a bad loss on a stage so big could quickly derail his ultimate goal.

The coach knew his team would face a tremendous challenge, yet he remained optimistic about their chances. Holtz faced many obstacles, i.e., his Razorbacks were plagued with injuries, leaving them weak in critical areas. Yet The Sooners had possibly the best offense in the nation, and their roster was packed with big-name 5 Star players.

Barry Switzer and his Sooners would be playing for a chance to win a *National Championship* with a win over the battered Razorbacks. Lou's Arkansas team was coming off a losing season from the year before. Plus, none of his players had experienced playing in a game of such magnitude.

Though the odds were stacked against him, the coach was confident his Razorbacks would make it a competitive game. However, the sports media did not agree! They also knew of Arkansas's challenges, and every sports commentator pronounced The Hogs dead on arrival. They all projected The Sooners would be much too powerful for the upstart Razorbacks. Holtz ignored their rhetoric and continued preparing his team for the impending battle.

Then, disaster struck! Three Arkansas players were found with a woman in their Miami hotel room two days before the *Orange Bowl*. They had broken strict team rules. And to make matters worse, they were the team's best offensive players.

Holtz was saddened by what occurred and burdened with a decision no coach would ever want to make. Two of the guilty players had produced 78% of "The Razorback's" offense that year. The team's chances against Oklahoma would dramatically increase if Lou allowed these players to stay. Yet if he sent them home, there was a good chance his team would be taken apart by the mighty Sooners. To add to his dilemma, the entire Razorback nation, the school's administration, and many influential Arkansas politicians urged Holtz to play the three offenders.

Lou knew sending the boys home would probably cost him his job and his Notre Dame dream. His decision couldn't have been easy; the team rules were clear, and the punishment was spelled out. Bravely, Coach Holtz chose to make the right rather than the popular choice and dismissed the players.

When the sport's media learned of Lou's decision, in unison, they insisted that The Razorbacks step aside and let a more worthy opponent play the powerful Sooners.

But despite enormous pressure, Holtz never gave a thought to the media or even his superiors. He pulled his team together and prepared them for the approaching monumental task. Lou clung to the hope that the game might still be competitive, with the right game plan and every Razorback's commitment.

But, according to the Las Vegas oddsmakers, Arkansas was an 18-point underdog before the suspensions. With the suspensions in place, the point spread rose to 24 points. The college football world was keenly aware the *Orange Bowl* would likely decide the *National Championship*, and it did!

On bowl day, the talking heads quickly pointed out why Arkansas didn't have a prayer of winning. They even belittled the coach for his selfish decision to compete.

But, once the game started, it was evident that the Razorback's Defense was tired of hearing how the Sooner's superior offense was too good for the little Arkansas team. Or, perhaps, those young men were inspired by a tremendously influential leader! Either way, those Razorbacks came to play that day!! And, they played with a mighty vengeance!!

Despite the Oklahoma O taking a significant beating, they still managed to move the ball up and down the field. Although anytime they approached the red zone (the last 20 yards before the goal line), the Razorback's D shut them down, or worse, forced them to fumble and took away the ball!

By the end of the first quarter, the Sooners had fumbled three times and given up the ball twice. After each turnover, the crippled Razorback Offense scored! Then, in the second quarter, if anything, the Arkansas defense got stronger. By halftime, the score stood 14 to 0 in Arkansas' favor.

The Sooners were still not too concerned, for the bigger and better team usually wears down the lesser team to make a strong showing in the second half. Only the Razorbacks had other plans and added an additional 10 points in the third period. When Oklahoma scored a touchdown early in the fourth, they failed to make the extra point which exhausted what steam the Sooners had remaining.

Yet the depleted Razorbacks hadn't finished. With another touchdown, their second and third-string offenses drove the last nail in Oklahoma's coffin. By the end of the game, Arkansas had matched the mighty Sooner's O yard for yard throughout the game.

The final score was Arkansas 31, Oklahoma 6. "The Razorbacks" ended their season ranked number two in the nation behind the Mighty Crimson Tide of Alabama (Roll Tide!). Oklahoma dropped to number four. That *Orange Bowl* game is still remembered as the biggest upset in Razorback football history.

Coach Holtz had made a statement that echoed throughout the college football world. Lou Holtz was not one to be taken lightly by his players, opponents, or the sports media. And more importantly, his Notre Dame dream was still alive.

Under Holtz, Arkansas experienced its best win-loss record in its history despite playing a demanding Southwest Conference schedule. During his seven seasons at Arkansas, the Razorbacks played in six bowl games and piled up 60 victories.

For years, Lou's decision to send the players home continued to haunt him even after that win. Then, at the end of his first down season, his political enemies pressured the university to let him go. But, with Lou's strong record, finding a new position was easy.

Unfortunately, the Notre Dame position wasn't available, so Lou accepted when a call came from the University of Minnesota to take over the Golden Gophers. But his acceptance had a few conditions.

Holtz agreed to become UM's coach with a back-door clause stating, *"If the Golden Gophers are invited to a bowl within two seasons and should Notre Dame call, Lou would be allowed to leave."*

Keep in mind that the Golden Gophers were coming off a 10-loss season, and the Irish hadn't indicated they wanted Holtz. So, those conditions must have seemed reasonable to Minnesota. Yet, two years later, after the Gophers earned a trip to the Independence Bowl, the Fighting Irish asked Holtz to become their new Head Coach.

Lou had achieved his dream. However, that's not the whole story. You see, though College football was important to Notre Dame, the school also wanted its players to be taught *honesty, character, integrity, and teamwork*. So their decision to hire Holtz was not a new one. It was made eight years earlier, in 1978. Yet it was not decided after that big Orange Bowl win.

It was decided *before* the *Orange Bowl* game when Coach Holtz chose to do the right thing and dismissed his best players. Notre Dame officials believed a man with such character and integrity would make an excellent coach for their beloved Irish, and they were right!

During Holtz's tenure at Notre Dame, his teams were victorious 100 times, only five wins short of Knute Rockne's record. The Fighting Irish won it all in his third season and were crowned the *National Champions of College Football*.

Lou's teams also broke school records with a 23-game winning streak from 1988-1989 and a 17-game streak from 1992-1993. 1991 through 93 saw the Irish register three consecutive bowl wins. Coach Holtz also took Notre Dame to nine straight bowls and won five of them.

When Lou retired, he'd coached the Irish in more games than any other coach in the school's history. He'd won one National Championship and had two near-misses. In 1977 and 1988, he was named National Coach of the Year.

Lou took every team he coached to at least one bowl game. He's the only coach in NCAA history who took six different teams to bowls, won bowls with five different teams, and had four different teams end their seasons in the top 20. Coach Holtz accomplished all that despite never inheriting a winning team.

Holtz also took 22 teams to bowls and won 12 (tying the fifth-best bowl record of all time). His career record of 249 wins placed him among the top ten coaches in college football history.

In 2008, Lou Holtz was inducted into the College Football Hall of Fame. Not bad for a guy who "Didn't have what it takes to be a college football coach!"

*"I don't think it's about who you play.
I think it's about who you are."*
~ Nick Saban

HE WANTED TO
BE ON TV

Summarized from a speech by Steve Harvey

Broderick Steven **"Steve" Harvey** was born, the youngest of five children, in the late nineteen fifties. His father, a coal miner, struggled to feed his large family. When Steve was still a small boy, the family moved to Cleveland in search of a better life.

With little money and many mouths to feed, neighborhood choices were limited, so Steve was raised in an undesirable part of the city.

Stevie, as he was called then, suffered from stuttering, a severe speech disorder. Because of this, the local kids bullied and made fun of him, causing him to stay home much of the time. The little boy loved watching television and dreamed he would be on TV one day.

When he was in the sixth grade, his teacher gave the class an assignment: *"Write what you want to be when you grow up."* Having always had a hard time in school, Stevie saw this as a chance to win a star. So he turned in, what he believed would be, the best answer in his class.

Confident that his teacher would be impressed, he wrote. *"When I grow up, I want to be on TV!"* Stevie couldn't wait for the teacher to see his paper because he was convinced he'd be getting a star. However, when the teacher called out the names, she called him last. *"Steven, come to the front of the class."* Smiling, he strutted to the front of the room to receive his award.

But instead of complimenting him, she told him that his dream was absurd, especially for someone who could barely complete a sentence. She even accused him of not taking her assignment seriously. Of course, the other children laughed. Then, as if things weren't already bad enough, the teacher called his mother and reported, *"Steven is being a smart aleck!"*

The child was devastated and knew he'd be in trouble at home. He was right! His mother angrily warned, *"You just wait till your father gets home, young man!"* Stevie was terrified. Although, when his father heard the story, he exclaimed, *"What's wrong with that?!"*

Waiting in his room while his parents talked, little Stevie was certain he'd be severely punished. But, when his father entered the room, he didn't seem upset. Instead, he hugged Steve and told him, *"Son, this is your paper. You take your paper and keep it in this drawer, and when you get up every morning, read it out loud. Then before you go to bed every night, read it again. That's your dream, Steve, don't ever let anyone take it from you!"*

The child diligently followed his father's instructions and read the paper twice a day until it was no longer needed. Eventually, he graduated high school and enrolled at "The University of West Virginia." However, he dropped out before receiving a degree to pursue a career in show business.

In the years that followed, Young Harvey worked many odd jobs. He sold insurance, delivered mail, and did some boxing. But, through it all, he read that paper daily. In his spare time, he developed comedy skits. And when he felt ready, he quit his job and started performing comedy routines. He even recorded an audition tape.

Despite his best efforts, by the age of 27, he'd hit rock bottom and was ready to give up show business. For the past three years, Harvey had given it everything he had, only to end up broke and living in his car. The young comedian decided to ask his father to let him move into his attic until he could find a job.

But, the last time he left home, his father told him he couldn't come back; and that he needed to learn to take care of himself. It seemed he hadn't learned much, as he was homeless and almost broke.

Steve visited high-class hotels with cloth hand towels in their restrooms to stay clean. There he could soap up with hot water, wipe off in a stall, and when the coast was clear, he'd grab more towels to dry.

But one day, Steve was trapped inside a stall when a convention ended early. Crying, he decided to beg his father to let him come back. Luckily, his parents allowed him to use their answering machine. So before calling home, he first checked his calls. To his great surprise, there was a message from *Showtime at the Apollo*. *"If you can come to New York on Saturday, you can be on TV on Sunday."*

"Wow, Showtime at the Apollo! That's my dream!!" Unfortunately, Steve only had $35.00, and New York was hundreds of miles away. So he couldn't even afford to buy the gas to drive there. Again, he cried, *"Oh God, how could you do this to me? I finally have a shot to be on TV, and I can't go? I've been waiting my whole life for this! God, can you please just give me a break?!"* And suddenly, he heard a voice saying, *"Steve, get up. I'm going to take you places you've never been."*

So Harvey called the answering machine again, hoping it hadn't said "this week." Listening closely, he heard… *"Steve Harvey, this is Chuck Sutton with 'Showtime at the Apollo.' We saw your tape and have an opening for you this Sunday. If you can get here, give me a call. We'd love to put you on TV."*

Sadly, he started to hang up the phone when he heard another beep. A new message! It was from Tom Sobel of the "Comedy Caravan." *"Steve, there's a gig available in Jacksonville on Friday night, and it will pay $150.00 if you want it."*

He thought, *"Friday, that's tomorrow--in Jacksonville! I can make it there!"* So the following night, Steve opened in Jacksonville and earned $150.00. Then the club owner told him, *"You're better than the guy I have now, and if you stay another night, I'll give you an additional $150.00."*

With $300.00 in his pocket, he called Chuck Sutton back to see if there was still an opening. Fortunately, there was, and Steve purchased a round-trip ticket to New York for $99.00.

Sunday morning at 11 am, Harvey showed up at the *Apollo Theater* in New York with everything he owned in a plastic bag. Since the theater was in Harlem, the manager allowed him to spend the day in a dressing room. That evening, the other acts began to arrive. They were all future big-name stars. Great comedians Jamie Fox, D L Hughley, Dwayne Johnson, and others.

That night's audience was ruthless; if they didn't like you, you were toast. Scheduled to go on last, Steve could only watch as every act was booed from the stage! But, he was determined not to waste this opportunity. And late that night, as he walked on the stage to face the brutal crowd, Steve flashed a big smile and proceeded to put on a show that tamed the savage beast.

When he finished, that rowdy horde rewarded him with a thunderous standing ovation adorned with hoots and whistles. Tears of joy ran down his cheeks as he stood in awe of what had just happened.

Only three days before, he was broke and ready to quit. Now, he had $1,000.00, and his star was rising. Sure enough, that night's triumph didn't go unnoticed.

A short time later, he was called back to the Apollo to MC their amateur night. Again, Steve was a hit. Then the theater hired him to host *Saturday Night at the Apollo*. Steve Harvey was on TV every weekend for the next eight years and became the show's longest-running host.

So Little Stevie, with the stuttering problem and the ridiculous dream, not only got his star, he was on TV! His dream came true, and today, Steve Harvey is the most-watched television personality in the United States and probably the entire world.

Oh yes, that sixth-grade teacher, the one who thought his paper was absurd; from that point on, every Christmas, "Stevie" sent her a new big screen television, so she could see him on TV!

"In my whole life, I have known no wise people who didn't read all the time! None!!"
~ Charles T. Munger

"*Education is the ticket to success.*"

Jamie Escalante

FULLER'S GAMBLE

A notable Black History superstar is the Mid-Twentieth Century industrialist **Samuel B. Fuller. Fuller** was one of the most respected businessmen of his time. But, all of his fame and fortune couldn't have happened had he not been willing to risk everything on a single gamble.

In 1895, Samuel B. Fuller was born into a family of nine. His Louisiana sharecropper parents struggled to get by as poor blacks in the Deep South. SB's mom often told him,

> "We are not poor because of God. We are poor because your father never developed a desire to become rich! And because no one in our family has ever desired to be anything else."

The young lad took his mother's guidance to heart and dreamed of becoming wealthy and successful one day. Forced to drop out of school after the sixth grade, SB supplemented his family's income with door-to-door sales.

While still a young man, Fuller hitchhiked to Chicago in search of better prospects. The big city did have more to offer, and in the following years, he worked for several companies in succession. Each job change represented a promotion until he was granted a quality management position in an insurance company. Fuller was doing well, but he knew he would never become wealthy and successful working for someone else. So, when the opportunity to purchase a direct sales business appeared, he resigned from his position, invested his savings ($25.00) in that business, and struck out on his own.

For twelve years, he worked to develop his customer base. Then, using $1,000 of his profits, he formed the "Fuller Products Company." The success of that company and SB's knowledge of his products earned him the respect of many business people in the Chicago area.

Although his company was small, Fuller continued to dream of making it big. He always saved a portion of his earnings to take advantage should another opening appear. That day arrived when SB learned that his supplier was selling their chemical manufacturing company.

The business was offered at $150,000.00, and the sale had to take place within two weeks. Fuller recognized this as his next big opportunity, so he immediately placed a down payment of $25,000.00 (everything he had, more than $360,000.00 in 2022 money). The purchase contract stated, *"The deposit will be forfeited should the sale not be completed in fourteen days."*

Everything was on the line, his money, his business, and his future. Yet SB was confident he could raise the needed $125,000.00 in the following two weeks. Fuller was a respected businessman with a good knowledge of his trade. So without much effort, he found several investors willing to take a chance on him. However, his list of potential lenders dwindled as the due date approached.

And, by the evening of the final day, he had exhausted every possible source of funds. Yet he'd only raised $115,000, leaving him $10,000 short (or about $150,000 in 2022 money).

Consequently, as the sun's light slowly evaporated from the streets of Chicago, SB's dreams were also diminishing.

Fuller's faith began to falter with the closing set for the following day. Then, the words of his mother came back to him. "*We are not poor because of God. We are poor because no one in our family has ever developed a desire to be anything else!*"

With that, SB adjusted his attitude, and with a new and even stronger determination, he resumed his quest. "*God, help me!*" He prayed. "*Where can I find that kind of money this late at night?*" Continuing to drive down the dark streets of Chicago, he had just turned down 61st Street when suddenly, in the distance, he spotted a solitary light shining from an office window. It was eleven p.m. when Fuller pulled over and exited his car.

As he approached the light, he realized he had been to this office before. It belonged to a contractor friend. As he knocked and slowly pushed open the door, a startled man inside called out, "*Is that you, SB?*"

Fuller announced himself and wasted no time getting down to business. He explained his plans for the new company and displayed the money he had raised from the other investors. When he finished, the contractor studied Fuller's face for a few seconds. Then he opened a drawer, took out a checkbook, and handed SB a check for $10,000.00.

"*I'm making you a loan on the condition you pay back this amount and an additional $1,000.00 in interest.*" SB agreed, thanked his friend, and purchased the chemical manufacturing business the following day.

A few months later, the loan and the $1,000.00 were repaid in full. In fact, each of his investors received excellent returns on their investments. SB Fuller propelled his soap manufacturing business into a multi-million-dollar conglomerate with more than $10 million in yearly sales and eventually opened offices in 38 states.

Fuller became so respected in the business community that he was made the first black member of The National Association of Manufacturers.

SB Fuller had a dream and the courage to make his dream come true!

*"In our space, in our time, we can and
must make a difference."*
~ SB Fuller

THE TEACHER

Alfonso Escalante Gutiérrez was born in La Paz, Bolivia, in 1930. His parents were both teachers. They separated when he was a small boy, and he was raised by his mother. In school, Jamie, as he was called, was a fast learner, mischievous, and often in trouble.

After high school and a short stint in the Bolivian Army, Escalante considered entering engineering school. Still, his burning desire was to teach and help young people better their lives. So instead, Jamie enrolled in the Bolivian State Teachers College. While there, he met and married Fabiola Tapia, a fellow student. After receiving his degree in education, he spent the following eleven years teaching math and science at three of Bolivia's finest schools. But Fabiola wanted her children to have a better life and pressed Jaime to move the family to America. At her urging, with only $3,000.00 and no English skills, Escalante left his excellent teaching positions and moved to Los Angeles.

Once in California, he searched for work. Yet his poor English made finding a good job difficult, but finally, he secured a position mopping floors in a diner. Fortunately, Pasadena City College, which taught language classes, was across the street from the restaurant. So, Jamie enrolled and focused on English. After a few weeks of cleaning floors, he was moved into the kitchen and received a pay increase. With his

English rapidly improving, he signed up for additional courses in math and physics.

After only a few months, he was accepted to an electronics company position. Though he enjoyed his new job and received excellent pay, he still had a burning desire to help young people.

However, he would need new degrees and a teaching certificate to teach in California. So Escalante studied during his free time. His excellent grades reflected his devotion, so when he applied to Cal State Los Angeles, they offered him a full scholarship.

Breezing through the education courses, Jamie earned his degree and teaching credentials the following year. At age 43, he chose to take a sizable pay cut to become a math teacher at Garfield High School in East Los Angeles.

A teacher's salary was a fraction of what he'd been earning, and his friends told him he was crazy. But he really wanted to help young people become successful. So Jamie chose to fulfill his dream over better pay.

The Garfield student body consisted of lower-income Mexican American students. A few years earlier, the school had almost lost its accreditation and the right to stay open. Other struggles included dealing with illegal drugs, gangs, and violence.

Escalante's first day was disappointing. He found he'd been scheduled to teach the lowest math level and that the textbooks were inadequate. But those things paled in comparison to his students.

His entire class lived in impoverished Latino neighborhoods with little or no family support. He also observed that their other teachers had no confidence in them and didn't believe them to be teachable. If those things weren't bad enough, discipline at the school was almost nonexistent.

Jaime soon realized that the last thing his students cared about was math!

After only one day, he seriously considered returning to his "good job." However, his desire to teach young people outweighed his disappointment. And when he found a dozen basic math students willing to take algebra, he decided not to return to the computer factory.

In his quest to realize his dream, Jamie faced many challenges. The children were far below their grade level in academic skills and had numerous social and family problems. They also faced constant negativity from their friends, relatives, and even the other teachers. Garfield's instructors were not interested in Escalante's dreams or their students. Yet, Jamie did have two allies. He had the support and encouragement of his principal and one school counselor.

Escalante swam against the tide for the next few years. He pushed the kids to work hard and told them, "*Basic math is too easy for bright young Latinos. You can do much more!*" He believed in them and told them they could be great if they had "Ganas" (a burning desire)!

Kemo, as the students came to call him (short for Kemosabe or trusted friend), worked to connect with his classes through encouragement and humor. After many months of patience and caring, he started getting through to some hard-to- motivate students. He told them, "*You don't count how many times you are on the floor. You count how many times you get up!*" Each year his pupils improved, and in his fifth year, he started an advanced calculus class for a small group of handpicked students.

Although these children were not adequately prepared, he taught the class anyway. He believed an Advanced Placement (AP) Calculus Course would motivate his lower-level math classes. The AP program was a college-level calculus course to prepare students for the nation's most challenging college entrance exam. A test so difficult that only

2% of the nation's graduating seniors would even attempt it.

Jaime's plan was a success, and in 1979, two of his five calculus students passed the AP test. The following year, nine tested, and seven passed. Then in 81, fifteen took it, and 14 passed. But what happened the next year was so incredible that Hollywood turned the story into the movie *Stand and Deliver!*

In 1982, eighteen of Kemo's students took the Advanced Placement Calculus Exam, and all eighteen passed! Of course, there were cheers, high fives, and chest bumps! But that celebration didn't last long.

When the Educational Testing Service officials looked at Jaime's students' scores and reviewed Garfield's history, they didn't believe the results were accurate. They even accused the kids of cheating and threatened to nullify the test's results!

Escalante was furious and asserted the AP representatives were prejudiced against poor Hispanics from a small school. But the officials would not back down. So, Jamie came up with an effective plan to refute their allegations. He asked his students to retake the test. And this time, AP administrators could watch. Though the reps initially shunned his plan, they reluctantly agreed when twelve students registered to retake the test.

With only 24 hours to prepare, his students retook the tests while AP administrators watched. Not only did they pass, but they also scored higher the second time!! With that, it became abundantly clear that Kemo's students were the real deal and that those "officials" had egg on their faces.

As newspapers and television networks picked up this story, Escalante was recognized as the exceptional teacher he was, and he received many teaching awards. And when the President of the United States read of his accomplishments, Jaime Escalante was awarded the *Presidential Medal of Excellence in Education*. Finally, the movie about his accomplishments served to inspire teachers throughout the world.

Kemo's kids eventually became engineers, scientists, and university professors. His advanced math program was even more successful in the following years. By 1987, one out of every four students in America who passed the AP Calculus exams were Jaime's students.

His dream of helping young people improve their lot in life was fulfilled. And, years later, when he became ill, the children he'd helped lift from poverty donated tens of thousands of dollars to pay for his medical bills.

> *"One of the greatest things you have in life is that no one has the authority to tell you what you want to be.*
>
> *You're the one who'll decide what you want to be. Respect yourself and respect the integrity of others as well. The greatest thing you have is your self-image, a positive opinion of yourself. You must never let anyone take that from you." Jaime Escalante*

"Education is the ticket to success."
~ Jamie Escalante

A BOY'S CRAZY DREAM

Arnold Schwarzenegger became Mr. Olympia, a Hollywood superstar, and the Governor of California. His accomplishments have been recognized worldwide, yet none of those successes came easy. As Arnold took on and overcame numerous obstacles, he never lost focus on his dreams.

Schwarzenegger grew up in a small town in Austria. His strict father, the chief of police, wanted him to also become a policeman. But Arnold didn't want to be a cop and rebelled against his father's rules. The young boy was good at sports, especially soccer and skiing, yet when he discovered bodybuilding at 15, he dropped the other sports.

He would frequent gyms, lift weights, and he loved reading articles and looking at pictures in bodybuilding magazines. He dreamed of one day competing and becoming a bodybuilding champion. Sometimes he would even break into his high school gym to work out.

One weekend Arnold saw the movie *Hercules*, starring Reg Park. Park was the greatest bodybuilder of the time, and Schwarzenegger wanted to be exactly like him. So, when he learned Reg used bodybuilding to become a movie star, Arnold developed a burning desire to do the same.

Think of that, a young boy in a small village, half a world away from America, having so bold a dream!

When Arnold told his friends, "*I am going to be the world's greatest bodybuilder,*" they laughed, "*You're just a skinny kid. You're crazy!*" Arnold ignored them and passionately stuck to his goal. Nothing was going to get in his way.

When a bodybuilder magazine published Reg Park's workout routine, Arnold resolved to adopt it for his own. The other weightlifters at his gym were puzzled by the extent of Schwarzenegger's workouts. They warned him that he might injure himself if he didn't slow down. However, Arnold did not listen. Their admonitions only made him work harder.

Schwarzenegger studied everything he could find about bodybuilding and developed a detailed plan for achieving his goals. Six days a week, he pushed himself to the limit. And he was making astonishing progress when his father stepped in. Concerned for his son, he asked, "*Why have you chosen to do bodybuilding instead of skiing or soccer?*"

"*I'm not interested in those sports, and I'm going to become Austria's best bodybuilder! Then, I'm going to America to become the World's Greatest Bodybuilder!*"

Laughing, his father replied. "*What do you expect to accomplish from that?!*"

"*When I become the world's best bodybuilder, I will become the most famous Movie Star 'eva'!*"

Arnold's father shook his head and believed his son was crazy. When his mother heard what he'd planned, she almost fainted. So his parents took him to a psychiatrist, where they were told, "*Such ridiculous dreams are common with youngsters; with time, he will adapt to the real world.*"

To discourage him, his father cut his gym visits to three a week. Not to be dissuaded, Arnold turned his home into a gym. Using whatever he could find as weights, he continued to exercise every free minute, even riding his bicycle in the bitter cold. Finally, his father realized Arnold couldn't be stopped and let him go back to the gym.

By the time he was 18, Schwarzenegger had become one of Austria's most muscular men and undoubtedly the biggest in his age group.

After high school, he joined the Austrian Army. Soon after enlisting, he learned of the upcoming *Junior Mr. Europe Competition*. Recognizing this as his opportunity to become a champion, he requested leave. When the Army refused, Arnold was crushed! Yet, on competition day, his desire was so strong that he defied orders and competed anyway.

To say the least, the army officials were not pleased, and when he returned, having won *Junior Mr. Europe*, they didn't know what to do with him. Though they jailed him for 15 days, he'd earned their respect, and they often told the other soldiers, *"You should be focused like Schwarzenegger."*

The *Junior, Mr. Europe* title, got him noticed, and a Munich gym owner offered to sponsor his training. The gym gave Arnold everything he needed to compete. He trained hard and easily became *Mr. Europe*. Arnold started becoming famous and was invited to London to compete in the *Mr. Universe* competition.

In his first contest, he came in second. Undaunted, he was crowned *Mr. Universe, Europe*, the following year. He was moving up, but he knew his next competition would be a more significant challenge. The IFBB contest attracted the greatest bodybuilders in the world.

The head of that organization recognized Arnold's talent and sponsored a work visa for him to compete in America. At the *Mr. Universe* competition, he came in second to Frank Zane. Seeing that

Frank wasn't his size, he wondered if the competition was rigged.

Although, when he saw Zane's picture, Arnold realized he was more ripped and defined. So Schwarzenegger determined he would work to develop more definition in his muscles. The next year, he surpassed Zane; the following year, he became the IFBB *Mr. Universe*. This time, he also defeated his idol, Reg Park. But he knew he was still not at the top. There was an even bigger competition called *Mr. Olympia*.

Schwarzenegger knew that to fulfill his dream, he would have to become *Mr. Olympia!* But, in his first competition, he lost in a close decision to Sergio Oliva. Then Arnold swore he would put in the necessary training and come back.

The following year, he defeated Sergio and became Mr. Olympia, the pinnacle of competitive bodybuilding. Still, he was not finished and continued to win the title until he won it more times than anyone else. Having fulfilled that dream, he retired from bodybuilding to concentrate on becoming a famous movie star. Again, this challenge would be even more difficult.

While Schwarzenegger was still a competitive bodybuilder, he acted in a low-budget movie, *Hercules*. It was a flop, and he was ridiculed. Knowing the film was horrible, he resolved to improve his acting skills.

The next year, Arnold was cast in a few movies and even won a *Golden Globe* for best debut in a small role in *Stay Hungry*. He was also the subject of an award-winning documentary, *Pumping Iron*. Yet, the idea of him becoming a major star was farfetched at best.

Even though his roles got him some attention, his agents were amused when he told them he wanted a leading role. They told him he was dreaming and didn't have a chance. They said, *"Your name can hardly be pronounced. People will laugh when they see it on billboards,"* and they suggested he change it!

Arnold refused! "*I will become a star and do so using my real name!*"

Then they said, "*You have a weird body and are overbuilt. Stars need to be slim, plus you have a weird accent. You can't become a leading actor with that accent, and no production company will risk having you play a leading part.*"

Arnold was disappointed in the agents but not in himself. They only caused him to become more determined! He vowed to accomplish his "crazy dream," regardless of what others thought.

Improving his heavy accent was his first objective. Next, he strove to make himself more visible, actually managing to become a media darling as a celebrity bodybuilder. He appeared on TV game and talk shows and labored to keep himself in the public eye.

His efforts did not go unnoticed, and all Hollywood producers knew him. Anytime a super muscular man was cast for a leading role, Schwarzenegger would be among the front-runners.

In 1980, movie director John Milius got his mega project, *Conan the Barbarian*, approved for production. Milius was seeking a lead actor with a super muscular build. When Schwarzenegger's name came up, he was asked to audition. This time, Arnold was prepared. He'd reduced his accent and greatly improved his acting skills. He had the right build, and his audition convinced Milius that he was Conan!

After a year and a half of filming, *Conan the Barbarian* hit the theaters. It was a blockbuster, and Arnold Schwarzenegger, the movie star, was the talk of Hollywood. Suddenly, he was lauded for his physique, acting, and dialogue. Then, what remained of Arnold's accent became famous catchphrases. He'd also earned the respect of the industry for his decision to stick to his original name.

Everything his agents told him would be liabilities became his greatest strength. And now that he was a big star, all the agents were chasing him. But when those who had discouraged him reached out, he ignored them.

Following the movie's super success, Schwarzenegger received numerous offers to star in major films. In 1984, he was cast as the *Terminator*, a role that would make him an international mega-star. With the release of his second blockbuster, his dream of becoming a superstar was realized.

The boy whose dreams had been ridiculed and laughed at turned those dreams into reality. In the 1990s, Arnold became Hollywood's most prominent and highest-paid movie star. After the turn of the century, Schwarzenegger had enough of Hollywood and dove into politics. He was discounted and told he lacked political experience. Everyone said that he had no chance. But he again proved his critics wrong. Arnold was elected Governor of the State of California, not once but twice.

The most incredible thing about Arnold Schwarzenegger wasn't his physique. But instead, his ability to focus on and achieve his dreams.

"The mind is the limit. As long as the mind can envision the fact that you can do something, you can do it, as long as you really believe 100 percent."
~ Arnold Schwarzenegger

"DO YOU BELIEVE IN MIRACLES?"

In 1980, a hand-picked group of college hockey players battled their way to the Olympic semifinals in Lake Placid. That young team experienced its share of struggles leading up to those games.

Their Coach, **Herb Brooks**, passed over some of the nation's finest college hockey players to pick these youngsters. They were selected because of their character, psychological makeup, and how well they played their positions. Brooks' selection process included a 300-question test that gave him insight into how each player would react under stress. Anyone refusing the test was eliminated from consideration. His screening process was so unpopular with the US Olympic Committee that it almost cost him his position. But Brooks stood firm, the committee relented, and he remained as the coach.

Brooks knew endurance was the key to recent Olympic victories. So, he initiated a rigorous conditioning program, constantly pushing the young players to their physical limits. If a player complained, he was dropped from the team. Still, after a time, even his own assistants questioned his techniques. Yet, Brooks persisted.

The United States had experienced a rough patch in the years leading up to these games. A severe recession had drained most Americans' bank accounts, and having to wait in long gas lines had demoralized the rest. It was a low time for the country. A Soviet invasion of Afghanistan led the American President to the brink of boycotting these Olympic games. But, at the last minute, he decided to allow the athletes to participate, despite the tensions. If America's teams could only win a few medals, it might help break through the darkness and give Americans something to cheer about. However, no one anticipated a medal in hockey, not that year!

The seventh-seeded Americans were assumed the least likely of all the nations to medal. Yet, the young lineup surprised everyone by making it through the opening rounds undefeated. So a faint glimmer of hope flickered in the breasts of some of the American fans. But, few believed these kids had any chance at all.

Nearing the end of the games, the US team was scheduled to meet the Soviet team, which hadn't lost a game in twelve years. Everyone assumed that the Russians would give the upstart Americans a hockey lesson. Even though the US had managed four victories and a tie leading to this game, they were not considered a match for Russia.

The Soviet team had won four consecutive gold medals. They were led by legendary players Boris Mikhailov, team captain Vladislav Tretiak, the best goaltender in the world, by general consensus, and the speedy Valeri Kharlamov. Every Russian player was experienced and talented.

On the other hand, the American team's players' average age was only 21, making them the youngest hockey team in US Olympic history. Of the 20 players on their roster, Buzz Schneider was the only one returning from the previous Olympics. The other players only had college experience. Nine had played under Brooks at the University of Minnesota. Four, including goaltender Jim Craig, and US team captain, Mike Eruzione, played against him in an NCAA championship series.

To make matters worse, three days before the defining games, the Soviets soundly defeated the US in an exhibition match. And, they hadn't just defeated them; they had humiliated them by a score of 10 to 3. In an Olympic-level competition, scoring 10 goals was almost unheard of. So, the American fans were hoping to at least see a less embarrassing showing.

Coach Brooks didn't seem concerned by the low expectations and told his youngsters to ignore the doubters. *"Those Russians are people just like us. We can beat them! And, we will beat them if we only 'play our game'!"* In the locker room before the match, Brooks insisted, *"We could play these guys 10 times, and they would probably win 9 of them, but not tonight! This is our night!!"*

The Russian and American teams were natural rivals due to the decades-long Cold War between the two countries. Consequently, the Olympic Arena was packed, mostly with Americans, but Russia had a respectable following. Before the match, the home fans waved United States Flags and sang patriotic songs. In the locker room, Coach Brooks, honestly believing his team would win, read them a statement…

> *"You were born to be a player, and you were meant to be here. This is your moment; it's going to happen!"*

The Soviets had a reputation for dominating in the final period. So, to save energy, Brooks instructed his players to limit their shifts to 40 seconds or less. Then, he asked the team doctor to track the ice time for each player.

With heads held high, the young Americans entered the ice to face the Russian juggernaut in a David vs. Goliath duel. Once play began, it didn't take long for the Soviets to score. Although, seconds later, a fifty-foot blast from Buzz Schneider found its way to the net, sparking some hope in the hearts of the US fans. And a few chants of USA were heard from the stands. But that hope was dashed when the Russians immediately took back the lead.

With his team down, US Goalie Jim Craig narrowed his focus and turned away a myriad of Soviet shots. Then, in the waning moments of the first period, Dave Christian fired a laser from 100 feet, and though the Russian goalie saved the shot, he misplayed the rebound. With the loose puck bouncing on the ice, Mark Johnson slipped between two Soviet defenders and fired it past a diving Tretiak. That tied the match with just one second remaining on the clock.

Then something remarkable took place. Because the Americans tied the score, Coach Tikhonov stunned his team by sending in his backup goalie, Myshkin, to replace Tretiak. Brooks immediately took advantage of the move, telling his players, *"You just sat down the greatest goaltender in the world!"*

Two minutes into the second, the Soviets scored a third goal. Myshkin shut down the American's offense, and Russia dominated, outshooting the US 12–2. At the end of the second, the Russians led 3–2.

Beginning of the Third

The third period started as a defensive battle, with both teams successfully defending their goal. Near the middle of the period, a Russian was called for high-sticking and sent to the penalty box. This gave the Americans, who had managed only two shots in the last 27 minutes, a rare power- play opportunity.

Late in the penalty, after two misses, as Dave Silk advanced into the Soviet zone, he was knocked to the ice causing the puck to bounce to Johnson. Mark turned and blasted a winner under Myshkin, tying the game.

Two shifts later, Pavelich slid a pass to an undefended Eruzione, who fired the puck past Myshkin and into the net, giving the US a 4-3 lead with 10 minutes remaining on the clock. When the Americans took the lead, their fans went NUTS, for lack of a better term!! Their cheers were deafening, and the bleachers swayed as the screaming home fans jumped for joy, screaming, "USA! USA!! USA!!!"

The Soviets, trailing for the first time, attacked ferociously and moments later found an opening. Their puck streamed toward the net but ricocheted off the right post. The Russian fans looked at each other with puzzled expressions. *"This isn't supposed to happen! These are only children!!"*

Nevertheless, they were not too concerned, for their team consisted of hardened professionals. And, ten minutes is an eternity, especially in the third period. The Soviets had dominated in that period for many years. Why should this game be any different? They knew their champions would soon show these kids who they were playing with. Although, these "Kids" were not the pushovers that everyone thought.

Time after time, the Russians attacked the goal, and each time, Jim Craig turned away their puck. Then the Soviets stepped it up, fighting harder and skating faster, yet the American's matched them stride for stride.

With the lead and less than 10 minutes remaining, everyone expected the Americans to go on defense. Yet, to the contrary, they staged an offensive attack. They upped their intensity, and play was fast and furious as each team chased the puck from one end of the ice to the other. Minutes passed like hours, and as time melted away, Coach Brooks repeated to the young Americans, *"Play your game. Play your game!"*

By the five-minute mark, the Soviets looked bewildered. In panic mode, they shot wildly at the net. Yet Craig was unflappable, calmly turning away everything they threw at him.

With under two minutes remaining, the Russians advanced into the American zone and found an opening. A powerful blast sailed toward the US net but veered just wide.

At the sixty-second mark, the world expected the Soviets to pull their goalie to add an extra offensive player. But they did not. They'd never needed to pull their goalie before, so they hadn't practiced it.

An eerie silence fell over the crowd as the final seconds ticked away. Both Soviets and Americans held their collective breaths. Every eye in the stadium was fixed on the speeding puck. A TV commentator asked, *"Is this really happening? Can these boys hold on against those giants?"*

With 33 seconds, Craig kicked away a Soviet slap shot, and although the Russians quickly regained control, a US charge freed the puck. At 12 seconds, amid a mad scramble, Johnson gained control and passed to Ken Morrow. With seven seconds remaining, Ken advanced the puck over the blue line. Then thundering from the bleachers came the countdown, 6 - 5 - 4.

Even the sportscasters picked up the count, 3 - 2 - 1. As the buzzer sounded, ABC's baffled commentator, Al Michaels, spoke these now famous words, *"Do you believe in miracles?!"*

As his team ran all over the ice in celebration, Brooks headed back to the locker room, where he was soon joined by the young Americans. Still joyous, the players spontaneously broke into a chorus of "God Bless America ." Brooks' prophecy was realized; it "was" their night! These US men had indeed achieved a miracle!

During the TV broadcast wrap-up, ABC's Olympic anchor, Jim McKay, compared the American victory over the Soviets to a Canadian college football team defeating the Super Bowl Champion, Pittsburgh Steelers.

Days later, the Americans defeated Finland to claim Olympic gold for their country. The totally unexpected David vs. Goliath win was the boost the country needed. It was the spark that ignited a new era of American pride and success.

But what about that exhibition game days earlier, when the Americans were humiliated 10 - 3? It was just that, an exhibition! It showed the Russians they had nothing to worry about from the upstart Americans. Was Herb Brooks that smart? Maybe not, but those humiliated upstarts didn't lose again throughout those Olympic Games.

"This is your moment. You're meant to be here!"
~ Herb Brooks

"The book you don't read won't help."
~ Jim Rohn*

"We become what we think about most of the time and that's the strangest secret."

Earl Nightingale

THE STRANGEST SECRET

Summarized from a speech by Mrs. Diana Nightingale

 In 1921, Earl Nightingale was born into a poor family in California. When he was seven, his father disappeared, and his family moved into a tent in Long Beach's "Tent City." At age twelve, Earl witnessed the country struggling through the Great Depression. But, he noticed that there were a few people achieving success. This puzzled him, and little Earl couldn't understand why some people were wealthy while others were poor. He often pondered, "What is their secret?"

So, the young boy made finding that secret his mission. He questioned many grown-ups but could never get a straight answer. Searching the Long Beach Public Library, Earl spent many hours reading and soon formed the habit of reading every day. He read books on a variety of subjects.

His mother, who also loved to read, taught him the value of knowledge. She frequently said, "Knowledge is everything, and everything you want to know has been written by someone, somewhere." Then she explained to him, "No single book has all the answers."

Young Earl pondered his mother's words but still thought there must be a book somewhere that could answer his question, and he was determined to find it. And even though his initial searches came up empty, he never stopped looking for "the secret of success."

In the winter of 1941, at age 17, Earl joined the United States Marine Corps and was stationed in Hawaii. There the weather was warm and the scenery beautiful. One Sunday morning, Earl was startled by a loud explosion at his station on the USS Arizona. Then, in rapid succession, many other explosions followed. As the ship beneath him trembled, a message boomed over the ship's intercom, "All hands, man your battle stations! This is not a drill."

Suddenly there was chaos, death, and destruction all around. The pounding continued until Earl was blown from the battered ship into the waters of Pearl Harbor. The seriously injured Marine witnessed wave after wave of Japanese planes scarfing and bombing the US Fleet. He could only watch as the mighty battleship, Arizona, succumbed to the barrage and disappeared beneath the sea.

Over 3,000 lives were lost that day, and 1,700 were from the USS Arizona. Earl was one of only twelve Marines on that ship who survived the attack. Therefore, he believed his life had been spared for a purpose. He committed what remained of it to find and fulfill his destiny.

During his long recovery and while still in the Corps, Earl volunteered to help at a local radio station. He enjoyed the excitement of being on the air. After the war, he found employment writing and presenting daily programs at a small station.

As his radio career developed, Earl became a celebrity as the voice of Sky King (a popular weekly national radio drama).

Even with his growing success, he continued to be haunted by those questions. "Why are some people rich while others remain poor, and what is the secret to success?"

Then one day, while browsing a small book store, Nightingale noticed a book with an interesting title. Skimming through its pages, he realized that he was looking at the book he'd searched for since childhood, which contained the answers to his questions! The more he read, the more excited he became! He later recalled, "Then it hit me like a bolt! It was as though I had been immersed in a bright light!"

Reexamining his discovery, he thought, "This is so simple, I've seen this in many forms in other books, but I had no idea what I was reading."

Earl had simply not been ready to accept or understand this most potent principle. But now it all made sense. Each cog fell perfectly into place, and he realized that the "six words" in front of him contained "the secret of success!"

   "People become what they think about."

Closing the book, he reread the title, *Think and Grow Rich,* by Napoleon Hill. "What an amazing concept!" Earl could barely contain his excitement. He couldn't wait to share his discovery with everyone. So, he wrote down his thoughts and recorded himself reading them. Earl quit his steady job and embarked on a new journey using his newly found principles. In a short time, he landed a new position that paid more than twice his old salary. Then, using this knowledge, he set new and more significant goals, increasing his income.

When Nightingale was 35, he purchased an insurance company where, in addition to broadcasting, he trained and motivated a sales force. Reaping the rewards of his hard work and success, he scheduled a short vacation. Before departing, he left instructions for his sales associates to listen to his recording.

Upon his return, he learned that his salespeople were so excited by his concepts that they wanted a copy of the tape. So, Earl asked a record company to record *The Strangest Secret* on an album. Shortly after that, he was surprised to be presented with a Golden Record.

His album sold more than one million copies with no advertising or promotion. His next move was to start promoting *The Strangest Secret*. His successful efforts gave birth to a new media industry, personal development.

Earl propelled himself from obscurity into one of the world's most recognized voices and names using his principles. His radio program became the most widely heard daily in America, Mexico, Canada, Australia, Guam, the Bahamas, New Zealand, Puerto Rico, and over thirty overseas countries.

Nightingale wrote and recorded over 7,000 radio, 250 audio, and many video and television programs during his lifetime.

"We become what we think about most of the time,
and that's the strangest secret."
~ Earl Nightingale

THE DJ

One of America's most sought-after motivational speakers, **Les Brown**, was born in an abandoned building in Miami. His birth mother gave him away three weeks later, and he was raised by an adoptive mother. As a child, Les was hyperactive and mischievous. School was a struggle for him, and in the fifth grade, he was held back and labeled "mentally retarded"; but Les never stopped trying.

While waiting for a friend, a teacher, Mr. Washington, mistook him for a class member and asked him to write something on the blackboard. Startled, Les replied, *"I cannot write on the board because I am mentally retarded."* Mr. Washington responded, *"Don't ever say that again! Someone's opinion of you does not have to become your reality!"*

Washington took an interest in this young student and became his mentor. *"What do you want to do with your life, Les?"* *"I want to become a disk jockey!"* So, Washington instructed his mentee to prepare himself to become that person. Then, when Les protested, he told him, *"It's better to be prepared for an opportunity and not have one than to have an opportunity and not be prepared."*

That day, Les Brown started studying to become a disk jockey. He worked on his delivery and planned what songs he would play. He listened to how announcers spoke and transitioned from one piece to another. Les imagined sitting in a radio control room, wearing earphones, speaking into a microphone, and managing the control board.

After receiving his high school diploma, he became a city sanitation worker. But Les continued to dream of becoming a disc jockey. He took a transistor radio to bed and listened to the smooth-talking DJs at night. He even created a mock radio station in his room. He practiced introducing records to his imaginary listeners using a hairbrush as a microphone.

When Les' brother and mother heard him through the thin walls, they'd shout, *"Quit flapping your jaws and go to sleep!"* But he ignored them and continued to imagine his dream.

Then one day, on his lunch break, Les boldly walked into WMVM in Miami Beach, his favorite radio station, and asked to speak with the station manager. *"Someone is here to see you, Mr. Smith."*

"Who is it?"

"It's a Mr. Les Brown." "What does he want?"

"He wants to apply to be a disc jockey."

The program director, Milton "Butterball" Smith, walked out and saw a disheveled young fellow in overalls and a straw hat. *"Hello, Mr. Smith, I'm Les Brown, and I would like to interview with you for a position."*

"Do you have any background in broadcasting?" "No sir, I don't, but."

"Do you have a degree in journalism?"

"No, sir, but please give me a chance to."

"Well, son, I'm afraid you're not qualified for any position at this station, and there isn't an opening anyway."

Les thanked him politely and walked out. Devastated, that afternoon, he visited his Mentor, Mr. Washington. After hearing what had transpired, Washington explained that he should not take it personally. *"Most people are so negative that they have to say no seven times before they say yes."* Then, he encouraged Les not to give up but try again.

So, the next day on his break, Les returned to the station, where he introduced himself again. The puzzled director said, *"Didn't I just turn you down yesterday? Why are you back?!"*

"Well, I thought maybe someone called in sick or quit!" The now annoyed Smith instructed him to leave and not to return!

But, as you probably guessed, Les returned the following day, only, this time, Smith looked at him with rage and said, *"Go get me a cup of coffee!"* Having found an opening, Les became the errand boy for the station's executives and DJs.

Brown did more than he was asked, bringing in lunch and dinner and keeping the station spotless. But at every opportunity, Les stood next to the control room, observing the DJs. He imagined himself in that seat, knowing his time would come one day.

Eventually, his enthusiasm for his work won over the directors' confidence. They even started sending him to pick up visiting celebrities in the station's Cadillac. He drove big names like The Temptations and Diana Ross and the Supremes. Little did they know that young Les had no driver's license.

Les did whatever was asked of him at the station and more. While hanging out with the DJs, he taught himself their hand movements on the control panel. He stayed in the control rooms and soaked up whatever he could until they asked him to leave. Then, back in his bedroom at night, he continued to practice and prepared himself for the opportunity he knew would present itself.

One Saturday afternoon at the station, a DJ named Rock was drinking while on the air. Les was the only other person in the building, and he realized that Rock was drinking himself into trouble. Closely observing the situation, Les walked back and forth in front of the Rock's booth window. His mind was racing, and he couldn't help but think, *"Drink, Rock, drink!"*

When the phone rang, Les pounced on it. It was the station manager, as he figured it would be. *"Les, this is Mr. Klein."*

"Yes, I know."

"I don't believe Rock will be able to finish his program." *"Yes, sir, I know."*

"Les, Would you call one of the other DJs to come in and take over?"

"Yes, sir. I sure will."

Les hung up the phone, thinking, *"He must think I'm crazy."* Les did dial the telephone, but it wasn't to call in another DJ. He called his mother first, then his girlfriend. *"Y'all go out on the front porch and turn up the radio because I'm about to go on the air!"*

A few minutes later, Les called Klein, *"Sorry, Mr. Klein, but I can't find nobody."*

"Les, do you know how to work the controls?" *"Yes, sir!"*

"Well, go in there and play some music? And, Les, don't you say a word!"

"Oh, no, sir!"

Les couldn't wait to get his hands on those controls. First, he put the Little Stevie Wonder record, Fingertips. And, as the music played, he took his place in the DJ's chair, lowered the music, and in a deep but resonating voice, articulated …

"This is me, LB Triple-P, Les Brown, your platter- playing popper.
There were none before me, and there'll be none after me!
I'm the One and Only, young and single, and I love to mingle.
Certified, bonafide, and indubitably qualified to bring you
satisfaction, And a whole lot of action.
Look out, baby, I'm yo l-o-v-e man!!"

Les' persistence and preparation paid off, and both the audience and station management were blown away. From that humble beginning, Les Brown enjoyed a successful career in broadcasting, politics, and public speaking.

"Imagination is the preview to life's coming attractions."
~ Albert Einstein

GETTING SOUTHWEST OFF THE GROUND

In the mid-1960s, an ex-State Supreme Court Justice, **Herb Kelleher,** moved to Texas to start a new business or a law firm. Not your typical entrepreneur, Herb was a fun-loving, chain-smoking, hard-drinking, Harley-driving, New Jersey Yankee.

One of his law clients, Texas business tycoon Rollin King and his banker, John Parker, also wanted to start a new company. They were looking for something big and different when Rollin came up with starting an airline. He visualized a carrier inexpensively flying passengers to cities in the South Western United States.

But Parker wasn't sold! *"Start a new airline? Have you lost your mind?!"*

Although, when Rollin said, *"I believe I know someone that might be just crazy enough to take on something so unusual,"* John relented.

So, a meeting was arranged with Kelleher at a bar to discuss their plan.

At that meeting, legend has it, Rollin sketched out his ideas for a different kind of airline on a cocktail napkin. King's appraisal of Kelleher was correct, and the plan intrigued the jurist. A short time later, the three set out to achieve the improbable, with Herb in the cockpit.

Here are only some of the things Kelleher faced on his first day in his new position. In addition to all the usual business startup issues, a myriad of additional challenges awaited him.

Including the airline industry was overly regulated and highly unionized. There were already three regional airlines serving the South West United States and three times that many national carriers.

Herb's to-do list included:
- Finding space at already crowded airports
- Dealing with route restrictions
- And attaining permission to take to the air from the US Government

Government permission meant dealing with politicians and national and state regulations. Add to that the tremendous costs of purchasing a fleet of safety-rated passenger airliners, storing the fleet, maintenance, maintenance facilities, jet fuel, and the salaries of highly trained safety-rated mechanics and pilots.

Unintimidated, Herb took over the operation and started making decisions. First, he limited flights to inside Texas to avoid Federal Civil Aeronautics Board price controls and market regulations; and to give Southwest the freedom to undercut competitors' prices.

It was never Herb's plan to keep the airline restricted to Texas; he secretly dreamed of building Southwest into a primary carrier. But, before he could hope to achieve that dream, he first needed to get the Southwest planes in the air. Yet, that turned out to be a more significant challenge than he could have possibly imagined.

By 1967 Kelleher had put all the pieces together, and the brand-new Southwest Airlines fleet was ready to fly. However, that was also when Herb's real problems began.

The second Southwest Airlines took shape; it was buried in lawsuits initiated by competitors, Braniff, Continental, and Texas International Air Lines.

Kelleher took on their challenges and met their highly paid attorneys countless times in court. The battles were long, arduous, and very expensive.

With the entire air transportation industry whispering, shaking their heads, and laughing, Herb stood firm despite their reservations. *"Who do they think they are, trying to start a new airline without any experience?!"*

For four excruciating years, Herb personally fought battle after battle. His quest finally reached a climax when he presented Southwest's case before the United States Supreme Court.

The war was won, but Southwest's passenger fleet had been sitting empty and unable to make a flight for four years. By the time they finally received permission to take to the air, their fleet was reduced to four Boeing 737s. Yet, with all roadblocks out of his way, Herb took the airline public. And in June 1971, 650,000 shares were offered at approximately $11 per share.

Although the stock's proceeds provided the airline some needed working capital, most of it went to pay the remaining legal expenses. For the next two years, Southwest struggled to even exist. And by 1973, the tiny airline was on the verge of collapse. But Herb sold one of the big jets rather than give in or lay off a single employee. Then he launched the uphill climb that would make him the talk of the airline industry for decades. But this time, there would be no laughing!

First, he instituted an unimaginable 15-minute gate turnaround. Then, in an unheard-of move, he convinced his flight crews to help clean and service the planes between flights, which allowed them back in the air much faster.

"Planes are only profitable when they are in the air!" Herb Kelleher

But Herb was only getting started; in one of the most masterful strokes of genius the airline industry ever witnessed, Kelleher initiated Southwest Cargo. Now Southwest planes carried passengers and paid cargo below, bringing in almost twice the revenue.

With Southwest's profits on the rise, Kelleher continued to innovate. He opted for efficiencies rather than costly frills, like forgoing a computerized reservation system saving Southwest twenty-five million dollars a year.

He strove to instill a culture of service in his employees, insisting on better and friendlier customer support. He told his managers, *"Quality Customer Support will result in additional profits and customer loyalty. Customer Support will eventually take us to the top!"*

CEO Kelleher often boarded flights, chatted with passengers, and asked for their feedback. He told them his company cared about what they thought. His brilliant ideas allowed Southwest to survive and thrive through a dip in the US economy. But I've yet to mention his most incredible accomplishment. Kelleher's phenomenal success couldn't have occurred without his fantastic relationship with his employees.

Working at Southwest Airlines wasn't only profitable; it was fun! Herb's spirit of friendliness and optimism became integral to the airline's culture. To maintain a light-hearted atmosphere, he appeared in various airline operations areas, dressed as outlandish characters. Once, he attended a board meeting in an Easter Bunny costume. He even boarded a flight in a stewardess uniform. Other costumes included Elvis and a leprechaun. But his most ridiculous stunt was when he showed up at a maintenance facility at 2 AM and climbed a locked fence to surprise his mechanics, dressed as a hooker.

Kelleher wasn't only a showman; he also cared for Southwest's employees. And though the rift between the Transport Workers

Union and other airlines' management was venomous, Herb's union employees loved him! They knew he was on their side because he repeatedly proved it by how he treated them. Good pay avoided strikes and resulted in a positive environment.

Southwest's optimistic tone translated into customer loyalty and higher profits for the airline. Herb once said, *"When you treat your employees right, they will treat your customers right!"* And even with its higher-paid employees, Southwest always managed to keep its fares low and profits high.

While Herb was Southwest's CEO, the airline never had a layoff, a furlough, or a pay cut. That was an unmatched feat, not just by the other airlines but also by anyone in the transportation industry.

Kelleher was the heart and soul of Southwest. His tireless efforts, victorious courtroom battles, and brilliant strategies earned him the respect and admiration of everyone the company touched. His stockholders, employees, customers, and suppliers all loved him. In fact, the only people who didn't love him were his competition. But even they had to respect the man.

Under Herb's leadership, Southwest Airlines was always a perennial choice for *Fortune Magazine's Most Admired Companies* list.

Herb's dream of little Southwest Airlines becoming a primary national carrier came true. At his death, the airline flew more than 120 million passengers a year, employing more than 58,000 people, and had shown a profit since its third year in business.

Now that's what I call getting Southwest off the ground!

"Never give up on what you really want to do. The person with big dreams is more powerful than the one with all the facts."
~ H. Jackson Brown, Jr.

25,000 BOOKS

Hilary Hinton **"Zig" Ziglar** was born in South Alabama in 1926, the tenth of 12 children. When he was five, his family moved to Yazoo City, Mississippi, where Zig spent most of his childhood. Growing up in Mississippi left Ziglar with an enduring southern accent.

As a young man, he made his living marketing cookware, selling enough pots and pans to earn a management position. Ziglar was so skilled in selling that he successfully made the challenging transition from direct marketing to motivational speaking.

A kind and generous man, Ziglar wanted to help people realize their potential. So, early in the 1970s, he decided to author a "how-to guide" to health, happiness, and success. Countless hours were devoted to his venture. He wrote about attitude, faith, courage, motivation, healthy living, selling, integrity, and winning. After many months of research, meditation and soul searching, his book, *See You at the Top,* was ready for publication.

With great enthusiasm, he submitted his manuscript to the major publishing companies of the day and gave them his best sales pitch. Unfortunately, none of them were interested in a book about success.

He then contacted other publishers, only to find they were also skeptical. Yet, Zig was not the kind of person to let a little rejection dampen his enthusiasm. As a salesman, he was accustomed to hearing "no." A "no" only strengthened his resolve and moved him closer to a "Yes!"

So, Ziglar submitted his manuscript to some smaller publishers. But alas, those companies also turned him down. Some even stated there wasn't a market for a book about "hype."

Thirty-nine no's later, Ziglar was disappointed but not ready to give up. Facing that kind of rebuff, most authors would have thrown in the towel, but Zig wasn't like most authors. He knew his book would sell if given a chance! He even believed it could become a blockbuster!

In his mind's eye, he envisioned *See You at the Top*, helping thousands of people become healthier, more productive, and enjoying the fruits of success. He anticipated lives being changed for the better because of the information in his book. So Zig Ziglar made an extraordinary and courageous move. He published the book himself!

Keep in mind that at that time, there were no print-on- demand publishing companies or websites to lead you through the complicated process of putting a book in print. Self-publishing was not a simple procedure. The printing cost alone would require a substantial financial risk.

Nevertheless, Zig located a company that would produce his book; but only if he prepaid for a thousand copies. However, with 25,000 copies, he would receive a substantial price break. Zig knew that most authors never even sell 250 books, much less 25,000! And certainly, no reputable publisher would've recommended placing an order of that size, especially for an unproven product.

But Zig Ziglar's desire to help people outweighed his fear, so he invested his money in his dream. Placing an order of that size must have taken a great deal of courage, but faith and courage were what his book was about. To Zig, the 25,000 books were only a first step toward helping millions of people. He knew to reach his goal, he would not only need to sell those books but also millions more. Zig was confident in his decision because he knew,

> *"You can have everything in life you want if you will just help enough other people get what they want." - Zig Ziglar*

A few weeks later, thousands of pounds of books were delivered to the Ziglar home. And Zig knew precisely what to do. He'd taught it in his speeches for years. It was time for him *to prime the pump!*

Zig often told the story of two friends driving their truck through South Alabama on a hot day. With the August sun beaming down, they became thirsty. So when they passed an abandoned farmhouse and spotted an artesian well with an old pump, one of them jumped out to get a drink of water.

Yet, when he tried the pump, nothing came out! His friend explained, *"To get anything out of that pump, you must first put something in!"*

"What do you mean?"

"Well, you have to prime the pump!"

So he found an old bucket and dipped it into a nearby stream. Then he poured some water into the old pump and said, *"Now try it."* Still, nothing came out.

"Don't stop! Keep on pumping and pump harder!" And though it seemed nothing was happening, the young man kept pumping.

> *"When you put something "in," the law of compensation says you'll get something "out." - Zig Ziglar*

After a while, the pump started to make gurgling sounds. Then, like magic, a stream of cool, clear water poured from the pump's spigot. The flow was steady and abundant. And to keep the water flowing now only took an easy, smooth stroke of the pump handle. The amount of water was plentiful, and the two young men enjoyed the fruits of their labor with a cool drink of water.

Ziglar knew that he must first put something in to achieve his goal. So, in addition to his investment of money, he devoted his time and energy to the project. Never expecting a quick return, he simply worked and embraced his faith.

Like Zig said in his story,

> *"You've got to sweat at it and pump away for some time before expecting the water to come. If you work hard enough, long enough, and enthusiastically enough, your rewards will start to flow."*

Day after day and week after week, Ziglar enthusiastically promoted *See You at the Top!* He was determined to do whatever was necessary to get his book into the hands of the people who needed it. And he never let the possibility of failure enter his mind.

After months of labor, the word began to spread about an excellent new book containing some valuable information. Then as suddenly as the water had appeared from that old pump, Zig's book began to take on a life of its own.

Sales organizations and marketing companies purchased large quantities for their sales forces. Parents bought it for their children. People looking to improve their lot in life descended on hundreds of book stores requesting Zig Ziglar's new book, *See You at the Top!*

Ziglar's plan worked, and his investments of money, time, and effort paid off. But he didn't slow down, he continued to promote until the first 25,000 books vanished, and he had to place a 2nd order. And still, he didn't stop pumping; he continued until a 3rd order had been depleted.

Finally, the book that "would not sell" was being sold in such quantities that keeping up with the printing became a problem. Then, something quite remarkable happened. Zig's phone started to ring. The people who insulted him now asked for a contract to handle *See You At The Top*.

The last time I checked, Zig's extraordinary book had sold over 1,600,000 copies in hardcover alone. And after 47 years, it's still going strong!

I genuinely hope this story makes you wonder what Zig said in that book! And if you choose to find out, I'll See **You** at the top!

Author's Note: I want to especially thank Ms. Laurie Magers, Zig Zigler's longtime Executive Assistant, for her help and support with this book

"You were born to win, but to be a winner, you must plan to win, prepare to win, and expect to win."
~ Zig Ziglar

"If I had to tell a young person or someone struggling, the one thing that would have the most impact on their life, that thing would be, form the habit of reading and listening every day!"
~ Dennis J. Henson

"You were born to win, but to be a winner, you must plan to win, prepare to win, and expect to win."

Zig Ziglar

HOGAN'S COMEBACK

Ben Hogan was one of the greatest professional golfers to ever play the sport. And, there's little doubt that he was the best of his time. At age 37, while at the top of his game, something happened that changed the course of his life.

One foggy morning, driving on a lonely Texas road, Hogan spotted an eighteen-wheeler headed directly for him. Swerving to avoid a head-on collision placed him in the path of a Greyhound bus. Realizing the inevitable, Ben bravely threw himself on top of his wife, saving her life.

The subsequent collision left Hogan gravely injured. His broken body was rushed to the nearest hospital. The doctors did what they could, but Ben's injuries were catastrophic. His pelvis, ribs, and shoulder were broken, his ankle was totally shattered, and a blood clot from his leg was making its way to his heart.

Hogan's only chance was emergency surgery. That operation saved his life, but the doctors told him he would never walk again, much less play golf. Listening to their predictions, he nodded and sighed. But Ben had no intention of allowing an accident to keep him down!

Although the following weeks and months were difficult, Ben's attitude remained positive. Day after day, he fought to regain the use of his body. His first significant hurdle was just to sit up. Having accomplished that, he focused on standing. Then to everyone's amazement, he began to regain his ability to walk. And even though he could only manage a few short steps, he began practicing his golf swing.

The pain he endured, from the cuts, bruises, and mending bones, was excruciating. His broken shoulder sent tremors throughout his body when he moved his arm. Putting weight on his shattered ankle was something an ordinary person couldn't have endured. But Hogan wasn't an ordinary person.

To the astonishment of his doctors and the sports world, he entered the *Los Angeles Open* eleven months after his accident. Still, no one actually believed that he would be able to compete. The consensus was he'd probably not finish the 72- hole requirement.

Yet, on Ben's first day back, he scored a 73. Over the next two days, he shot rounds of 69, and by the end of the 72nd hole, he was tied for the lead. And finally, he competed in a playoff round. Although he didn't win that tournament, he proved to the world that Ben Hogan was back and still a pro.

His next goal was to win the *US Open!* Once again, everyone doubted that he could do it. But on opening day, he shot a 72 and followed that the next day with a 69. However, that night, Hogan's body gave out. He suffered from nausea and dizziness. Though he soaked in a hot bath to relieve his strained muscles, his symptoms persisted.

The following morning, he shot a 72, but his pain was unbearable by the afternoon. Ben's legs were so numb that he considered dropping out. Then he remembered the letters he'd received from his fans struggling with disabilities.

He pondered what it must mean to them to see him playing. Realizing that he was their champion, Hogan continued.

Fighting off the pain and playing through numbness, he ended the round within 2 strokes of his morning score. The next day, feeling much better, Ben shot a 69 and won the tournament by 4 strokes. Although he was excited about winning, he was more pleased that he hadn't disappointed his fans.

That US Open win represented Ben Hogan's reemergence, and he once again became the dominant player in golf. In 1953, Ben completed the famous *Hogan Slam* by winning three consecutive major tournaments. His post-crash golf swing is recorded on film and is still used as an example of near-perfect mechanics.

Hogan's unshakable optimism saved him from a life in a wheelchair and turned him into one of the world's most admired sports figures.

"It's not how many times you get knocked down,
it's how many times you get back up!"
~ George A. Custer

A LITTLE GIRL'S GOAL

Rachel Beckwith of Seattle, Washington, was a bright, eight- year-old with shoulder-length reddish-brown hair and green eyes. Her smile would light up a room. Everybody loved Rachel, and she loved everyone back. Although she only weighed about fifty pounds, her heart must have been made of pure gold.

Rachel and her family attended a 4,000-member Community Church near downtown Seattle. One Sunday, her youth group's featured speaker told them that children in parts of Africa do not have access to clean water. They further explained that they either have no water or must drink water filled with dirt, bacteria, parasites, and animal remains. He explained, *"Consequently, many develop severe health problems, and some die of thirst."*

Little Rachel was so moved that she asked her mother if she could forgo her 9th birthday party to raise money to help those children. Now, giving up your 9th birthday party, all the attention, the cake, and the wonderful presents was no small matter for a little girl! Yet, that's what Rachel wanted to do. So, with her Mom's help, a webpage was developed that read…

"On June 12th, 2011, I'm turning 9. I found out that millions

of people don't live to see their 5th birthday. And why? Because they don't have access to clean, safe water, so I'm celebrating my birthday like never before. I'm asking everyone I know to donate to my campaign instead of gifts for my birthday."

Rachel set a goal of $300.00 and went to work promoting her project. After telling her friends, family, Sunday school teacher, and pastor, she watched as donations trickled into her website. When her birthday arrived, she had raised $220.00; $80.00 short of her goal.

Little Rachel was terribly disappointed. Her mother comforted her by explaining that a $220.00 donation wasn't bad and that she could try again next year. So Rachel resolved that for her tenth birthday, she would raise more than $300.00. Only her tenth birthday never came.

A few weeks later, Little Rachel was riding with her sister and mother when a semitrailer jackknifed into a logging truck, causing a chain reaction. The big truck rear-ended the car carrying Rachel's family, and she was critically injured. Although she was rushed to a nearby hospital and the doctors did what they could, her life support was discontinued the following day.

Her family was devastated! And as they despondently prepared a memorial service, her mother thought it would be fitting to reopen her daughter's web page. She remembered how much Rachel wanted to help the children by raising $300.00. So the next afternoon, the website was again taking contributions.

More than a thousand people attended Rachel's memorial. And as part of his eulogy, her pastor mentioned little Rachel's birthday goal. He told the gathering how disappointed she had been for falling $80.00 short, then he gave her a webpage.

In days the site received pledges of more than $200,000.00. Yet Little Rachel's dream didn't end there. When the local media learned of a nine-year-old girl who wanted to help the children in Africa, their press coverage inspired more than 32,000 people to give to Rachael's project!

But when her story was picked up by the national media, more than 80,000 people contacted "Charity Water." They offered to forgo their birthdays for Little Rachel's kids.

The tiny nine-year-old with a heart of gold had started a movement, and more than 1,000,000 people joined her cause. Rachel's dream came true as hundreds of new wells with powerful water pumps were installed. Over 9 million impoverished people were given access to a continuous supply of fresh, clean water, saving countless thousands of lives. And, when the little girl's website eventually closed, $1,270,000.00 had been donated in her name. More than $6,000,000.00 was raised because of a little girl's goal.

"A Dream Is a Wish Your Heart Makes."
~ Lily James

PUTTING GREEN BAY ON THE MAP

Have you heard of Green Bay, Wisconsin? I imagine so. It is the home of the National Football League's Green Bay Packers franchise. Today's Packers are well respected and have a rich football history, although, in 1958, they had neither. That season's record was a dismal ten losses, one win, and a tie. Things were so bad that the franchise was in danger of being dropped by the NFL. And the people in Green Bay were so upset that they hung their coach in effigy.

Vince Lombardi, a 45-year-old assistant coach with the New York Giants, was tagged as the new person to take over The Pack. After learning about his new position, he told his family he had a big announcement. *"We're moving to Green Bay, Wisconsin!"*

When she heard her father's statement, his young daughter, Susan, replied, *"Where's Wisconsin?!"*

So, the next day, Lombardi brought home a map. *"Susan, here is the State of Wisconsin!"* But to his dismay, Green Bay didn't appear on his map.

Little Susan was mortified, *"I'm not moving to a place that's not on a map!"*

But her father calmly replied, *"When I am done, it will be on the map, and everyone will know exactly where it is!"*

Over the next nine seasons, Lombardi's Packers won five NFL Championships (three of those were in the newly formed *Super Bowl*). The Packers won so many games and titles that Green Bay became known throughout the sports world as *Titletown*.

In 1966 when the National Football League created the ultimate prize for the winners of their Championship Game, *The Super Bowl*, they named it *The Vince Lombardi Trophy*.

And, one other thing, Green Bay is prominently displayed if you look at a map of Wisconsin today.

"Winning is not a sometimes thing; it's an all-the-time thing. You don't win once in a while; you don't do things right once in a while; you do them right all of the time. Winning is a habit. Unfortunately, so is losing."
~ Vince Lombardi

"THREE LITTLE SISTERS"

Their profound influence extends even today, with such pop idols as Bette Midler, The Pointer Sisters, Barry Manilow, Manhattan Transfer, The Star Sisters, and Christina Aguilera embracing their style.

They were the defining sister act of all time. And their reign as the most popular singing group of the 20th Century was only eclipsed by The Beatles.

However, their road to stardom was fraught with obstacles and disappointments. And, but for a remarkable coincidence, their talent and brilliance may have gone unnoticed. This is the extraordinary story of three wonderfully talented girls who simply refused to give up.

Childhood

In 1910 a young couple, Peter and Ollie Andrews, moved to the USA from Greece and opened a restaurant in Minneapolis. The following year their first daughter, LaVerne, was born. Maxine arrived in 1916, then Patricia Marie (Patty) in 1918.

The family loved music and purchased a piano for the girls. LaVerne, a child prodigy, started playing by ear at an early age. She could hear a musical arrangement and play it back almost exactly. And though she read music and was an accomplished pianist, she rarely used a written score.

As a young teenager, LaVerne loved playing and singing the songs of the Boswell Sisters (a famous girl's trio). And in 1925, when Patty was only seven, LaVerne brought her little sisters together and taught them to sing harmony.

Maxine was a natural soprano, while Patty's voice fell in the mid-range, and LaVerne had a rich, low alto voice.

In addition to singing, their parents enrolled them in dancing school. And once they'd perfected several numbers, Ollie signed them up for a local talent contest. When asked the name of their act, they replied in unison, *"We're The Andrews Sisters!"*

The Andrews Sisters performed at parties, school dances, and every Minneapolis talent contest that Ollie could find. Most of the time, they brought home first prize and won so many contests that they became local celebrities.

The girls loved singing together and practiced constantly. The more they practiced, the better they became. And after a short time, they developed a beautiful, distinctive sound.
Their voices blended so perfectly, and their timing was so precise that their harmony almost gave the impression of being a single beautiful voice.

A Sixth Sense

There is a magical mystery usually associated with twins or triplets. It is that they possess a unique relationship that appears to endow them with telepathic qualities. Conversely, a similar bond among sisters born years apart is not only uncommon but extraordinary.

Yet the Andrews Sisters possessed that sixth sense. This connection allowed them to precisely match each other's phrasing and movements during challenging musical numbers with little or no practice.

On top of that, they were able to, without the aid of written music, immediately put in place three-part harmonies that would challenge the most gifted arranger. In other words, the girls were simply amazing!

> For a great example of their ability, listen to their recording of Tico Tico.

Musicians in the bands of that day relied on sheet music comprised of: notes and their duration, rhythms, phrasing, rests, repeats, dynamics, accents, tempo, time and key signatures, and sometimes lyrics.

Compare that to the sisters whose only crutch was a lyric sheet. And even LaVerne, who could read music, did not rely on written music when performing with the girls.

On The Road

A favorite pastime in Minneapolis was to attend Vaudeville shows at the *Orpheum Theater*. The sisters enjoyed watching and dreamed of one day having an act of their own.

So when Larry Rich, a big-name entertainer, held a competition in 1931 to find new acts for his show, the girls jumped at the chance. After performing a number made famous by the Boswell Sisters, the trio was selected to join Larry's troupe.

The show was an evening of theater that included dancers, magicians, comedians, singers, and skits. It traveled extensively, performing in many major cities.

Patty, only fourteen at the time, wore lots of makeup to avoid trouble for working at such a young age.

Over the next 10 months, the girls performed their act more than a thousand times. That year their expression and precision improved immeasurably. They also developed stage presence and learned to draw in their audiences by convincing each member they were performing for them alone.

The trio's act was always well received; however, the country was struggling through a great depression. And with Vaudeville in a death spiral, Larry disbanded the troupe, and the disappointed sisters returned to Minneapolis.

Nevertheless, the trio wasn't ready to give up their dream. In 1934, Peter closed his restaurant, and he and Ollie spent the next three years on the road with the girls. They traveled from town to town, picking up gigs anywhere they could, often completing an engagement and traveling a hundred miles to the next.

The jobs paid very little, and travel expenses ate up most of their income.

Things got so tough that even feeding the family was a struggle. Sometimes they were forced to make one chicken last an entire week. The girls practiced and practiced to keep their minds off their hunger. Their criteria for choosing a place to stay was,
"How close is it to a piano?"

Their hard times continued until 1936 when Leon Belasco hired them to sing with his band. Belasco wanted to incorporate Swing into his mostly ballroom show. New York was where swing was all the rage, so he asked the girls to meet him at the New Yorker Hotel that October.

Not only did their records with this band receive mixed reviews, Belasco decided to retire. So once again, they found themselves out of work. Things had never looked so bleak, and returning to a life on the road was simply not feasible.

However, one Belasco band member helped the sisters book a radio broadcast from the Edison Hotel in the Big Apple. Though the gig only paid $15.00, it was $15.00 they didn't have.

Then, to take a line from Disney, *"fate stepped in."* The first night, as they sang, Jack Kapp, the founder of Decca Records, was in a taxi and overheard their broadcast. He was so impressed that he sent his leading publisher and agent, Lou Levee, to *"find those girls!"*

"Who Wants to Know?"

After completing their radio spot, the trio stopped at the hotel's lounge to discuss their future. Their long faces exemplified their futility. When seemingly out of the blue, a well-dressed gentleman entered the lounge and began to inquire if anyone knew where he could find The Andrews Sisters.

With a bit of an attitude, Patty quipped, *"Who wants to know?"*

Turning to face the girls, the man replied, *"Jack Kapp of Decca Records wants them to come for an audition!"*

Immediately jumping to their feet, the siblings, in perfect unison, exclaimed, *"We're the Andrews Sisters!"*

The trio performed song after song at the recording studio the following day. Kapp was already looking for a group to replace the recently retired Boswell Sisters and was captivated by what he heard. And without hesitation, he signed the girls to a Decca recording contract (1937).

To Me, You Are Beautiful

Although the trio's first record failed to make the charts, the studio was still optimistic. Their second release was to be a Gershwin song from a popular Fred Astaire film, *Nice Work If You Can Get It*. However, no decision had been made for the B side of the record.

The girls spent long hours in the studio practicing and trying out new material. Then one day, Kapp overheard them phonically singing a Yiddish tune. He liked the song and arranged to have the lyrics translated and a musical score written for its background.

He asked the sisters to do it again, this time in English. After hearing it, Jack saw it was placed on the flip side of their new record. The song *Bei Mir Bist Du Shein (To Me, You Are Beautiful)* didn't immediately appear on the charts; however, it wasn't long before it began to move.

Then early one morning, Peter rushed into their bedroom and urged, *"Get up, girls and get your clothes on! Hurry now. There's something you have to see!"*

Puzzled, they did as their father asked and accompanied him to Broadway and 7th Ave.

There they encountered a crowd so large that it was blocking traffic on both streets. A local record shop had placed a speaker in front of their store. The music it was blaring was *Bei Mir Bist Du Shein.*

The Andrews family joined the crowd and watched in awe as they witnessed what was to be the beginning of two decades of the girls' dominance in the newly formed swing era. No one in the crowd knew they were standing next to the singers. *Bei Mir Bist Du Shein* became the Andrews Sisters' first Gold Record and was the song that put them on the map.

> *Two weeks after appearing on Your Hit Parade (January 8, 1938), the song rose to number 1 and held that slot for 5 weeks. Bei Mir Bist Du Shein was the Andrews Sisters' first million-selling record and the first gold record by a female singing group in history.*

Unfortunately, the terms of their contract paid them a flat fee per recording and no residuals. So for that first million- selling record, the girls received just $50.00.

It Wasn't Sophisticated

Following the success of *Bei Mir Bist Du Schon*, Jack Kapp asked the trio to record *Beer Barrel Polka*. However, they resisted stating, *"That song isn't sophisticated!"* Nevertheless, at Jack's insistence, they relented, and the *Beer Barrel Polka* became their second gold record.

A Unique Combination

By the late '30s, almost every restaurant in America featured a jukebox. There were more than a half million, and Decca Records dominated those machines. The younger crowd often pushed back restaurant chairs and tables to make room to dance.

Big Band music controlled the charts, yet the Andrews Sisters had such a unique sound that their listening audience quickly moved them near the top.

Going head to head with the big bands was impressive. But when music director Vic Shorn created the unique blend combining the girls with those big bands, the trio's records shot to the top.

The Sisters would sing a phrase accompanied by only drums and bass. Then between those phrases, the bands would rotate, punctuating their parts with trumpet, trombone, or sax fills. As a climax, the entire band joined the sisters to add an exclamation point. And for the next two decades, that remained an unbeatable combination.

> For a great example of this technique, listen to their recording of *Sing, Sing, Sing*.

Swing was the new music of the day, and the girls' music embodied that genre.

A New Day

Throughout the 1930s, Bing Crosby was the country's top solo singer and a successful movie personality. As Decca Record's number one artist, he received huge residuals from his recordings. And though the girls had recently turned out seven smash hits in a row, they were still struggling to make ends meet. Per their contract, they'd only earned a few hundred dollars.

One morning, upon their arrival at the studio, the receptionist informed them that Mr. Kapp would like a meeting. Wondering if they'd done something wrong, they make their way to the office where Kapp was waiting. They cringed as Jack took their contract and ripped it to pieces as they took a seat.

But to their great surprise, he handed them a new agreement. However, this arrangement contained terms almost identical to the ones in Bing Crosby's contract. There was, however, one exception. This new agreement was made retroactive from their first day.

But Jack wasn't finished. As the sisters looked at each other in disbelief, they were also given a check. The number on the amount blank of that check contained so many zeroes; the girls couldn't believe that much money existed.

Some might consider this a generous move on Kapp's part. However, in the following decades, the Andrews Sisters were instrumental in turning Decca Records into one of the most successful labels in the music industry.

Unmatched Talent

Patty, the sexy, vivacious blonde and personality of the group who always sang lead, is one of the most talented singers ever to take a stage. The timbre of her voice was piercing and endearing at the same time.

However, the glue that held the sisters together was the fiery redhead, LaVerne. Her natural musical ability and rich low voice were the basis of their sound.

Maxine, the beautiful brunette, not only flawlessly sang the upper parts; she was the most physically attractive of the three.

The girls produced a sound that has often been copied but never matched. When they wanted to sing with power, they sang in unison. Then when they broke into parts, it only emphasized their splendor. Yet, their sound was just the beginning of their talent.

Before them, most singers and singing groups simply sang and sometimes swayed to the music. However, the Andrews Sisters incorporated striking choreography in their performances. Adding that to their immaculate harmony, high energy, and sixth sense precise timing set them apart from any other group.

Seeing them perform could be compared to viewing a three- ring circus. A lot was going on, and their audiences simply couldn't get enough. From 1938 through 1951, their hit records established the trio as bona fide stars, which brought them extensive radio and personal-appearance work.

"I'll record with them any time they want!"

In 1939, Jack Kapp approached Bing Crosby (who also did not read music) about recording with the Andrews Sisters. Crosby wasn't interested and turned him down. However, Kapp remained persistent and eventually convinced Bing to do one session with the girls. That recording produced Ciribiribin and Yodelin' Jive. Afterward, Crosby told Kapp, "I'll record with those girls anytime they want. And they can pick the material."

Thrilled, the girls not only took him up but also convinced Mr. Crosby to use their musical director, Vic Schoen, and their orchestral arranger and conductor, John Scott Trotter. Those first two recordings' massive success spawned a new era for the trio. After that, they worked with every big-name singer of the day, turning out hit after hit.

Here is just a partial list of the hit songs they did with Crosby over the years:

- Ciribiribin
- Yodelin' Jive
- Pistol Packin' Mama
- Jingle Bells
- Santa Claus is Coming to Town
- Ac-cent-chu-ate the Positive
- Route 66
- There's No Business Like Show Business
- Here Comes Santa Claus
- Have I Told You Lately That I Love You?

In all, Crosby and the trio recorded 47 songs, with 23 ranked high on the Billboard chart, demonstrating that the team was among the most successful pairings in show business history.

The Glenn Miller Radio Program

Soon the big bands came calling. And after recording some of their best songs with band leaders like Jimmy Dorsey and Paul Whiteman in 1940, they were invited to share a radio show with the greatest of them all, Glenn Miller.

However, as that show took shape, its sponsors were not sure the Glenn Miller Band was a big enough attraction. So, their advertisements gave the Andrews Sisters top billing. That's a great example of how popular the sisters had become.

The Swing Era

The "Swing Era" (aka The Big Band Era) lasted from 1933 through 1947. The girl's intricate vocal arrangements and rhythmic ability mirrored the sound of the big bands.

Some notable groups that became popular during that time included: Glenn Miller, Benny Goodman, Tommy Dorsey, Jimmy Dorsey, Count Basie, Artie Shaw, and Woody Herman. However, the group who truly personified swing was the Andrews Sisters.

Movies

The trio's talent didn't go unnoticed by Hollywood. Universal signed them to star in several musicals, starting with Argentine Nights in 1940. Then, as America prepared to become embroiled in a world war, they were slated to star in several patriotic films.

From 1940 -1948, they appeared in 17 movies, including lending their voices to two animated features for Disney.

Buck Privates (1941) featured *I'll Be With You in Apple Blossom Time* and *Boogie Woogie Bugle Boy* (the song that endeared them to America's troops).

Boogie Woogie Bugle Boy was nominated for an Academy Award for Best Original Song and is ranked No.6 on the Songs of the Century.

Apple Blossom Time

The ballad, I'll be With You in *Apple Blossom Time*, was initially rejected by the producers of *Buck Privates*. They believed it would slow down the picture; still, the girls insisted. Then the studio refused to pay for its rights.

Undaunted, the girls paid the $200.00 themselves, and *Apple Blossom*

Time became another massive hit. The song was eventually adopted as their theme song!

Pennsylvania Polka

The *Pennsylvania Polka* was recorded for their 1942 film, *Give Out, Sisters*. And though it was slow to gain attention, over time, it grew to become one of their better-known numbers.

One day Patty received a call from the polka's composer, Zeke Manners.

During that call, he shared with her how the tune came about. On his way to a horse race in Pennsylvania, a radio station played *Roll Out The Barrel*. That inspired him to create another polka for the Andrews Sisters.

That same day at the track, he heard the trumpeter's *Call To The Post* before the start of each race. Then it hit him; that bugle call would make an excellent polka melody. Once he got the tune in his head, he couldn't stop thinking of it. So that evening, Manners composed the *Pennsylvania Polka*, especially for the sisters.

In their next movie, Private Buckaroo, the girls put on a show for service members singing, Don't Sit Under the Apple Tree with Anyone Else But Me.

The War

From the end of 1941 to 1945, with the nation embroiled in bitter combat, the sisters' upbeat and optimistic nature made them the perfect boosters for the country's war effort. While performing Boogie Woogie Bugle Boy and in other movies, their dress in military uniforms endeared them to the GIs fighting overseas.

The USO

The United Services Organization (USO) was a collaboration between show business professionals and the military to bring morale-boosting entertainment to the troops during the war. Funded by public donations, it initially brought shows to the bases where young men were trained before going overseas.

Most shows were performed on flatbed trucks that could be driven from base to base. They featured the day's top talent, such as Bob Hope, Bing Crosby, Dorothy Lamour, Ginger Rogers, Betty Grable, Abbott & Costello, and Clark Gable, along with the music of Tommy Dorsey, Glenn Miller, Benny Goodman, and of course the Andrews Sisters.

Thanks to the girls' Vaudeville background, they held their own with the best of them. And during the war years, they performed in hundreds of shows.

For the GIs, the Andrews Sisters represented home and the comforts they had left behind. When the young girls sang *I'll Be With You In Apple Blossom Time*, a hush fell over the recruits who were already missing their loved ones. Yet, when they launched into *Boogie Woogie Bugle Boy,* those same GIs rose to their feet to dance and clap to their music.

Throughout the war, the girls volunteered to entertain the enlisted and wounded. They sang for war bond rallies and USO Canteens. The Canteens were staffed by famous stars, who waited tables, washed dishes, and provided entertainment for the boys. While working with the USO, the girls often joined three random GIs for dinner.

For a war-torn country, the trio provided a musical security blanket thru their records, films, radio, and personal appearances. Their motto was to emphasize that *"America is strong and proud!"*

Their optimistic, upbeat war campaign instilled hope, joy, and allegiance through song, comedy, and lively movement. Time magazine called them the *Queens of the Jukebox,* and the New York Times stated that *"the Andrews Sisters are in a class by themselves."*

In addition to their war efforts, the girls played to civilian audiences, setting attendance records during a national tour in 1942. They also had a Sunday night radio show, appeared in more than a dozen films, and continued to do recordings for Decca. By 1944 the Andrews Sisters had sold more than 30 million records.

After three years of lobbying the USO, the girls were finally allowed to participate in an 8-week tour. On tour, they entertained thousands of service members in North Africa and Italy, often performing in war zones only a short distance from the front lines.

America's Sweethearts

Second, only to Bob Hope in commitment and extensive touring, the girls earned the title of *America's Sweethearts.* However, it was more than just a title to the young men living in fox holes and fighting on foreign soil. Those boys were not only dirty, tired, and scared as they faced the real threat of death, they were desperately homesick.

Pinup girls, like Betty Grable, Rita Hayworth, and Lana Turner, were nice to look at, but few of those GIs could imagine them as their sweethearts. However, the attractive but less glamorous Andrews Sisters reminded them of the girls back in Pine Grove, Springfield, Madison, or wherever they called home, the ones they saw in school and church.

The trio looked like their own sisters, cousins, and friends. The boys could easily see themselves returning home to marry someone who looked just like them.

V- Disks (records) of the trio were produced, especially for those serving. So the recruits could see their pictures, hear their voices, and experience their personalities.

The GI's love for the Andrews Sisters was as real as any they'd had or would ever experience. And the girls realized that there would never be another sweetheart for many of them. So they gave them a show they would never forget. Their performances were always followed by thunderous applause, whistles, and shouts. Thousands of letters were mailed home from war zones saying, *"Mom, I saw the Andrews Sisters, and they were incredible!"*

Eight-to-the-Bar Ranch

Eight-to-the-Bar Ranch was a western-themed radio program hosted by the trio and co-hosted by Gabby Hayes (the most famous of all the Sidekicks in western movies). It ran from 1944 to 46 and featured a new guest every week. Big stars like Frank Sinatra, Bing Crosby, Bob Hope, Eddie Cantor, Carmen Miranda, Judy Garland, Ethel Merman, Rudy Vallee, and other prominent celebrities were featured.

Their movies continued to experience box-office sellouts. And they remained in great demand for on-stage and personal appearances nationwide.

Drinking Rum and Coca Cola

One afternoon in December of 1944, a friend brought a new song to the studio for the girls' consideration. And though less than an hour was spent reviewing it, they believed it might have merit. The following day, after completing all their sessions, 20 minutes remained of studio time.

Taking advantage of those minutes, the sisters recorded the song from the night before. Without having access to a musical arrangement, Laverne played the tune a couple of times for the studio musicians. Then, after talking over who would sing what and when, and with the other musicians' ad-libbing their parts, the girls recorded the song in a single take.

Believing the song might be something they would rerecord later, they forgot about it. However, when Jack Kapp heard that take, he declared, "*That's it!*" That single was placed on the group's next record. When *Drinking Rum and Coca-Cola* was released, it immediately rose to the number one position and remained there for seven weeks.

During that time, millions of copies were sold! And when many radio stations considered it too risqué and refused to play it, the record became even more desirable. When you tell teenagers they can't have something, they will move heaven and earth to get it!

A Shortage of Shellac

How big was *Drinking Rum and Coca-Cola*? In 1945 phonograph records were made of shellac. And, because of the war, that material was tightly rationed. Typically, that wasn't a problem because each record company was allowed a sufficient amount to produce their albums.

However, the demand for *Drinking Rum and Coca-Cola* was so strong that Decca ran out of shellac and was about to be forced to stop making records altogether. Fortunately, the other record companies gave up some of their quotas so the public could enjoy hearing their new favorite song.

> *Drinking Rum and Coca-Cola introduced Calypso music to the nation and was the hit of the year in 1945.*

Post War Success

Once the war ended, the sisters formed a corporation to handle their finances and permanently relocated to Los Angeles. 1946, found them in demand on radio, on stage, in clubs, and in the recording studio.

Even Disney used the girls' voices in the cartoon features *Make Mine Music and Melody Time*. The following year CBS Radio signed them as regulars on *Club Fifteen*, where they appeared three times a week for five years as alternating hosts with Bob Crosby and Dick Haymes.

The trio again topped the charts in 1948 when they were ranked Recording Artists of the Year. They also appeared in that year's highest-grossing film, *Road to Rio*, with Crosby, Hope, and Lamour.

Compared to the hectic pace of the war years, their lives in the late 40s were more settled. However, their singing was still magic, and their shows and recordings continued to be popular.

I Can Dream, Can't I?

Their next big hit came in 1949 with *I Can Dream, Can't I?*. The song, a solo by Patty with her sisters providing backup, reached gold status and hit number one in January 1950.

The trio continued to record for Decca through the end of 1953, when Patty left the group for a solo career. Yet, Maxene and LaVerne continued to perform as the Andrews Sisters. However, the mid-fifties ushered in a new generation of listeners that replaced the teens of the '30s, '40s, and early 50s. Swing music fell by the wayside and was replaced by the music of artists like:

1. Chuck Berry
2. Little Richard
3. Fats Domino
4. Ricky Nelson
5. Jerry Lee Lewis
6. Buddy Holly
7. Bobby Darin
8. The Big Bopper
9. Ritchie Valens
10. Elvis Presley

End of the Ride

In 1950, the *Andrews Sisters Series* TV pilot was produced, yet it was not picked up by a network. The girl's final performance was on the *Dean Martin Show* (September 29, 1966), ending their forty-one years together. Though their singing career was over, they continued to be loved by their millions of fans.

For the balance of their lives, they constantly received the honor and respect they so richly deserved. And even these many years later, the Andrews Sisters remain an integral part of American music history.

One Day in May

The sisters may be gone, but their spirits live on as their music continues to bring joy to both young and old. They will always be remembered as the Sweethearts who brought comfort and delight to their country's fighting men in their darkest hours.

And, one wonderful day in May, I know we'll see them again. *"When? In Apple Blossom Time."*

Accomplishments

The Andrews Sisters' reign was remarkable because they brought in a new and different style of music. Their material was upbeat and often borrowed from other cultures.

They recorded over 1,700 songs and 113 of those topped the charts. They sold over 80 million records, and 19 of their titles achieved golden status. Their 18 movies were box-office hits, and they regularly appeared on radio and television.

The girls remained at the top of their industry for almost three decades.

Patty's solo *I Can Dream, Can't I?* was one of the most artistic and memorable songs ever recorded. They were and still are the most successful female singing group in history. And they were the top-selling group of the 20th Century until they were overtaken by The Beatles.

"Music gives a soul to the universe, wings to the mind,
flight to the imagination, and life to everything."
–Plato

"The Law of Attraction says that you will attract into your life whatever you focus on. Whatever you give your energy and attention to will come back to you."

Jack Canefield

Famous Failures

These men and women failed numerous times, yet they ultimately prevailed because they developed the habit of persistence. They did not let their failures define them; but instead, used them as stepping-stones for improving their lives.

GOOD GRIEF, SPARKY

Charles Monroe was born the son of a Minneapolis barber in the early 1920s. A few days later, his uncle nicknamed him *Spark Plug,* and the name stuck. Spark Plug was smaller than other kids his age. And though he was kind- hearted, he never seemed to fit in. His insecurities often caused him problems; you might say "*his anxieties had anxieties.*"

Charles constantly over-analyzed everything and never felt liked or respected. To avoid being around other children, he spent a lot of time at home. While watching TV, he imagined himself participating in the plots of programs and cartoons. His only close friend was his dog, Spike.

Sparky did well in elementary school, so well, in fact, he skipped two grades. Yet being around older kids caused him more anxiety.

Junior High was different. He failed all his eighth-grade subjects, causing the other students and even some teachers to consider him a loser. Still, little Sparky never stopped trying; he was just unsuccessful at everything he tried.

Miserable, he retreated into a dream world and spent most of his time doodling. But after examining some of his sketches, one teacher offered him some encouragement. Charles relished her compliments and dreamed of one day becoming an artist.

Making a new attempt to gain acceptance, he enrolled in several sports. After failing all his tryouts, he was finally accepted to his school's golf team. Yet, he lost when he got the chance to help his team win in a tournament. Then, in a consolation game, he failed again. Hanging up his clubs, Sparky focused solely on art.

As for his high school social life, he didn't have one. Due to his shyness, Charles never even approached a girl. He thought about it but believed he would be rejected, so he didn't dare.

Charles believed his artwork was good. And when *Ripley's Believe it, or Not* (a nationally syndicated feature) published one of his drawings, he began taking art more seriously.

With his mother's encouragement, he completed a correspondence course for artists. In his senior year, he submitted a few of his drawings to the school's yearbook staff. Yet they chose not to use them.

After high school and a short stint in the military, the young man set his sights on becoming a professional artist. While in college, he submitted drawings to many syndicators. They all turned them down, and their rejections were often insulting. Yet, Sparky persisted, even sending some of his work to Walt Disney Studios, but they also turned him down.

While still on campus, he finally mustered the courage to speak to one of his classmates, Donna Mae Johnson, a stunning redhead. Soon the two seemed inseparable. Then, when Charles learned of a breakthrough from a syndicator, he took the opportunity to propose marriage to *"the love of his life."*

Donna Mae not only turned him down; a few weeks later, she married someone else. The following week, his art studio and all of his art supplies burned to the ground. Poor Sparky, totally devastated, had never felt so low. But rather than giving up, he worked harder to produce more and better pictures.

After graduation, his alma mater hired him to teach painting. Along with his teaching, he supplemented his income by providing intermittent one or two-panel cartoons to the *Saturday Evening Post*. The Post's panels got him noticed, leading to a more lucrative position drawing three-panel strips for the St. Paul Pioneer Press.

Sparky based the stories on his life and called his strip *Li'l Folks*. In *Li'l Folks*, he described himself as a loser and a chronic underachiever. That script was so good that a major publishing company engaged him to provide it to several newspapers.

Although Sparky was thrilled, there was a problem. His new publisher didn't like the name *Li'l Folks*. So, the publisher gave the strip a new name without Charles' consent and to his great dismay.

At that time, there was a popular TV show, *Howdy Doody*.

The show's host, Buffalo Bob Smith, called the kids in the show's audience The Peanut Gallery. And for that reason, Sparky's publisher named his comic strip *Peanuts!*

You see, Charles (Sparky) Monroe's last name was Schulz. Charles

Schulz, the creator of Snoopy, Lucy, Linus, and his lovable alter ego, Charlie Brown, the little boy who could never fly a kite or kick a football. Sparky's cartoon characters became famous and loved throughout the world!

And that resilient young man, the one who'd failed over and over and over again; the same person whose artwork was so often rejected, became the most famous and the highest-paid artist in the history of the world.

"Success is stumbling from failure to
failure with no loss of enthusiasm."
~ **Winston Churchill**

"I DREAMED A DREAM"

Susan Boyle, the youngest of eight siblings, spent her childhood in a small village in Scotland. Complications during birth resulted in what was believed to be mild brain damage.

She was thought to have learning disabilities in elementary school, and her classmates often teased and called her *Simple Susan.* A subsequent examination revealed Susan actually suffered from a minor developmental disorder.

At age 12, she became interested in singing and participated in musical productions at school. Recognizing her talent, her music teacher encouraged her to sing.

After high school, Susan briefly worked as a cook before enrolling in *Edinburgh Acting School.* Yet, music was her first love. She dreamed of being a professional singer and took every opportunity to perform. She sang at church and karaoke clubs and recorded a CD for charity. In 1995, she unsuccessfully auditioned for the talent show *My Kind of People.*

Having received excellent reviews on her CD, Susan spent her savings on a professional demo. She then mailed the tape to television and radio stations, record companies, and talent competitions. Yet, when her dear sister died unexpectedly, she didn't feel like singing for almost two years. Then, when she started back, her mother also passed away. For the next several years, Susan completely withdrew.

One day she recalled how her mom encouraged her to audition for *Britain's Got Talent*. So, to honor her mother, she signed up for the 2008 pre-screening. That preliminary went well and earned her a spot on the live TV show.

Simple Susan, the unemployed charity worker who lived alone with her cat, strutted onto the stage for her live audition. She was obviously nervous. In her past, the largest crowd she'd performed for was at her church. Her appearance left much to be desired, a portly middle-aged woman dressed in less than flattering attire.

When the judges saw her, their body language let everyone know they were not impressed. Simon Cowell asked her name and age. Trying to be brave, Susan told her age and made a poor attempt to say something funny. Simon rolled his eyes, and the audience laughed and whistled, but not with her, at her.

Simon: *"What's your dream, dear?"* *"I'd like to be a professional singer!"*

Simon, unimpressed, asked sarcastically. *"Why hasn't it worked out before?"*

"I haven't been given a chance before, but here's hoping it will all change."

Simon's face registered his skepticism. *"And who would you like to be as successful as?"*

Susan boldly proclaimed, *"Elaine Page."*

The sneers and gasps of the audience could be clearly heard. Yet

Susan put on a confident face and nodded for the music to start. BGT cameras panned the massive crowd for the next few seconds, stopping on two young girls who were giggling. Unfortunately, the judges were also amused.

As the orchestra's intro began, silence fell over the auditorium, and Susan smiled sweetly. Then to everyone's amazement, she began to sing, *"I Dreamed a Dream of time gone by..."*

It only took about two seconds for the crowd to react. The muffled sneers were replaced with cheers. The judges looked at each other with dropped jaws. Two young hosts, just off stage, looked at a camera, *"You didn't expect that, did ya?"*

As Susan continued, the audience got more involved; some even rose to their feet. Simon put his hands atop his head and smiled with approval. Before she completed the first verse, the entire audience was clapping! Susan smiled and kept singing. Throughout the song, wave after wave of applause echoed through the auditorium.

As the volume dropped and then rose into the song's climax, the crowd stood and clapped in unison; this time, two judges joined them. A loud roar followed a long and enthusiastic ovation when the music ceased. Susan smiled and began to walk off stage. But she was quickly escorted back to hear the judge's comments.

Piers Morgan; *"Without a doubt--that was the biggest surprise I have had in my three years of this show! When you stood there with that cheeky grin and said, 'I want to be like Elaine Page,' everyone was laughing at you! No one is laughing now! That was stunning!"*

Amanda Holden; *"I am so thrilled because I know everybody was against you. I honestly think we were all being very cynical, and we got the biggest wake-up call ever! And I just want to say it was a complete privilege listening to that."*

With sarcasm, Simon Cowell quipped, *"Susan, I knew the minute you walked out on that stage, we were going to hear something extraordinary, and I was right!"*

Susan received three yesses and advanced to the next phase of the competition. Videos of Boyle's debut were viewed on the internet by an estimated 100 million people. Although a few weeks later, she placed second in the finals, by then, she no longer needed to win. Her future as a professional singer was already secure. Her first studio album, *I Dreamed a Dream*, debuted at number one on the *Billboard* charts in 2009. It was the second best-selling album of the year, selling more than 3.1 million copies.

In 2012, *I Dreamed a Dream*, a stage musical based on Susan's life, toured the United Kingdom, with Boyle occasionally making cameo appearances. Her autobiography, *The Woman I Was Born to Be*, was published in 2010.

Despite being rejected time after time, Susan never gave up on her dream. And today, she's won numerous awards, and her voice has been heard around the globe. Those years she spent failing have only made her successes more enjoyable.

*"There comes a special moment in everyone's life,
a moment for which that person was born."*
~ Winston Churchill

FROM THE BRINK
OF DISASTER

In 1887, **Conrad Nicholson Hilton Sr.** was born into a wealthy New Mexico family. He learned about business while working at his father's hotel and general store as a boy. When he was young, he entered politics and was elected to New Mexico's first State Legislature. Although, by the end of his term, he was done with public life and chose banking as his new career. Yet Conrad didn't intend to work in banks; he planned to own them. As I mentioned, he came from a wealthy family.

At the height of the oil boom, Hilton spotted a listing for a bank in Texas. Contacting the broker, he signed a purchase contract. But when the deal fell through, he instead purchased the Mobley Hotel in Cisco, Texas.

The Mobley was an excellent investment. Because of its massive success, Hilton began to purchase and build hotels throughout the Lone Star State. Things were going so well that in 1926, he vowed to build a new hotel every year.

Outperforming his own plan, Conrad averaged building three per year over the next few years. And, by 1928, he held more than six hundred rooms.

Already holding investments of more than three million dollars, in the fall of 1929, he bought a one million seven hundred fifty thousand dollar, three hundred-room hotel in El Paso. Unfortunately, two weeks later, the US Stock Market crashed, marking the beginning of the Great Depression.

The depression hit the hotel industry hard! Almost 80 percent of the hotels in the country either went bankrupt or were lost to foreclosure. With hundreds of empty rooms and a myriad of payments, Hilton struggled to hold on.

He made adjustments by closing entire floors, removing phones, and asking his staff to work for room and board. Yet, the economy continued to deteriorate, with no sign of recovery.

Conrad remained optimistic and believed that things would get better if he could just hold out a little longer. Unfortunately, he was wrong, and things got worse. Under enormous pressure, Conrad Hilton turned to prayer to give him the strength to continue.

Desperate for options, he accepted a meeting with the wealthy owners of American Life Insurance, WL Moody, and his son, Shearn. Even though Hilton knew these men were shady, at this point, he believed them to be his only hope. The Moody's agreed to loan Hilton $300,000 if he'd pledge his hotels as collateral. And though that loan provided some breathing room, it was short-lived. Meanwhile, The Great Depression persisted.

"If I could just find another $200,000.00, I think I'll be okay." But, banks were not lending, and his friends were also facing hard times. Hilton was so deeply in debt that his accountants and attorneys urged him to file bankruptcy. But he felt obligated to those who believed in him and invested in his dreams. So, he refused to give up and used every penny at his disposal to save his hotels.

One day, walking through a lobby, one of his bellboys handed him

$300.00 (the man's entire life savings), "*I believe in you, Mr. Hilton!*" Later, at a filling station, a young attendant told him, "*I was ordered to cut off your credit Mr. Hilton, but I've paid for your last two tanks with my own money.*"

Things deteriorated until Conrad had no money to keep his home or even buy food. Consequently, he moved his family into the El Paso Hilton to provide them with food and a place to stay. He was reduced to borrowing travel money from his associates to visit his own hotels. Yet, Hilton never gave up and remained determined to come up with solutions. He believed he could turn things around, despite everything that was happening.

One morning, on a train car, Conrad was thumbing through a magazine when he spotted a picture of a hotel. It was a drawing of plans for the fabulous Waldorf-Astoria. The Waldorf was to be built in New York City and become the world's largest hotel. Then something astonishing happened! Hilton removed the picture from the magazine, and before placing it in his pocket, he jotted a note, "One day, I will purchase this!"

> *Just imagine Conrad Hilton sitting in a train car during The Great Depression, paying for his ticket with borrowed money. He was totally broke, deeply in debt, and had no idea what to do. Seeing a picture of what was to become the world's grandest hotel, saved it and resolved that he would one day own it! What a powerful expression of Faith!*

The Moody's saw no way out for Conrad and threatened to call their loan and take his hotels. Hilton knew he was on the brink of disaster! If the Moody's followed through, he would lose everything, leaving his family homeless and destitute. But rather than give up, Conrad Hilton prayed for guidance. Then, with renewed energy, he went to Galveston to meet with WL Moody.

The older Moody was a shrewd businessman and realized that Conrad

Hilton was a much better hotel manager than he or his son would ever be. So without informing the younger Moody, WL agreed to meet with Connie.

Note: Moody's hotels were also failing!

At that meeting, the Old Man presented an offer. He proposed merging their hotels and forming a new company, The National Hotel Company. Then he suggested that Connie take over management of the new company's properties. In return, Hilton would own one-third of the new business, receive an annual salary of $18,000.00, and share a third of any company profit.

Conrad struggled to contain his excitement. While maintaining a poker face, he requested a single caveat; a clause stating that should their partnership dissolve, Hilton would retain one-third of its hotels. Incredibly the older Moody inserted that clause and signed the agreement. Conrad's prayers had been answered. And the following week, he started back to work with a renewed passion.

Once his salary checks began, he paid back the bellboy and the gas station attendant. He also gave them shares of his stock (which paid them dividends for the rest of their lives). Then, while still providing their room and board, he restarted the salaries of his remaining employees.

While Conrad successfully managed the combined chain, he never stopped purchasing and building his own hotels. The younger Moody resented the partnership and, after a time, caused it to become toxic. So Conrad dissolved the business and exercised his clause.
A fierce legal battle followed, but Hilton eventually gained control of his third of the hotels. Over the next few decades, Conrad Hilton's holdings expanded throughout the United States and the civilized world.

Then, as he'd resolved, on that Texas train (while broke and facing financial disaster), Connie purchased the Waldorf Astoria (the world's largest hotel) and renamed it the *Conrad Hilton*.

Throughout his life, Hilton continued to dream big dreams. And, at the time of his death, most of his dreams had been realized. Even today, the Hilton Hotel chain continues to span the Globe.

"To accomplish big things…
you must first dream big dreams."
~ Conrad Hilton

SWEET SUCCESS

There are few more recognizable names in America than Hershey. It would be difficult to approach a check-out counter in any grocery, drug, dollar, or convenience store without seeing a candy bar that bears that name. A simple glimpse of one of those chocolate delights might cause one's mouth to water. Yet had it not been for a young man's refusal to give up on his dream in the face of numerous failures, those delicious morsels would not be available today.

Milton Snavely Hershey inherited an entrepreneurial spirit from his dad. When he was a small child, his family moved from town to town while his father attempted various business ventures. All those moves caused Milton's early schooling to be haphazard, and it stopped altogether after the fourth grade.

At 14, young Milton went to work as an apprentice for a newspaper. But he was fired after dropping a tray of type that had already been set. His second position was as a confectioner's apprentice. There he learned to make candy and ice cream.

Milton loved making candy and vowed he would own a candy company one day. So when he was 19, he borrowed $150.00 from his uncle and started a small taffy and caramel business. After preparing the portions, he sold them from a pushcart.

Hershey worked day and night for the next six years to keep his business afloat. But even his young body could not sustain that kind of punishment. So, one day, he collapsed from exhaustion. Physically unable to continue, he was forced to close his shop.

At that time, the Colorado Gold Rush was the talk of the day. So Milton set out to seek his fortune prospecting for gold in Denver. And like most gold rushers, he failed to find very much gold. Badly in need of income, he found work in the Denver Candy Company. While there, he learned a better toffee-making process. But Hershey wasn't happy working for someone else and wanted to own his own business.

He then moved to Chicago, where he and his father opened another candy company. Even though the two made a gallant effort, that business also failed. And though New Orleans looked promising, a similar fate awaited him there. Undeterred, Hershey packed up and moved to New York City to pursue his dream.

Once in the Big Apple, he opened Hershey's Fine Candies. The company got off to a promising start. But things quickly changed when sugar prices drastically increased. Suddenly, his company was losing money, and when a group of kids stole all of his stock, Milton was bankrupt. This time, he lost everything, including his machinery.

Dejected, Hershey returned to Lancaster to start over. Considering his past failures, even his uncle refused to loan him money this time. Luckily, he ran into an ex-employee from a previous venture. Together, they scraped up enough capital to start the Lancaster Caramel Company.

Using what he'd learned in Denver, he devised a new candy formula that included fresh milk. The result of that was Hershey's *Crystal A Caramels. Crystal A's* were popular, and when an English importer chanced by and tasted one, he placed a $2,500.00 order. With that windfall and growing revenue, Milton convinced a bank to advance him $250,000.00.

That money was used to expand the caramel company. Then Milton began to experience the sweet taste of success. Over the next few years, his business did so well that he opened another plant in Pennsylvania and two more in Illinois.

He was shipping caramels all over the nation, and his workforce grew to over 1,400 employees. Hershey's persistence had finally paid off, and this would prove to be only the beginning.

Years earlier, he had viewed an exciting demonstration at the *World's Colombian Exposition* in Chicago. It was a new system of making chocolate using special machinery from Germany. That experience sparked a new determination in him, causing him to resolve, *"Caramels are a fad, but chocolate is permanent. One day, I'm going to be in the chocolate business!"*

With the caramel business booming, Melton took the opportunity to move to chocolates. So, he began construction on the Hershey Chocolate Company. This mammoth and modern facility would use the same machinery he'd observed at the exposition. Little did he know this new plant would soon change the course of the candy industry forever.

The new company experienced rapid success. So much so that Milton decided to sell Lancaster Caramel. The sale brought an astonishing one million dollars! He then turned his full attention to making the nation's finest chocolate.

Soon, the Hershey Chocolate Company produced more than 114 different chocolate candies. Still, Milton was obsessed with the idea of developing "milk chocolate."

Back then, chocolate was a delicacy only the rich could afford.

Hershey wanted to change that and dreamed of perfecting delicious milk chocolate anyone could afford. So he concentrated his energy on developing a new, delicious, inexpensive chocolate bar. Yet, achieving that dream would be no small feat.

His confectioners faced a major dilemma as they strived to create Hershey's ambitious formula. And their success did not look promising. Attaining their goal involved a delicate balance of the candy's taste, consistency, color, and cost. But every time they achieved one feature, significant problems appeared in the others.

Months of experimenting turned into years. Failures were followed by more failures, yet Milton Hershey was no stranger to setbacks. So he did what he'd always done. He persisted. After hundreds of disappointments, the confectioners finally experienced a breakthrough. And the famous Hershey Milk Chocolate formula, as we know it today, became a reality.

The Hershey Bar became an instant phenomenon and would be the product that would make Hershey a famous name all over the world! Milton Hershey's path to sweet success and worldwide fame was fraught with obstacles and setbacks. But through his perseverance, ingenuity, and an admirable ability to bounce back from failure, he was able to build one of the great American fortunes!

Hershey brought joy to millions worldwide with his delicious assortment of affordable milk chocolates. *"One is only happy in proportion as he makes others feel happy."*

"Give them quality. That's the best kind of advertising in the world."
~ Milton S. Hershey

"When you wish upon a star, it makes no difference who you are. Anything your heart desires will come to you!"

Ned Washington

GRANDMA'S CHICKEN SOUP

Motivational speaker **Jack Canfield** often used interesting narratives to inspire his audiences. In the early 90s, after almost every speech, someone would ask if they could get a collection of his stories. But Jack had to tell them no.

Then, he came up with the idea of producing a book of encouraging tales to fill that need. When he mentioned his plan to his friend Mark Victor Hansen, Mark loved the idea so much that he asked to be part of the project.

Jack agreed, and the two got busy compiling one hundred and one of the best stories they could find from around the globe. That was no minor undertaking; however, after months of searching, calling, typing, and editing, their manuscript was finished.

Then, their new book only needed a compelling title to entice their patrons to read it. Yet, they struggled to come up with a name. Nothing they considered seemed to fit.

So, the two resolved to meditate on a title for one hour each day for seven days. On the third day, Jack visualized a green chalkboard and a hand reaching down to write Chicken Soup. Yet, neither Jack nor Mark knew why that would be relevant.

The only thing that came into Jack's mind was his grandmother's chicken soup and her promise that "it would cure anything." He recommended, "*Our title needs to imply that the book will cure anything that troubles the soul.*"

"*I think you have something there!*" Mark replied. "*What do you mean?!*"

"*Chicken Soup for the Soul,*" and the two got chill bumps.
With the script in hand, Jack and Mark found an agent and spent the next 14 months looking for a publisher. But no one wanted their book. The agents would say, "We *are not interested in a collection of short stories.*"

"*That is a stupid title!*"

"*Chicken Soup for the Soul? What does that mean?*" "*People don't buy short story collections.*"

"*No one has ever been successful selling anything like that.*"

Eventually, even their agent returned the book, saying, "*I can't sell this!*"

In all, the original *Chicken Soup* was rejected by 144 publishers. With few options remaining, they took their book to the National Book Sellers Convention in Anaheim, California, where four thousand publishers were represented. Then for the following three days, Jack and Mark went from booth to booth asking, "*Will you publish our book?*" Only to hear, "*No! No! No! No! No! No! No!*"

Late on the third day, the owner of a Health and Wellness publishing company in Florida agreed to read the book. Three days later, he said "*Yes*" to publishing it.

When Jack asked, "*How many copies do you think we will sell?*" The publisher said, *"Maybe 20,000 if we are lucky."*

Then, when the two told him their goal was to sell a million and a half copies in a year and a half, the man laughed out loud!

In June 1993, *Chicken Soup for the Soul* went to press. By the end of December, it was a holiday favorite. The people who received the book as a gift spread the word about this wonderful new book, and sales grew. The new buyers loved it and told their family and friends, and sales grew more...

Finally, the book took on a life of its own. In a short time, with little conventional publicity, word of mouth propelled *Chicken Soup for the Soul* to number one on the New York Times Best Seller List. Then to the amazement of everyone, it remained in the number one position for the following four years, a feat unheard of in the book marketing industry.

Today, the first title alone has sold more than 10 million copies and is still going strong. It continues to provide a cure for souls that need hope, motivation, and inspiration, one short story at a time.

The Chicken Soup Series now has 147 titles in print in 47 languages. Total sales have eclipsed 115,000,000 copies. More than one billion dollars worth of *Chicken Soup* books have sold worldwide.

Letters and emails continue to pour in from people whose lives have been changed by the motivational stories in *Chicken Soup*, which only proves... Grandma was right!

"The Law of Attraction says that you will attract into your life whatever you focus on. Whatever you give your energy and attention to will come back to you."
~ Jack Canfield

THE PHILOSOPHER'S STONE

Joanne (Jo) Kathleen Murray always dreamed of becoming a published author. As a young girl, she made up stories to entertain her younger sister. But as a teenager, her parents encouraged her to pursue other interests. Jo majored in French in college but preferred reading Dickens and Tolkien to school work.

Still anxious to become a writer, she convinced her school to publish one of her essays. After graduating in 1986, she accepted a position with Amnesty International. And though she found this work important, Jo couldn't resist spending her work time typing book ideas. During meetings, she developed character names and jotted down plots. Needless to say, that position did not work out.

One day on a train ride from Manchester to London, an idea came to her mysteriously, and in a flash, a fully formed boy took shape in her head. She could see him clearly, a skinny, dark-haired lad wearing glasses. The revelation gave her a rush of excitement. She had never felt that way about anything before.

Not having access to a pencil or paper, she was forced to sit through the train ride as hundreds of characters and plot lines rushed into her mind.

Getting off the train, Jo felt as if she had met a new friend and relished the thoughts of their future relationship. As soon as she arrived home, she started writing.

After marriage, Joanne became pregnant, but when she miscarried, a dark depression consumed her. A year later, she had a child, which paused her dream of becoming an author. Then her depression became even more severe with the loss of her mother. But the worst was still to come. Once her marriage abruptly ended, Jo was left with nothing but a baby to support.

With little money and no job, Jo depended on government assistance to get by. She often skipped meals to feed her daughter and borrowed money from her friends to pay the rent. She sometimes waitressed at her cousin's short order cafe to bring in a few more dollars, where she would jot down a few pages on napkins between shifts and breaks.

After the baby was asleep at night, she wrote into the morning hours.

Jo took every opportunity to write for five years, mostly while sitting in cafés. When her manuscript was completed, her hopes for its success were high. However, book agents and publishers told her, *"It's too long for children, and it won't be of interest to anyone else!"* Disappointed but not defeated, Joanne sought out other outlets.

Then, a remarkable event provided her with the break she'd needed. An agent agreed to review her manuscript and took the first three chapters to read. Upon arriving home, he dropped the manuscript on a table. A short time later, his 8-year-old daughter Alice said she was bored. So to appease her, he asked if she would help him review a new book.

When Alice agreed, the agent, hoping to divert her attention for a while, handed her a partial manuscript of *Harry Potter and the Philosopher's Stone.* Later that night, Alice returned, insisting that she must read more.

Puzzled, the agent began to quiz his daughter. It was apparent that the little girl was mesmerized by the story. So the next day, the astonished man contacted Joanne and took her on as a client.

Subsequently, he convinced Bloomsbury to publish *Harry Potter*. And though the publisher paid Jo 2,500 pounds for the right to take on the story, their editor was not enthused. He even warned her to *"keep your day job!"* But Jo would never need a job again.

Harry Potter took the world by storm. And, as you probably deduced, Joanne, whose last name was Rowling, became a world-famous author under her pen name, JK Rowling.

> *Jo's pen name is a combination of her first name (Joanne), her grandmother's name (Kathleen), and her maiden name (Rowling).*

Joanne Murray, the single mom, struggling author, and diner waitress who depended on welfare and borrowed money realized her dream and became a published author. Oh yes, she also became the world's first woman billionaire.

> *Don't give up on your dreams, and don't stop trying. One day, you may end up like J.K. Rowling, achieving your goals in the face of everything life places in your way.*

"Had I really succeeded at anything else,
I might never have found the determination to succeed in the
one area where I truly belonged."
~ JK Rowling

HE'D NEVER WORK IN HOLLYWOOD AGAIN

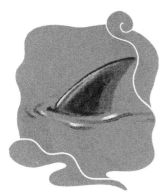

Steve Allen was not a good high school student. His grades were so bad that his applications to the University of Southern California were rejected three times. After failing to gain entrance to USC, he enrolled at California State University. However, he wasn't a very good college student either, so he dropped out to pursue a movie career.

He made numerous attempts to break into the industry again, facing rejection. Even though he was determined to make movies his career, he settled for TV shows and short films. Noticing his excellent work, Universal Studios granted him an internship. After some of Universal's executives previewed one of his short films, they signed him to a seven- year contract.

Despite being the youngest director ever hired, he was able to amass many commercially successful and critically acclaimed credits.

His first major film came in 1974 when he was only 27 years old. However, that production was plagued by every imaginable problem. The word in Hollywood was that the young director had lost control of the project. And he had! The cost of the film skyrocketed, causing him to overspend his budget by 300%. Even worse, his shooting schedule of 55 days drug on for more than twice that long.

When the movie was finally in the can, rather than being elated, Steve suffered an anxiety attack. It's easy to see why! He was sure that he'd never work in Hollywood again.

Yet, without his knowledge, the Universal Studio executives took a unique approach to promoting his movie. Shortly before it hit theaters, they placed numerous 30-second prime-time TV spots.

So, in June of 1975, three nights before the release, every major television network's air was flooded with prime-time trailers. The results were astonishing!! Steve's first major film, Jaws, quickly brought in over 100 million dollars and broke the records of both the *Godfather* and the *Exorcist*. *Jaws* ultimately grossed 260 million dollars in the US alone. And Stephen Allen Spielberg became one of the most influential directors in cinema history and one of the world's wealthiest filmmakers.

His early work in television and short films paid off by laying the groundwork for the wellspring of talent that dazzled audiences for many years. And the University of Southern California, who'd rejected his applications three times, awarded him an honorary doctorate and made him a member of their Board of Councilors.

Author's Note:
If you are enjoying these stories,
more are available at dennisjhenson.com

"I don't dream at night, I dream all day;
I'm dreaming for a living."
~ Steven Spielberg

"THE DREAMER"

For many, simply hearing the name Disney sparks delightful memories.

Walt Disney's creations have entertained children and grownups alike, from cartoons, movies, books, toys, TV shows, theme parks, cruises, or a simple Mickey™ Mouse™ Watch. Yet Walt's ascent to the pinnacle of Big Thunder Mountain wasn't an easy climb; his ups and downs were more exciting than those in any amusement park. So, climb aboard, buckle up, and in just a few moments, we will begin our trip to the wonderful world of Walt Disney. Enjoy the ride!

Once upon a time, in 1901, in Chicago, Walter Elias Disney was born, the fourth son of Elias and Flora Disney. When Walt was two, a baby sister, Ruth, was added to the family. When he was three, his family moved to a small farm near Marceline, Missouri.

"The Happiest Time in My Life"

Walt and little sister Ruth experienced many exciting adventures on the farm. However, farm life wasn't easy for Elias. Financial challenges caused his demeanor to be harsh and unpleasant.

In 1907, Walt's brothers, Herbert and Raymond, ran away and moved back to Chicago. Still, young Walt loved the beauty and freedom of the countryside. He enjoyed fishing, watching passing trains, and visiting downtown Marceline under the supervision of his remaining brother, Roy.

Walt's grandmother often read fairy tales to him and Ruth at bedtime. As she read, Walt would drift off and become part of the stories.

Another thing that he really enjoyed was being around and playing with the farm animals. He gave each animal a name and carried on imaginary conversations with them, bestowing them with human-like qualities. His best friend was a pig named Porker. Porker was intelligent and enjoyed playing with him. She even allowed Walt to ride on her back.

"I guess I really loved that pig. . . . She had an acute sense of fun and mischief. . . . Do you remember the foolish pig in The Three Little Pigs? Porker was the model for him."

Yet, drawing was Walt's true passion. His sketches were popular with his family and nearby neighbors. Once a doctor friend paid him a nickel for drawing a sketch of his horse. Yet, Elias wasn't impressed by Walt's art and thought he should spend more time on farm work.

On the other hand, Flora encouraged the boy and convinced his father to purchase a set of colored pencils and a Big Chief Tablet. Overjoyed with his gift, young Disney spent much of his time copying cartoons from newspapers and the pictures in his grandmother's fairy tale book.

Despite Walt's later remarkable success with his art, Elias never considered it a real profession.

While living on the farm, Walt became infatuated with trains. He and Ruth loved to watch them pass by on the nearby Santa Fe Railroad. By putting his ear on the tracks, he could hear an approaching locomotive a mile away. The children's Uncle Mike, an engineer, would often bring them a bag of candy when his train passed near the farm. And sometimes Uncle Mike would allow Walt to pull the cord and blow the train's whistle.

Main Street

Walt, Ruth, and Roy formed a lifelong bond while enjoy- ing the happiest times of their lives in Marceline. The little town's main street was a beehive of activity with shops, restaurants, dry goods stores, and a theater. For the most part, it was a typical early 20th century, mid-western city.

If you've ever walked Main Street in Disneyland™ or Walt Disney World™, you've seen a glimpse of the way Walt remembered Marceline.

The siblings took every opportunity to spend time in the city. Buffalo Bill Cody's Wild West Show was in town on one visit.

Cody, who had been a rider for the Pony Express, an Army Scout, and a buffalo hunter, headed up a popular circus-like Wild West Show that traveled from city to city in the early 1900s.

A parade was scheduled to draw attention to upcoming performances. When a large crowd gathered, lining the entire length of Main Street, Buffalo Bill himself appeared, driving the lead wagon. As the procession began, Bill spotted a small boy gazing in amazement. Cody asked if he would like to ride. Walt climbed up and sat beside *The Greatest Showman of the Old West.* Throughout the route, Walt smiled and waved to the crowd. After that first experience with a celebrity, he commented…

"I was mighty impressed!"

On other visits to downtown Marceline, Walt attended a circus, a movie, and a live play (Peter Pan). Between the farm, going downtown, and fishing, Walt and Ruth couldn't have had it much better.

Despite their bliss, the stress of running a farm was more than Elias could handle. So, to the children's dismay, he sold the farm and moved the family to Kansas City.

Kansas City

At the tender age of nine, Walt found himself a stranger in a big city. But all was not lost because he discovered a spectacular distraction, *Electric Park,* a few blocks from his new home."

"Electric Park"

In 1910, electric lights were still a rarity. Only the very rich had them in their homes. Consequently, a large light display drew a crowd, especially in the American heartland. Kansas City's *Electric Park* featured more than 100,000 lights. It was designed to depict a small German village. It included a merry-go-round, a roller-coaster, and ten other rides.

There was a shooting gallery, a penny arcade, a bandstand, a dance pavilion, a performance theater, a bowling alley, and animal attractions. But the thing that most captured Walt was the scenic train ride encircling the park.

At night, strands of lights outlined every attraction. A luminescent fountain served as a stage for nightly live shows, with actors dressed in colorful costumes. Finally, the park featured a massive fireworks display each evening just before closing.

The Vision

When the young boy first saw the park at night, the vision left a lasting impression. Long strands of lights raised from their centers by poles of various lengths were placed throughout the park. Viewing the scene from a distance, those lofty lighted spheres, and ornate turrets amid the illuminated structures rising high into the black, star-filled

Midwestern sky were magical.

That mystical site reminded Walt of the magnificent castles in the fairy tales that his grandmother read to him. The scene, augmented by the flashes of shooting roman candles and exploding rockets was one he'd never forget. Young Walt's impression of that fairy tale castle was one he would never forget. And decades later, his reconstruction of that vision would become an integral part of Disney magic.

Elementary School and a Newspaper Route

Elias, strict as always, frowned on playtime, sweets, toys, and especially amusement parks. He purchased two *Kansas City Star* newspaper routes with the money from the farm sale. Walt and Roy were assigned the daily responsibility of delivering newspapers. For the next few years, in worn-out shoes, the two boys delivered papers from 4:30 AM until school started, then from the end of the school day until the evening routes were completed.

Walt found classes at *Benton Grammar School* challenging, often nodding off and missing parts of the lessons. When awake, his class time was spent daydreaming of fairy tales and distant castles or sketching animals and locomotives.

Three positive things happened during those school days.

First, Walt was cast to play *Peter Pan* in the school play. And, when it was time for Peter to fly, Roy hoisted him by pulling a rope, a remarkable foreshadowing of things to come!

Second, the *Kansas City Star* rewarded its paperboys with a pass to the black and white silent movie *Snow White and the Seven Dwarfs*™. And lastly, he met and befriended Walter Pfeiffer. Walter's father liked young Disney and allowed him to accompany his family to Vaudeville shows and motion pictures.

Disney subsequently spent more time with the Pfeiffers than with his family and couldn't get enough of Vaudeville or the movies. He visited Vaudeville acts so often that he memorized the gags and shared them with his schoolmates.

First Attempt at Animation

When Ruth became bedridden with measles, Walt was assigned to take care of her. Anxious to keep her entertained, he made his first attempt at animation by creating a series of drawings. When flipped, the pictures appeared to move.

The Young Entrepreneur

As the newspaper routes grew, they became more than Walt and Roy could handle, so Elias paid other boys to help make the deliveries. Yet, he never compensated Walt or Roy for their work.

"That is their part as family members."

So, when Roy finished high school, he'd had enough, and in 1912, he left the family home to work for his Uncle Will.

Conversely, Walt was industrious and earned his own money. While still running his paper routes: he charged businesses to deliver packages, purchased additional newspapers to sell independently, and, in exchange for haircuts, drew customer caricatures for a barber.

The young entrepreneur then spent his money on candy, snacks, and train rides at *Electric Park*. He also enrolled in a correspondence course on drawing cartoons and attended art classes at the *Kansas City Art Institute*.

When Walt was 15, Elias sold the paper routes, invested the profits in the *Chicago Jelly Company*, and moved to Illinois. But this time, Walt chose to stay behind and moved in with Roy.

News Butcher

On his own for the first time, things didn't go that well. Roy helped Walt secure a position as a news butcher for the Santa Fe Railroad and loaned him the required $15.00 bond. For the next two months, Walt enjoyed the romance of traveling along sprawling lines to cities in a half-dozen states. His blue serge uniform, brass buttons, cap, and badge made him feel important. As trains rolled into each station, he stood beside the conductor, offering to sell passengers magazines, peanuts, candy, apples, and soft drinks.

And though Walt loved working around trains, he couldn't resist eating his products. And when he failed to collect the soft drink bottles after one trip, he lost all of the money for their deposits. Soon he was broke and was forced to rejoin his parents.

While living in "The Windy City" and working at his father's Jelly Factory, he decided that art would be his future.

Needless to say, Elias wasn't impressed with that decision. Nevertheless, he arranged for him to take classes at "The Chicago Academy of Fine Arts."

High School and WWI

At 16, Walt entered McKinley High, where he became the school photographer and produced drawings for their newspaper. But, World War I was raging, and when Roy enlisted in the Navy, Walt dropped out of school to follow suit. Unfortunately, he was rejected for being underage. Yet when one of his friends learned that the Canadian Army was accepting younger volunteers, the two boys planned to sneak across the border to enlist. However, when his friend's mother found his packed suitcase, she called Walt's mother and ended their plans.

Still determined, his friend learned that the American Ambulance

Corps would accept volunteers as young as 17. So Walt, still 16, took a black pen and altered the birth year on his notarized passport application, making him appear 17 He then enlisted in the Red Cross Ambulance Corps on September 16, 1918. While his parents were unhappy about him going overseas, they reluctantly agreed.

A Very Close Call

Simultaneously, the horrific Spanish flu epidemic was raging. Nearly one-half of the deaths it caused were among young adults. Hospitals were overwhelmed and had neither the staff nor the medicine to treat the onslaught of sick patients.

More US soldiers were dying from Spanish flu than being killed in battle.

When the epidemic hit Chicago, thousands of young adults were stricken, and many died. Walt and two others in his barracks became so sick they were released to be hospitalized.

When the ambulance arrived, the driver asked, *"Kid, do you live in Chicago?"*

"Yes, I do."

"Then, let us take you home. If we take you to the hospital, you won't come out alive."

So the driver took him to his parent's home and delivered him to his visibly shaken family on a stretcher. Flora put her son in bed and brought in a local doctor who treated him with heavy doses of quinine. Then she nursed him through weeks of high fever and delirium, wrapping him in poultices and treating him with a mother's love and more quinine.

Disney remained delirious for more than a week, then slowly regained his strength.

Would Walt have survived had the ambulance not taken him home? There is no way to know for sure, but as the driver predicted, the two boys admitted to the hospital died a few days later.

When Disney attempted to return to his company, he found they'd sailed without him. By the time he reconnected with his unit, the war was over. Yet, drivers were still needed to help evacuate troops, so Walt was stationed in Paris on November 11, 1918, just days after the Armistice.

While in France, Disney earned money by drawing cartoons for soldiers to send home to their loved ones. He also used his skills to paint animal characters on his truck. On a larger scale, the military newspaper *Stars and Stripes* used some of his drawings in their publications.

Driving his ambulance throughout Europe for the next 12 months gave Walt a broader world perspective.

Back to Kansas City

Returning to the States in 1919, Walt turned down an excellent position at the Chicago Jelly Factory and moved to Kansas City. There, hoping to pursue an art career, he took a job at the Pesmen-Rubin Commercial Art Studio. The position paid $50 a month, but Walt was laid off after only a few weeks for *"lack of creativity."* But that episode wasn't a total loss; while at Pesmen-Rubin, he met and befriended a fellow artist, Ub Iwerks.

Iwerks-Disney Commercial Artists

Both now jobless (in 1921) Ub and Walt formed Iwerks- Disney Commercial Artists. And though the two were talented at drawing ads and cartoon panels, their selling skills were nonexistent.

Consequently, a few weeks later, that project also failed. Nevertheless, their next move would not only reset the course of their lives but also spark the creation of an entirely new industry.

Meanwhile, at the Jelly Factory, things were not panning out, so Elias, Flora, and Ruth returned to Kansas City. And for the first time in a long time, Walt enjoyed having his family close again.

The Kansas City Slide Company & Animation

When Disney learned of a position at the Kansas City Slide Company producing cartoons, he submitted his application and was hired. The company was so impressed with Walt's work that they asked him if he knew of others with similar skills. And when Walt told them of his friend Ub, he was also hired.

Disney was so intrigued by the slide company's technique of bringing characters to life that he vowed to improve his animating skills. So, visiting the Public Library, he pored over Edward Muybridge's *Human Images in Motion* and other books on animation. Using the information he'd gleaned from these books, Walt created the illusion of movement on multiple images.

Then, after convincing his boss to lend him an old camera, Disney converted his brother's garage into a makeshift studio. There he spent every spare minute creating animated shorts. Walt's devotion to hard work and education didn't go unnoticed by Roy, who later stated...

"Long after everyone was in bed, Walt was out there still, puttering away, working away, experimenting, trying this and that."

Meanwhile, at the Jelly Factory, things were not working out, so Elias, Flora, and Ruth returned to Kansas City. And for the first time in a long time, Walt enjoyed having his family close again.

Laugh-O-Grams

While working at the slide company, Walt attempted to expand his customer base. His first short cartoons were sold to a small Kansas City theater chain, Newman Theaters. And, though his costs were more than his pay, Disney gained something better than profits: education and the exhilaration of being a local celebrity.

Newman commissioned Walt to create 12 cartoons, this time for a profit. So, he set up a production company called *Laugh- O-Gram Studio*. Working at the slide company during the day and producing *Laugh-O-Grams* at night, Disney eventually earned enough to buy a camera and rent an office.

Realizing that producing animated films was not a one-man operation, he hired local art students and co-workers as animators.

While at *Laugh-O-Gram*, Walt started to dream of becoming someone important in the movie industry.

Good Times

Things started looking up in 1922 when Laugh-O-Gram Studio signed a distribution contract for 6 animated shorts with Pictorial Clubs of Tennessee.

Six Cartoon Shorts for Pictorial Clubs:

1. "The Four Musicians of Bremen"
2. "Little Red Riding Hood"
3. "Goldilocks and the Three Bears"
4. "Cinderella"
5. "Puss in Boots"
6. "Jack and the Bean Stalk"

Pictorial Clubs agreed to pay Laugh-O-Grams" $100.00 upfront and $11,000.00 once the shorts were completed.

Walt had the ammunition to persuade investors to purchase stock in his studio with his current customers and this new contract. He raised $15,000.00 of badly needed capital. Brimming with success, Disney bought new equipment, hired Ub, and brought in five additional animators.

Laugh-O-Gram's future looked bright. For the first time, Walt had money to spend. Suddenly he could wear nice clothes, watch plays, enjoy good meals, and have dates or go out with his friends.

Walt's favorite pastime was movies, where he was treated to a newsreel, a cartoon, a short, and a full-length feature. Except for an enthusiastic pianist, these features were silent.

He also frequented *Electric Park,* where he took his dates to the dance pavilion and enjoyed the rides with his friends and fellow artists.

Note: During one visit to Electric Park, Disney is rumored to have told Rudolph Ising... "Someday I will own one of these!" (Referring to the park)

Laugh-O-Gram Studio was buzzing and flush with people. His studio churned out eleven Newman films, numerous local advertisements, and the Pictorial Clubs shorts. Walt hadn't felt this good since he left Marceline, savoring the activity and seeing only smooth sailing ahead.

A Huge Disappointment

Unfortunately, his euphoria wouldn't last. Roy contracted tuberculosis, and in an attempt to save his life, the Navy placed him in a TB Sanatorium in Los Angeles.

Then Elias, Flora, and Ruth moved to Portland. So, except for his staff, Walt was all alone. And, Disney received the devastating news that Pictorial Clubs had declared bankruptcy. And, though they had received all of the Laugh- O-Gram shorts, they would not be paying their $11,000.

If that wasn't bad enough, when Pictorial Club's assets (including the shorts) were sold to a New York company, that company assumed no responsibility for that debt. As you can imagine, Laugh-O-Gram stock took a colossal hit. Soon Walt's employees were working without pay. And, though they loved the work and probably would like to have stayed, one by one, they took other jobs that included paychecks.

A Glimmer of Hope

The handwriting was on the wall, but Walt refused to go down easy. He worked day and night desperately trying to save his business. A glimmer of hope did appear when the Deener Dental Institute offered Laugh-O-Gram a contract to produce a short about dental hygiene.

Taking heart from this, Walt rehired some of his artists. Although the project paid $500.00, Disney invested in a new film, *Alice's Adventures in Wonderland,* instead of paying his debt. At the time, it looked as though he had made a terrible mistake, but that move turned out to be one of the best choices he'd ever make.

Alice's Adventures in Wonderland incorporated live-action along with animated characters with background. It was an excellent demonstration of the advancements made at the Laugh-O-Gram Studio. Nevertheless, it only added more debt to an already struggling company without a paying customer. It was too late; Walt's costs were more than he could handle by then. He couldn't even pay his own rent.

Last Days in Kansas City

Strapped for cash, Disney gave up his apartment and moved into his office. He slept on the floor, showered at the train station, and survived on an occasional $30.00 check from Roy. His diet was cold beans from a can and water. Still, even an empty bean can bring good fortune if you have a big enough dream.

An Uninvited Visitor

With the studio empty and Walt all alone with his thoughts, an uninvited visitor appeared. It was a tiny mouse, probably attracted by the smell of the cans in the trash. Startled by the intrusion, Disney jumped, and the frightened mouse scurried away. But the next day, as Walt worked at his drawing table, the mouse reappeared and looked at him with a questioning stare.

Still, a little taken aback, Walt said *"Hi"* and proceeded to do what he'd done so many times back on the farm. He struck up a conversation with the little critter. He imagined the mouse saying, *"Hi, I'm Mortimer, but you can call me Mort."*

Happy to have some company, Walt replied, *"My name is Walt Disney, but my friends call me Diz."*

That night Walt left out a few beans and some water, hoping to keep his new friend coming back. Disney became quite fond of that mouse, and the little guy seemed to enjoy sitting on Walt's drawing board, watching him draw. Walt took solace in Mort's company and found him a sympathetic creature. Eventually, he poured out his soul to Mort as if he were an actual person.

Relating his successes and disappointments to the critter, Walt imagined the little fellow replying, *"Gosh"* or *"Oh boy!"* Then for the really depressing stuff... *"Aw, gee!"* And when Disney told Mort his dreams for the future, the mouse simply replied, *"That sure is swell!"*

Disney appreciated Mort and would again one day recall these conversations. But their friendship would soon be terminated. His studio was out of options, and young Disney accepted his third major disappointment. Laugh-O-gram Studio was finished.

Note: Although it may seem Laugh-O-Gram was just another failure, that little studio incubated talent, which would have a tremendous influence on the film industry for decades to come. Each of these notable animators and producers got their start in Kansas City at the Laugh-O- Gram Studio: Ub Iwerks (Oswald the Lucky Rabbit™ and Minnie™ Mouse), Friz Freleng (Porky Pig, Tweety, and Sylvester), Hugh Harman (Bosko), and Carman Maxwell (Loony Tunes).

A New Direction

Walt wasn't just broke and out of a job; he was barefoot and soon to be homeless. He did own some shoes but didn't have enough money to retrieve them from the cobbler shop.

Defeated and despondent, Disney was forced to sell his most prized possession, his camera. With the money from that sale, he bailed out his shoes and purchased a train ticket to Los Angeles. His Uncle Robert (who lived in Hollywood) agreed to let him stay with him until he could find work. Disney believed that in Southern California, more people should be interested in his talent. And he could visit Roy, who was convalescing in a Tuberculosis Sanatorium there.

On the train to Hollywood, a passenger asked him, *"What business do you have in Hollywood?"*

When Disney replied, *"I make cartoons,"* the passenger, with a scowl, said, *"Oh."*

Arriving in California

Stepping off the train in Hollywood, Disney's only possessions were:
• The clothes he was wearing: shirt, pants, sport coat that didn't match his pants, and shoes with patched holes
• A cardboard suitcase containing an extra shirt, briefs, drawing materials, and a partially completed reel of the Alice short
• $40.00
• And a burning desire to make it in the film industry.

Walt wanted to make it big in Hollywood, but he wasn't sure how. Maybe he would become an actor or a director. Even though his true passion was making animated films, he believed he'd missed his chance; because the New York studios were so far ahead.

After settling in at Uncle Bob's, he methodically visited each movie studio and applied for acting and directing positions. But Walt was just one of the thousands seeking those jobs. Nonetheless, while at the studios, he spent the entire day asking questions and learning about the movie-making process.

After being rejected for his initial applications, he re-applied for any available work, only to be turned away again. After several weeks without success, Uncle Bob asked him when he would get a job. Walt concluded that finding work in the film industry wasn't in the cards. So he talked his uncle into allowing him to convert his garage into a studio.

Fate Stepped In

After setting up a makeshift office, he sent the "Alice" short to the New York film distributors, hoping to generate some interest. Then, *fate stepped in!*

When Margaret Winkler, the owner of Winkler Pictures, received Walt's film, the timing couldn't have been better. She had been promoting Out of the Inkwell and *Felix the Cat*™ cartoons. And, when Walt's film arrived, Out of the Inkwell had informed her that they were not renewing their contract. So she was looking for a replacement, and after viewing the *Alice* short, she immediately sent Disney a telegram.

Her wire contained an offer for six *Alice* shorts and stated that Winkler Pictures would pay $1,500.00 for each short (about $22,000.00 in today's money). Walt couldn't believe "his luck."

Roy Disney

In the early 1920s, tuberculosis (TB) was another deadly illness with a high mortality rate. It was certainly not something to be taken lightly. Roy Disney, a U.S. Navy World War One Veteran, contracted the disease. And in an attempt to save his life, the Navy placed him in one of the nation's top TB sanatoriums near Hollywood. Having been deathly ill, Roy convalesced in his hospital room when Walt appeared. The younger Disney was beside himself with both excitement and panic.

"Oh, Roy, I don't know what to do! I received this offer from Winkler Pictures, and it's the opportunity of a lifetime! I'm sure I have the knowledge to create the films, but I don't have the resources or the business skills to pull this off!" Handing Roy the telegram, he asked again, *"Roy, what am I going to do?"*

The older Disney read the telegram, then turned and studied his little brother's face. He remembered Walt's hard work and the time he'd spent researching and developing his skills back in Kansas. The older Disney was also impressed that Walt realized he couldn't do this project alone and needed the help of someone possessing business skills.

A Miracle?

Roy then got out of his sickbed, put on his street clothes, and the two brothers left the hospital together. The following day, they formed Disney Brothers Studio (the first cartoon studio in California).

Note: Roy lived 48 more years, outliving Walt, and never again exhibited any symptoms of tuberculosis.

Eight years Walt's senior, Roy was a wise and kindly man who understood business finance (having worked in banking).

He possessed the ability to raise capital, deal with employees, see to all other business matters, and somewhat control Walt's spending. His presence allowed Walt to do what he did best--be creative.

Note: Without Roy's help, the name Disney would probably not be recognized today.

Disney Brothers Studio

On October 16th, 1923, the "The Disney Brothers Cartoon Studio" was formed. Their first order of business was to sign the contract with "Universal Studios" that "Winkler Pictures" had brokered. They then rented a small room in a Real Estate office and purchased a used camera for $200.00. Walt did the animation, and Roy operated the camera.

At first, their only income was $85.00 from Roy's monthly Navy disability check. Walt knew that animation would be too time-consuming and that his focus should be on development and direction. So in anticipation of the payments from Winkler, he offered Iwerks a small salary and 20% of the company if he would join them in Hollywood.

He also hired and trained other young artists to do the tedious work of animating and two girls for inking and painting the celluloids. One of those girls was Lillian Bounds. Walt then focused his energy on story development and directing. And in March of 1924, the first

Alice Comedies reached theaters.

Marriage

After the payments started arriving, Walt purchased a small car, and most evenings, he offered his employees a ride home. And though the other workers lived farther away, Walt always dropped Lillian Bounds off last. Walt and Lillian began dating and were married in 1925.

The brothers placed a down payment on a large lot one week before their marriage. That purchase was the first step toward building a studio to house the *Alice* series production.

Note: The brothers didn't sell stock in their studio until 17 years later.

Meanwhile, Margaret Winkler also married one of her employees, Charles Mintz. And once she became pregnant, Mintz took over the management of Winkler Pictures.

This caused a shift in the two company's working relationship. Mintz never shared Margaret's enthusiasm for Disney's work and took every opportunity to downplay it.

Oswald the Lucky Rabbit ™

Around the same time, Universal executives decided that they would like to replace Alice with a new cartoon character, possibly a rabbit. So, they asked Winkler Pictures to make that happen.

Margaret wanted to give the project to Disney. However, Charles disagreed; but Margaret, who still owned the company, offered it to them anyway. Walt concurred that *Alice* had run its course and was excited to accept a new challenge.

Iwerks created a rabbit character that Mintz approved. When Universal executives came up with names they liked, they couldn't agree on which one.

So they had a drawing and literally pulled *Oswald the Rabbit*™ out of their hat. Since a rabbit's foot was believed to bring good luck, the character was ultimately named *Oswald the Lucky Rabbit*™.

In 1926, at Roy's urging, the studio was renamed Walt Disney Studios. Roy believed the new name fit better because Walt was the visionary. That same year the studio moved to a new building on Hyperion Avenue, the birthplace of some of Disney's greatest films, also known as Hyperion Studio.

Walt Disney studios devoted 100% of its effort to the production of *Oswald*™. And, almost immediately, audiences and critics alike warmed to the lucky rabbit. Nine *Oswald*™ shorts were released in 1927 alone.

With the series an incredible success, Walt convinced Roy to allow him to bring in additional animators. He hired many of his Laugh-O-Gram artists and supplemented his studio with local talent. Additionally, he bought the latest state-of- the-art equipment and taught animation night classes to the new animators.

The expansion, and the demand for more shorts, caused production costs to soar. To save money, Walt split the artists into groups to develop two cartoons simultaneously. Yet despite their success, Mintz continually downplayed Disney's work.

Trouble Brewing

With Walt spending most of his time trying to improve the business, he was oblivious to the behind-the-scenes chaos brewing. Rumors were rampant that George Winkler (Mintz's brother-in-law) was conspiring with Disney's animators. Still, Walt was too busy to bother with gossip and dismissed the idea.

As the *Oswald*™ contract wound down, Disney's production costs surpassed their income. Nevertheless, the series' popularity had Walt and Roy convinced that their agreement would easily be renewed and include a pay increase.

A Trip to NewYork

Unaware of the betrayal, Walt and Lillian traveled to New York to renegotiate. Mintz had already secured a new *Oswald*™ deal with Universal. When Walt arrived at Winkler Pictures, he was optimistic about the future. But his optimism quickly vanished when Mintz proposed a 20% reduction in pay for retaining Disney.

Walt couldn't believe what he was hearing and threatened to drop the project altogether. However, Mintz reminded him that contractually, all characters appearing in the shorts were the property of Universal Studios. And, as was the custom in those days, Disney's contract relinquished those copyrights.

But the worst was yet to come; Mintz had successfully coerced 19 of Disney's 22 animators to sign contracts with him. And, even though Walt attempted to make a separate deal with Universal, Winkler Pictures already had a signed contract.

Universal suggested that Mintz be allowed to take over Disney's studio to salvage Disney. Walt rejected that idea and walked away from *Oswald*™, resolving to retain the future rights to his characters.

A Prophetic Warning

Before leaving New York, Walt met with Mintz a final time and gave him this prophetic warning, *"Be prepared! If those guys desert me, they will do the same to you!"*

As usual, Disney was correct. The following year, two of those same animators met with Universal executives in an attempt to take over

Oswald's™ distribution from Mintz.

Consequently, Universal, sick of all the bickering and politics, took *Oswald's*™ distribution in-house and assigned it to Walter Lantz (Woody Woodpecker's eventual creator). But before Lantz accepted the assignment, he checked with Walt and received his blessing. The two gentlemen remained friends for the balance of their lives.

Since Universal's involvement meant Walt's films were shown in larger, more prestigious theaters and the cartoons were a hit with audiences and critics alike, Disney greatly benefited from the exposure he received.

Back to Square One

No longer owning the characters that he created and having lost the vast majority of his animators, a devastated and saddened Walt Disney yet again faced an imminent business collapse.

The Train Ride Home (1928)

He had taken those struggling artists with raw talent and trained them to be professionals in a new form of media. He considered them friends and loved them like family. Disney's heart was broken; he'd been betrayed and lost his characters. With these things weighing on his mind, he and Lillian boarded the train to Hollywood.

Determined not to be destroyed or to face Roy and Ub without a single character, Walt took a notepad and began to draw. Cats were out. There were too many cat cartoons already. And though he sketched a raccoon, a dog, a possum, a bear, and even a frog, nothing seemed right; and his feelings of depression persisted.

But the motion of the moving train, the ringing of the bell, the rhythmic clacking, and the occasional blows of the whistle helped to soothe his ruffled spirit.

Before long, the sweet relief of sleep overtook him. While drifting off, he recalled the last time he'd felt so low. Soon he found himself back at his Laugh-O-Gram office, commiserating with Mort.

A jolt of the train woke him from his dream. Then, "like a bolt our of the blue," it hit him; a mouse! *My character will be--a Mouse!* Now wide awake, Walt looked at Lillian.

She sensed the change in his demeanor. *"What is it, Walt?" "I have it! My new character; will be a mouse, Mortimer Mouse!"*

Although Lillian managed a faint smile, Walt could tell she had reservations.

"What? You don't think a mouse is a good choice?"

"Oh, it's not that. It's the name. It should be happier and friendlier; maybe Mickey™ would be a better fit."

Walt looked at his wife for a few seconds, then as a big smile covered his face, he said the name for the first time… *"Mickey Mouse™? Mickey Mouse™! I think you may have something there."*

And so was conceived the most famous cartoon character ever to grace the silver screen. "Mickey Mouse™!" He couldn't wait to tell Roy and Ub.

Walt Disney often said, *"I only hope that we never lose sight of one thing—that it was all started by a mouse."* But I sometimes wonder, *"Which mouse?"*

Of course, I don't know what really happened in that train car. Still, none of the evidence I have uncovered disputes anything in this story.

Mickey Mouse™ Takes Shape

By the time that train ride ended, Walt had mapped out a plan to produce *Mickey Mouse™* cartoons. And upon Walt's return to Hollywood, Iwerks took the lead in implementing that plan.

Unfortunately, Disney's optimism wasn't shared by the big movie houses. When he showed *Mickey™* to MGM, they were unimpressed and remarked, *"A giant mouse on the screen would terrify women!"* and *"Nothing about this character stands out above any others."*

So, despite Walt's considerable effort to market *Mickey™*, no one was interested. *Mickey™* was just another character competing for screen space with F*elix the Cat™* and even *Oswald the Lucky Rabbit™*. His first two cartoons, *Plane Crazy* and *The Galloping Gaucho* failed to find distribution. But Walt's belief was strong, so he moved forward with a new and different approach.

Steamboat Willy™ (1928)

The previous fall, audiences had been blown away by the *Jazz Singer*, which featured a new synchronized sound technique. Disney reasoned that the novelty would sell if he could produce talking cartoons. So the Walt Disney Studio started creating their first synchronized sound cartoon, *Steamboat Willie™*, starring *Mickey Mouse™*!

Once the animation was complete, Walt needed a sound system and a distributor. Finding nothing on the West Coast, he visited New York City. Delivery systems in the Big Apple were costly and low quality. Then, he met Pat Powers.

Powers was well known in the industry and owned a sound recording business. His system, Cine-phone™ (which allowed theaters to run sound films), operated at a fraction of the cost of the heavyweights like RCA.

But the kicker was if Walt agreed to use Cine-phone Sound™, Powers would distribute *Mickey Mouse*™ cartoons through his company, Celebrity Pictures.

"Cine-phone" was an optical sound-on-film system that allowed sound to be recorded directly onto the film strip. This system became the industry standard and was the predecessor of every sound system used today, such as Dolby Digital™.

Pat offered Walt $2,500.00 upfront and 10% of gross earnings from each *Mickey Mouse*™ cartoon. Although Disney should have been wary of Powers, he desperately wanted his sound system and needed a distributor (having been rejected by all the others). So, Walt signed an agreement with Celebrity Pictures.

Even using the lesser expensive Cine-phone™, adding sound was costly. Walt and Roy drew money from anywhere they could, including their personal money.

Unfortunately, their first attempt to synchronize a cartoon with music and sound effects was a total disaster. Yet, Walt refused to give up.

Having exhausted every other available source of funds, he instructed Roy to sell his most valued possession, his *Moon Roadster* sports car.

The roadster sale brought in enough money to complete a second attempt. However, nothing had really changed, and the probability of another catastrophe loomed.

Although the brothers knew a second failure would mean the end of Walt Disney Studios, they continued to move forward.

Then, *"fate stepped in again!"* Wilfred Jackson, a Disney animator whose mother was a piano teacher, suggested creating a metronome by adding a bouncing ball to the film. This simple change made synchronizing the music and sound effects achievable. After implementing that technique, their next attempt was a smashing success.

On November 18, 1928, *Steamboat Willie*™ opened at the Colon Theater in New York. It was billed as *"the first animated cartoon with Synchronized Sound."* To say that it was a hit would be an understatement. As Walt had predicted, the cartoon thrilled audiences, and the press gave it glowing reviews.

Mickey Mouse™ quickly overtook *Felix the Cat*™ as the world's favorite cartoon character. The phenomenal success of *Steamboat Willie*™ challenged every other cartoon studio. It established Disney as a major player in the animation industry.

Mickey™'s popularity continued to skyrocket. Walt replaced all the animators he'd lost to Winkler, and he couldn't wait to use them to begin new and more challenging projects. *Steamboat Willie*™ not only brought Walt his first major success but also his first Academy Award.

It's interesting to note that the sale of Walt's Moon Roadster was made only two weeks before Steamboat Willie™ *debuted.*

That same year, 1929, the Walt Disney Studio changed to Walt Disney Productions, Ltd. It established its subsidiaries–Walt Disney Enterprises (for merchandising), Disney Film Recording Company, Ltd. (for music), and Liled Realty and Investment Company (for real estate). But, eight years later, the subsidiaries merged with their parent company Walt Disney Productions.

As Disney's studios cranked out *Mickey Mouse*™ cartoons, Walt moved forward in an entirely new direction. Until then, cartoons were based on individual characters and had predictable plots. Walt's *Silly Symphonies*™ broke that mold.

Using animated pieces set to classical music allowed Disney animators the freedom to experiment. The *Skeleton Dance* was first. It featured macabre bones and skulls dancing through a graveyard by moonlight.

However, Pat Powers wasn't impressed and was confident that musical cartoons would not sell. Yet, Walt prevailed, and the *Silly Symphonies*™ were not only profitable but also helped to advance the art of animation.

Another Takeover Attempt (1930)

From the beginning, Walt believed that Powers was more interested in promoting Cine-phone™ than Disney cartoons. And, since he needed Pat's sound system, Walt failed to thoroughly read the agreement with Celebrity Pictures.

Unfortunately, the contract allowed Powers to advance a small amount (sound familiar?) on each film from expected profits. Yet, it didn't require Pat to produce any receipts showing the earnings. Nevertheless, with business booming, Walt was confident that the cartoon's revenues would be more than enough to fund the studio's growth.

However, Roy started to notice that the royalty payments from Powers were arriving erratically and were for considerably less than he'd anticipated. And, after a year of success with *Mickey Mouse*™ and *Silly Symphonies*™, Roy told Walt of his concerns.

When Walt confronted him, Powers didn't deny owing more. To the contrary, he admitted he'd been withholding cash all along. Powers believed that Disney's Studio would not survive unless he took over. So he had withheld money to expedite the company's demise.

Walt wouldn't stand for it and engaged an attorney. Then once again, he again began searching for that elusive honest distributor.

Powers believed that Iwerks was the secret to Disney's success. So he provided Ub the funds to start his own studio and a distribution contract for anything he produced. And though Iwerks accepted and resigned, Walt refused to give in and continued without Ub.

Note: Iwerks sold his 20% interest in Disney back to Walt for around $2,000.00, a decision he'd lived to regret. (Just think what 20% of Disney was worth 10 years later).

Walt and Roy lost almost $150,000 from their association with Powers, money that Pat promised to pay if they would extend his contract. But it was too late. Walt had moved on.

Note: Ub did form a studio, but he and Powers never saw eye-to-eye. None of his cartoons caught on, and the Iwerks Studio lasted less than 2 years. Ub eventually returned to Disney, where he worked for the balance of his life as an employee, not a part-owner.

After Iwerks Departure

Walt regretted losing his friend and best animator. Still, Mickey Mouse™ was already a national sensation, and Merry Melodies had already caught on. This time finding a distributor was easy. Columbia Pictures was happy to start distributing Disney's products.

So, in contrast to Pat Power's belief that Disney would fold, the studio thrived and moved on to even more challenging projects. Walt discontinued relations with Powers' company but couldn't afford a lawsuit. So, he walked away from a $150,000.00 commission.

The first Mickey Mouse™ product was a paper tablet. The Big Chief's picture was replaced by a color picture of Mickey Mouse™. Also, in 1930, the first Mickey Mouse™ doll was released.

The Original Mickey™ Mouse™ Club

The famous TV *Mickey Mouse™* Club was not the first to bear that name. The original club started in 1930 in Ocean Park, California's

Fox Dome Theater. The club quickly expanded throughout the USA and to other countries.

Mickey Mouse™ made his first newspaper appearance on January 13, 1930.

By 1931, *Mickey Mouse™* Club memberships surpassed one million, and *Mickey™* was recognized in every civilized country.

The original "Mickey Mouse™ Clubs" grew to over 2,000,000 before being phased out in 1935.

Despite its national popularity, the studio still found it challenging to stay afloat. The struggles with Powers, his wife Lillian's miscarriage, and his work schedule were more than Walt's body could handle. Consequently, in October 1931, Walt suffered a nervous breakdown, causing his doctors' to insist that he take a break.

Reluctantly, Walt took Lillian on a cruise to Cuba and Panama. However, that trip was what was needed. And when Disney returned to Hollywood, he came up with a bold new idea.

Technicolor™

Walt's timing was perfect, Technicolor™ had just developed a 3-color procedure, and Disney immediately incorporated it into his films. And, though his studio was in the middle of producing *Flowers and Trees,* a black and white short, Walt halted its production; and redid it in Technicolor™. *Flowers and Trees* was the first animated Technicolor™ film, and it won an "Academy Award" for "Best Short Subjects, Cartoons ."

After that, Walt signed an exclusive three-year contract with Technicolor™, making it impossible for other cartoon studios to compare their color quality. Disney then produced a plethora of products that its competitors couldn't match.

That same year, in 1932, Lionel Toy Co., hit hard by the depression, was on the verge of bankruptcy. However, after licensing *Mickey's*™ and *Minnie's*™ likenesses for their toys, they sold 253,000 Disney-related products in the following 4 months; Lionel credited their reemergence to their affiliation with Disney.

In November of 1932, Walt hired Chouinard Art Institute teachers to give his artists and animators classes.

That summer, Disney requested Columbia increase their cartoon advances to $15,000.00. But when that request was turned down, United Artists stepped up, agreed to pay their price, and took over Disney Cartoon distribution.

The Three Little Pigs

Previously rejected by distributors for too few characters, the *Three Little Pigs* was released through United Artists. It debuted in 1933 and was a hit. Its original song, *Who's Afraid of the Big Bad Wolf?*, became the anthem for The Great Depression.

As mentioned earlier, *Flowers and Trees* received an Academy Award for Best Short Subjects: Cartoons. It was the first cartoon to ever receive an Academy Award. The second in that category was *The Three Little Pigs*.

On December 18, 1933, Lillian gave birth to Diane Marie Disney, their first child. And that year, the first Mickey Mouse™ *watch was released.*

Walt's Big Dreams

By 1934 Walt Disney Studios was turning out quality shorts and making a good profit. The company was growing, and its future looked bright. Still, Walt wanted a lot more.

He envisioned bringing in more artists and providing them with schooling. He pictured developing new innovative equipment to make his films look more realistic. And he wanted to automate and speed up the drawing process.

Walt visualized a massive state-of-the-art studio, a place where children and their families could come to meet his characters. He wanted better sound and brighter colors.

But most of all, Disney craved the respect of his Hollywood peers. He dreamed that one day all of Hollywood would turn out for the premiere of one of his films.

In less than a decade, Walt Disney Studios progressed from the crude Steamboat Willie™ to the award-winning Technicolor™ shorts Flowers and Trees, The Three Little Pigs, and The Old Mill.

Snow White and the Seven Dwarfs™

Walt knew he could never realize his dreams by making shorts. His path to success was feature films. So he set his sights on producing a full-length animated feature.

His first challenge was finding a good screenplay. It had to be a story that contained the elements of a great movie and one that could hold people's attention for more than an hour. As he pondered, he remembered how he loved listening to the fairy tales his grandmother read him back on the farm.

1. Cinderella
2. Snow White and the Seven Dwarfs™
3. Hansel and Gretel
4. Rapunzel
5. Little Red Riding Hood
6. Rumpelstiltskin

Disney recalled being captivated by the movie *Snow White and the Seven Dwarfs*™ as a boy in Kansas City. So he visited nearby libraries and read every version of *Snow White* he could find.

To his surprise, there were numerous variations of the plot. But every version contained the elements of an entertaining film; a jealous evil queen with mystic powers and a magic mirror, a lovely young princess whose life was in danger, seven dwarfs who rescue her, and the handsome prince that saves her and takes her to his castle to live happily ever after.

Having immersed himself in many scenarios of the same story, Walt developed his own ideal screenplay. In his version, he gave each dwarf a name and matching personality, making them likable and easier to animate. He also made his story family-friendly.

The names and traits of each of the movie's characters were easily recognizable, and music was written to further emphasize those traits.

Over the next three years, Walt spent much of his time developing what he believed to be a perfect story. In 1934, he called a meeting of his top artists and animators to explain his plan to create a full-length feature of *Snow White and the Seven Dwarfs*™.

At that meeting, Walt mesmerized his team by acting out the entire story and demonstrating the parts and personalities of each character. He also explained that this would be the first full-length animated film and that it would make motion picture history.

At the end of his presentation, the room was abuzz with excitement. No one there doubted that they would produce Walt's movie. However, Hollywood had a different opinion. They believed that Disney had lost his mind. None of the major studios would have even attempted a project this bold.

Even Roy and Lillian weren't enthusiastic about taking on such a risky venture during a depression. But Walt was optimistic and saw their skepticism as just another obstacle to overcome. He believed the depression was temporary, and things couldn't get much worse.

Unfortunately, he was wrong on both counts. Nevertheless, he set his sights on creating a full-length animated color feature. But as the word of Walt's plan spread, the Hollywood elites were not only skeptical; they laughed and mocked him, saying, *"People will not sit through a 90-minute cartoon; the bright colors will hurt their eyes."* And they even dubbed his project *"Disney's Folly."*

Only Walt and his animators believed his plan could succeed. The consensus in Hollywood was that Walt was about to destroy his company.

Walt Disney gambled his personal fortune and risked the future of his business to produce a cinematic masterpiece that would change the course of the entire movie industry.

Original cost estimates for *Snow White* were a quarter-million dollars. Still, Roy believed it would take at least twice that amount. However, Walt had neither the time nor inclination to pursue the funding. So he concentrated on production and left the finances to his brother.

Even with money tight, Walt spared no expense in pursuing a film that would meet his expectations. He experimented with special effects, new processes, and techniques in his quest to produce realistic animation.

The Disney staff grew to 187 employees, and Mickey Mouse™ first appeared in Macy's Thanksgiving Day Parade as a 30-foot balloon.

Walt was determined that everything in the film would be perfect. Staying at the studio day and night, he constantly inspected and critiqued each phase of the picture. In the summer of 1935, the pressure of producing such a major project got to him. He was irritable and had trouble sleeping.

He worked so hard that Roy, concerned about his health, sought to avoid another breakdown by insisting they take a European vacation.

With Walt in Paris, work on *Snow White* ground to a halt. But when the brothers happened on a theater that had strung together several *Mickey Mouse*™ cartoons and ran them as a feature, Walt returned to Hollywood more excited than ever.

Upon his return to Hollywood, he began the casting for the voice of *Snow White*. The first person to interview was Andrina Castilatte, whose father was a singer and voice coach.

Although 150 other young women also interviewed for that position, once Walt heard Andrina's voice, he knew she was *Snow White*.

Also, that year (1935) Disney phased out the original Mickey Mouse™ *clubs as they had become too large and awkward to handle.*

A New Distributor-RKO (1936)

Disney's next major challenge was to find a company willing to risk promoting his *"folly."* Distributors had always been a sore spot. However, when RKO agreed to take on the film, it created an even bigger problem.

Part of RKO's contract included a timeline. The movie had to be ready before the Christmas season of the following year (1937).

In 1936, Walt's reluctance to give his television rights to United Artists led to RKO also taking over the distribution of Silly Symphonies™.

On December 21, 1936, Lillian and Walt adopted Sharon Mae Disney.

Under the Gun

In January of 1937, after almost 3 years of work, the movie wasn't even close to being finished. But now the clock was ticking, and Walt realized he had to step in. Among other things, he initiated a bonus system for the faster animators. Then he instituted an assembly line process for moving drawings along faster. Although, the thing that had the most impact was hiring additional artists and animators. In just a few weeks, the Disney studio staff swelled to over 500.

A Technological Advancement

Walt was determined for his first feature film to look realistic. But there was a big problem, how could he make a two- dimensional picture appear as three dimensions on film. However, the Disney engineers came up with an amazing solution. It was a multi-plane camera. This technology allowed things in the background to remain large while the objects in the forefront got smaller.

It had up to seven different layers and gave the film a sense of depth and dimension. Nothing like it had ever been seen before. It was tested in the *Silly Symphony*™, *The Old Mill*, and approved for use in *Snow White*. Though this technology slowed production, the results were worth it to Walt.

Twenty-five songs were written for *Snow White,* but only eight were kept in the film. The same was true for many scenes; if they didn't move the story forward, they were dropped, despite the hundreds of hours of work that had gone into their completion.

All of these things were very costly. But Walt spared no expense. He knew this would be his only chance, and everything had to be perfect.

Also, in 1937, Donald Duck™ got his own series of short films

The Financial Burden

All the new salaries created an astronomical financial burden. Originally estimated at $250,000.00, the film's cost had already surpassed that by $1,000,000.00. Walt and Roy had leveraged everything of any value they owned; their homes, cars, life insurance, and even their beloved studio. Still, they ran out of money. The brothers were in so deep that should the film fail, they would lose their business, fortunes, and reputations.

By the summer of 1937, most of the studio was working around the clock to finish *Snow White*. With time running out, there was still much to do, and it looked like the film couldn't be completed on time. But what happened next made even that seem insignificant.

Bank of America Scare (1937)

The bank, who'd been lenient until then, was becoming concerned. Roy met with Walt and explained that, even though they had spent $1,250,000.00, another $250,000 would be needed to complete the movie. He told him Bank of America insisted on seeing the progress of their investments. Walt would not hear of it. He declared that he would not show an incomplete film to anyone. "It would be suicide to show them *"bits and pieces!"*

But Roy explained that the film would never be finished without another loan, and another loan would require a screening. With his back to the wall, Walt relented. He scheduled a showing with the bank's vice president, Joseph Rosenberg.

Rosenberg showed up on a Saturday afternoon, and he and Walt entered the projection room. Disney then gave the signal to roll the film.

What was presented to the banker was a patchwork with sections of completed color and long spans of sketched drawings. The sound flickered in and out. Parts were beautiful and complete, while other parts were only animated line drawings. Walt talked through the entire movie, explaining the storyline and describing the scenes. The showing took about 2 hours, and Walt talked the whole time.

During the screening, Rosenberg remained silent and expressed no emotion. When the movie ended, the two exited the screening room. For Walt, everything rested on Rosenberg's next words. He was extremely nervous, but Rosenberg started to talk about the weather, sports, and anything other than the movie he'd just witnessed.

Poor Walt just stood there, dumbfounded, with his entire life resting on what the banker thought. But Joe just got into his car, shut the door, and cranked the motor.

Disney's head dropped, and as tears welled in his eyes, Joe rolled down his window and said, *"Well, so long Walt, you boys are going to make a boatload of money on that film."*

The Final Stretch

With financing assured, the production of *Snow White* continued! Unfortunately, Walt left the most difficult scenes for last. With time running out, the pressure to complete Snow White by Christmas was incredible. So Disney again stepped in and took more drastic measures. He put his entire staff on 12-hour shifts, implemented bigger bonuses for the faster animators, and made additional changes to speed the process. Yet despite his efforts, more people were needed. So within weeks, the studio grew from around 500 employees to almost 1,000.

The most challenging part of the process was animating the humans. The dwarfs and animals were relatively easy, but the problem was that people have certain expectations for how a human should look and move. Walt hired actors to demonstrate each part so his animators could see their movements. He sent the animators to life drawing classes to learn to better emulate human actions. The results were incredible. The animation was absolutely life-like when compared with anything produced in the past.

This would be the first full-length animated cartoon, and Disney was adamant that everything had to be perfect. Every detail was inspected and re-inspected, and every frame was reviewed. Walt also oversaw the music, sound effects, and even the ink colors! He personally approved everything that went into the film.

Nearing the end of the process, Disney noticed that *Snow White*'s complexion was too white and talked to the ladies in "Ink and Paint" about giving her face some color. Once a solution was found, Walt was concerned that the inkers wouldn't be able to apply her makeup precisely the same on each slide. One of the ladies turned to him, saying, *"Mr. Disney, what do you think 'we' do every morning?"*

Things were still being changed and corrected days before the movie was to open. Sometimes, that meant dropping sequences that were already approved. These choices were not popular with those who stayed up nights for months producing them. But Walt remained stalwart, and if something didn't add to the story, it was cut.'

Can a Cartoon Make You Cry?

The most critical scene was when Snow White's dead body was lying in state, and the Dwarfs came to pay their respects. It was the most important scene Walt had ever done. His biggest concern was that the audience wouldn't feel sadness at the Princess's death. He wondered…

"Can we, with two-dimensional drawings, reach through people's souls and pull out the desired emotions? We all know that a cartoon can make you laugh. The question is, can a cartoon make you cry?"

Walt knew that if the audience wasn't moved by the scene where the Dwarfs cry over the death of Snow White, the film would be a failure.

The doomsday prediction of the Hollywood elite appeared to have been proven accurate when during a pre-release screening for college students, over half the audience walked out halfway through the movie. However, it turned out that the college girls simply needed to return to their dorms for curfew.

The Premier

On December 21, 1937, Shirley Temple, Judy Garland, Charles Laughton, Marlene Dietrich, Hedy Lamar, Charlie Chaplin, Mickey Mouse™, Minnie Mouse™, Donald Duck™, and other famous stars of the time gathered at the Carthay Circle Theatre to watch a cartoon. Also in attendance were Hollywood's elite directors, producers, and studio executives.

A live orchestra played selections from the movie's soundtrack outside the theater. A long line formed at the theater entrance, witnessed by a massive crowd of on-lookers.

In addition to Hollywood royalty, Disney's artists, who'd worked so hard to put this film together, were in attendance. And finally, Hollywood's Media showed up in force. Walt's critics, most of whom had long predicted his failure, were also there.

And though one of Walt's dreams was realized, when Hollywood turned out for the premiere of his movie, with so much at stake, he was extremely nervous. Disney was not sure what the audience would think of his film. He realized that the entire world would immediately know if it bombed.

Having done everything he could, Walt Disney entered the theater and took his seat. As the lights in the auditorium dimmed, the curtains opened, and the projector rolled, all Walt could do at that point was watch and wait.

But from the moment the first image was projected on the screen, the viewers were entranced by his creation. They laughed at its gags and oohed at the visual effects.

They swayed to the music and snickered at the dwarfs as the film came together to create a visual experience they'd never imagined.

But the true test came near the end as *Snow White's* dead body lay in state. The Disney artists, dispersed throughout the auditorium, watched as the Seven Dwarfs took off their little caps and knelt beside her casket while teardrop-shaped wax fell from giant candlesticks mimicking their tears. At that point, the artists heard the people around them sobbing, crying for a cartoon character they had created.

When the Prince broke the dreadful spell with his kiss and carried *Snow White* away to live happily ever after, the audience erupted in applause. Only then did it become clear to Disney's team that they'd created something magnificent and that they had made cinematic history.

Reaction to the Premier

The premiere of Snow White was a blockbuster success, and the film's reviews were spectacular. The critics couldn't find enough superlatives to describe what they had witnessed. Here is just one example…

Variety, December 28th, 1937

Snow White and the Seven Dwarfs™

There has never been anything in the theatre quite like Walt Disney's Snow White and the Seven Dwarfs™, seven reels of animated cartoon in Technicolor™, unfolding an absorbingly interesting and, at times, thrilling entertainment. So perfect is the illusion, so tender the romance and fantasy, so emotional are certain portions when the acting of the characters strikes a depth comparable to the sincerity of human players, that the film approaches real greatness." – John C. Flinn Sr.

Suddenly, Snow White and the Seven Dwarfs™ dolls, games, toys, and music soundtracks were everywhere. Walt had gambled that the movie would be a hit, and he wasn't wrong!

Walt Disney had a dream and risked everything to make it come true: his fortune, business, fame, and health, for that is what dreamers do.

After Snow White

Snow White was released to the public in February 1938, and it became the most successful film, not just of that year but of all time. It ultimately grossed almost $8 million and did so at a time when most theater tickets were 20 cents and children's tickets were less. Even today, it's still one of the highest-performing animated films ever made.

Currently, Snow White has had a lifetime gross of $480,000,000.00.

When the Academy Awards came out, there wasn't a category for animated films, so they created a unique Oscar for *Snow White* which was presented by Shirley Temple. The trophy consisted of one regular Oscar and seven small ones (representing the seven Dwarfs).

Snow White changed the course of movie-making history and secured Walt Disney Studios the funding to build the greatest animation empire the world has ever known.

The movie premiered in 49 countries, debuted in 21 languages, and was the 1938 *Movie of the Year*. More importantly, Roy paid off all the studio's debts, and they lived happily ever after… Well, not exactly. You see, Walt wasn't finished dreaming.

Disney received 59 Academy Award nominations and won 26 Oscars, the most ever. His dream of gaining the respect of his Hollywood peers had come true.

Snow White and the Seven Dwarfs™ was the turning point in Disney's career and one of the most influential films in cinema history.

A New Studio

Realizing that more space was needed to increase film production, Walt and Roy decided to use some *Snow White* profits to build a state-of-the-art studio. Setting aside 3 million dollars, they began searching for a location. A few weeks later, Roy made a $10,000.00 deposit on the land, which would become Walt Disney Studios in Burbank. The $100,000.00, the 51-acre tract was purchased from the Burbank Dept. of Water and Power and had previously served as a polo field for the Black Fox Military Academy.

During the facility's construction, Walt was involved with every element, from the layout to the design and contour of the animator's chairs. Nothing was left to chance. The studios were beautiful and, as Walt would say, *"An ideal place to work!"* A job there not only paid well, at first, but included numerous employee amenities, such as cafeterias, theaters, sleeping areas, ping pong tables, a gym with personal trainers, private parking, and even a gas station.

Also, in 1938, work began on Disney's second full-length feature, Pinocchio. Walt brought in Leopold Stokowski to collaborate on Fantasia™, a movie that weds animation to classical music.

After the move, the studio's animation staff had their plates full with productions of Fantasia™, Pinocchio, Bambi™, Alice in Wonderland, Peter Pan, and the ongoing Mickey Mouse™, Donald Duck™, Goofy™, and Pluto™ cartoons.

Walt believed that should one feature film fail, the next one could restore the studio's cash flow. He never imagined four could fail in a row.

All the studio's awards were wonderful, yet the business still depended on profits for survival. And in 1939, the competition got very stiff. Imagine going up against this line-up...

- Gone With the Wind
- The Wizard of Oz
- Mr. Smith Goes to Washington
- Goodbye Mr. Chips
- Stagecoach
- Wuthering Heights
- The Hunchback of Notre Dame

Just to name a few.

The combination of those remarkable films, the war in Europe, and the poor economy caused the studio to lose money on their subsequent four films. But, rather than letting go of his staff, Walt kept them and cut their pay and benefits, which proved disastrous a short time later.

Construction on the Buena Vista Street studio was completed in 1939.

Mickey Mouse™ Park

In the late 1930s, Daddy's Day was every Saturday. That's when Walt spent time with his three and six-year-old daughters. He took them to ride the Merry-go-round, the Zoo, and any other attractions he could find. The problem was that there were not many things for kid's to-do near Hollywood, and the ones there were, were neither clean nor family-friendly.

Each day's mail at the studio contained cards and letters from children wanting to know where they could meet Mickey Mouse™, Donald Duck™, and the other characters. In the past, Walt had considered setting up a tour of his studios but realized there were just not enough exciting things to see.

Disney also took up a new hobby to help him deal with stress: trains. He often thought about how much fun it would be to have a place where parents and children could enjoy a short train ride together.

Walt's eureka moment came while sitting on a Griffith Park bench, waiting for his girls to finish their ride on the carousel. That day he envisioned an amusement park where parents and children could enjoy doing things together.

A few days later, while looking at a drawing of the studio's acreage, he realized a sizeable triangle-shaped area was not being used. He brought in two of his character designers. He asked them to draw some sketches for a park-style attraction that the whole family could enjoy and where they could meet their favorite characters. He named the project Mickey Mouse™ Park.

Also, in 1939, Mickey Mouse™ was set to star in The Sorcerer's Apprentice™, and Leopold Stokowski volunteered to conduct the music.

Simultaneously Bambi™ was started but was released much later due to the time necessary to draw the animals.

Mickey's™ first cartoon, Plane Crazy, was remade with added sound and became a hit.

Storm Clouds Gather

The money from *Snow White* helped create more cartoons, and the full-length features Fantasia™ and Pinocchio were both released in 1940. Also, that year, Disney moved to the new Burbank Studio and released *The Night on Bald Mountain*.

Fantasia™ introduced a new technology, Fantasound™, which preceded stereo and surround sound by 20 years.

Unfortunately, none of these films were commercially successful. Although *Fantasia*™ became a success decades later, the 1940 audiences were put off by its lack of a story, and the *Night on Bald Mountain* was considered unfit for children. *Dumbo*™ was produced and finished in one year after cutting many corners but only made a small profit.

Due to the losses on these films and the mounting costs from the new studio, the company was forced to make a public stock offering, something neither brother wanted. Yet, with no other immediate option, 600,000 shares of common stock sold at $5.00 per share. The stock offering sold quickly and temporarily kept the studio afloat.

EtTu, Brute

After the devastating losses from the past four feature films:
1. *Pinocchio*– Lost half a million 1940
2. *Fantasia*™ – Lost more than Pinocchio 1940
3. *Dumbo*™ – Was barely Profitable 1941
4. *Bambi*™ – Also lost money in 1942

The studio's future was in peril, and if Disney didn't already have enough problems, more were on the way.

After the other movie studios unionized, two unions sought to organize Disney's cartoonists. And on May 29, 1941, Disney's Employees walked out and a picket line formed in front of the studios. Walt couldn't believe what was happening. He looked at his employees as family and was crushed by their betrayal. This stress caused his health to falter, and he needed to get away.

He accepted when the US State Department offered him a film-making and goodwill tour of South America.

The movies Saludos Amigos and The Three Caballeros resulted from that trip. These films were successful in both North and South America.

With Walt in South America, Roy took over the studio's affairs and settled with the employees and their union. But the relationship between Walt and the animators was never fully resolved.

World War II

Then on December 7, 1941, the Japanese bombed Pearl Harbor, and the United States entered World War II. The next day the US Army requisitioned half of the studio to house troops assigned to protect a nearby Lockheed plant. The draft took one-third of Walt's artists.

For most of 1942, the US military partially occupied the luxurious new complex. Disney's animators, who were not away fighting America's enemies, produced training and morale-boosting films for the US government.

Overseas markets, which usually generated significant profits, were out of reach. The money the studio received from the government hardly covered its costs. And, there was nothing like *Snow White* in the pipeline to act as a savior.

For the following 4 years, the studio worked exclusively for the government. During World War II, more than 4,000 profitless war films were produced. And Disney's debt to the Bank of America continued to grow.

By 1944, Walt Disney Studios found itself in need of funds and re-released Snow White. That move generated some much-needed revenue and started a pattern of re- releasing their animated feature films.

The studio did not quickly return to normal when the war finally ended. The company was slow to rebuild, and MGM and Warner Bros, having noted Disney's success, took on animation in a big way.

In 1945, when the public flocked back to the movies, it wasn't Disney movies they were watching.

Another Close Call

To make matters worse, the studio still owed Bank of America more than four million dollars. And without the knowledge of Walt or Roy, a board meeting was called to consider calling the Disney loans. Fortunately, one executive took the floor and said he'd been watching the company. In his opinion, it would be in the bank's best interest to give the studio time to rebound. The board agreed, and the loans were renewed. So the Walt Disney Studios once again survived an extremely close call.

Reviving a Dormant Dream

That same year (1945), Walt attended a Steam-up Party at the home of an employee, Ward Kimball. Walt was shocked to see that Ward had a miniature railroad in his backyard, the Grizzly Flats Railroad. As Walt and Kimball ran the locomotive and blew the whistle, Walt recalled his uncle's visits and his experiences at Electric Park. Then, the dormant plans for Mickey Mouse™ Park took on a new life.

In 1945, The Three Caballeros was released as the first combined live-action and cartoon film.

For the most part, 1946 was a good year to be in the movie business. The war that had brought suffering, death, and hardship to so many was in the past. Theaters were flooded with moviegoers, and 19 pictures earned $4 million or more in the US; before that, only 25 Hollywood feature films had achieved that milestone.

And even though Disney released *Song of the South*, it was only mildly received, earning just $226,000 in profits.

However, Zip-A-Dee-Doo-Dah was named Best Song by The Motion Picture Academy, and James Baskett won an Oscar for his portrayal of Uncle Remus.

Disney needed money, lots of money. Roy urged his brother to start cutting staff and expenses, but as usual, Walt resisted. And by the end of 1946, their debt to the Bank of America had surpassed $4.3 million. To avoid a complete collapse, Roy secured a $1 million loan from RKO and planned to lay off 400 of its 1,000 employees.

After 20 years of portraying the voice of Mickey Mouse™, Walt stepped away from that role.

Deadly Turbulence

In preparation for his next full-length feature, Alaska, Walt took a flying tour of that state. But, minutes into the flight, heavy thunderclouds surrounded the small plane, and visibility vanished. The turbulence that followed rendered the tiny craft's instruments useless. In the two hours that followed, Walt could only hold on and pray. Surrounded by high mountains and running low on fuel, the flight was in peril.

Then as suddenly as the episode had begun, the clouds parted, and the pilot found a suitable place to land. It was yet another close call, but "fate" was kind again to Walt that day.

After reviewing the *Alaska* films, Disney started a feature based on the life of seals. The resulting movie did not appeal to RKO (Disney's film distributor at the time). They felt that audiences would not sit still for a nature film. So Walt convinced a friend at Pasadena's Crown Theater to show the film for one week. That allowed *Seal Island* to be considered for an Academy Award nomination.

Though the movie was much longer than usual short subjects, the audience loved it.

So, it wasn't just nominated; it won an Oscar for Best 2-reel Documentary. The following day Walt took the award to his brother's office:

"Here, Roy. Take this over to RKO and bang them over the head with it."

Later that year, while recuperating from a severe polo injury, Walt decided to get away from the studio. So he invited Ward Kimball to accompany him to the Chicago Railroad Fair. He and Ward received a grand welcome and were even allowed to run some of the steam locomotives.

The pair not only attended the railroad fair but also visited *Greenfield Village*, a living history museum in Michigan's *Henry Ford complex*. That outdoor museum featured historical buildings, moved from their original locations, and arranged in a village setting with an adjacent steam railway.

The trip inspired Disney to begin work on his ideas for a theme park. Upon his return home, Walt told Lillian, *"That was the most fun I ever had in my life."*

Mickey Mouse™ Park Revisited

After the war, tourism to California increased. Studies showed that one of the top three things tourists wanted to do, was to visit a movie studio. Walt was quoted as saying to his friend Ward Kimball...

"You know, it's a shame people come to Hollywood and find there's nothing to see. Even the people who come to the studio. What do they see? A bunch of guys bending over drawings. Wouldn't it be nice if people could come to Hollywood and see something?"

Although the war delayed further discussions of a park, it didn't stop Walt from thinking about one. And after his trip to the Chicago

Railroad Fair, he renewed his interest in creating an amusement park. So for the following nine years, he studied entertainment venues, from Knott's Berry Farm and the Los Angeles County Fair to smaller venues such as Beverly Park, with rides designed for children.

Then in August of 1948, Walt started in earnest, formulating plans to build Mickey Mouse™ Park. He sent Dick Kelsey, the studio's production designer, a memo outlining his ideas.

Amusement parks in those days were primarily disorganized, rowdy places that were not well kept and certainly not family- friendly. Disney wanted his park to be different. He initially conceived a small park with a train ride, a boat ride, and a few themed areas. He planned to build it on an empty lot adjacent to the Burbank Studios.

Unfortunately, despite Walt's best sales pitch, the Burbank City Council refused to consider putting an amusement park in their city. And worse, neither Roy nor the Disney directors wanted a park. Finally, when Disney's Board of Directors told him that they didn't consider his plan in the stockholder's best interest and that it wasn't in the company's charter, he replied…

"Fine, I'll start a new company, and then you won't be able to tell me what to do."

Then, to Roy's dismay, Walt did what he'd promised! His separate company was initially called Walt Disney, Inc. But to avoid confusing it with Disney Productions, it was renamed WED, Enterprises (for Walter Elias Disney).

Disney then transferred his name and likeness rights to the new company and started charging Walt Disney Productions for their use. That gave him enough money to work on developing his park without worrying about shareholders.

He then stepped up his visits to other parks for inspiration; as his ideas grew, more designers were recruited, and his plans quickly outgrew the projected location. Consequently, he located a more suitable and affordable space in Anaheim; 160 acres of orange and walnut tree orchards. With all the new changes, Walt sought to give the project a new name. *Disneylandia* was considered among others, but *Disneyland*™ was his final choice.

The Walt Disney Music Company was formed in 1949. In 1950, the release of Cinderella marked the first commercially successful feature since Snow White. Treasure Island, the studio's first completely live-action movie, was also released. And by November of 1950, Disney Studios' debt was reduced to $1.7 million.

Alice in Wonderland followed Cinderella but lost over $1 million. The next cartoon in production was Peter Pan. Disney had purchased its rights 12 years before and was turning it into a cartoon since purchasing it. That year, it also licensed Disney characters to the Ice Capades.

In 1951, NBC hired Walt to produce *One Hour in Wonderland* to air near Christmas. It was a huge success, and Disney was impressed with TV's ability to attract large audiences.

The production of *Lady and the Tramp* began again in 1952, after being dormant for almost a decade. And that year, Walt chose to take on *20,000 Leagues Under the Sea*, a project that would ultimately cost the studio 4.2 million dollars. Then, *Seal Island* was completed due to the success of True-Life Adventures.

Then, when RKO started experiencing their own problems, Roy feared they might not be up to handling the marketing for these three films. So Walt Disney Productions *finally* established its own distribution company, Buena Vista. Not only did their new company successfully market *20,000 Leagues*, but the film also became one of Disney's all-time money-makers. After that, Buena Vista became Disney Films, exclusive distributor.

On February 5, 1953, *Peter Pan* was released and well received. For the balance of that year, Disney continued visiting parks, fairs, carnivals, and circuses. He studied their attractions and questioned their owners.

To his amazement, most of those owners doubted his park would be successful. They even warned him not to spend money on a project that would probably fail. But Walt's dream was much stronger than any discouraging words from a park owner.

"Tivoli Gardens"

In the early 1840s, Copenhagen, Denmark, opened the gates to *Tivoli Gardens*. Guests were immediately impressed by the elegant mix of an amusement park and a beautiful garden. By the early 1950s, the park had evolved into something quite unique. It offered immaculate, colorful gardens, expansive lawns by day, and strolls under thousands of lights reflecting off a gorgeous pond by night. Its fairy-tail castles, roller coasters, flume rides, and ornate stages were favorites of children of all ages. It was clean, orderly, and beautifully manicured like the rest of Copenhagen.

So, Walt traveled to Denmark to visit the world's oldest amusement park. And, unlike other less classy attractions, *Tivoli's* clean and orderly appearance, safe rides, and cheerful family atmosphere were just what he was seeking.

Art Linkletter, who accompanied Walt on that trip, recalled...

"Disney walked through the amusement park scribbling down notes about the seats, gardens, rides, food, and every other detail he noticed."

Upon his return from that trip, Walt again borrowed against his life insurance to assemble a planning staff. Then, in a single weekend, he and Herb Ryman drew up a plat that could be used to sell the park's concept to potential investors. That design called for a single entrance, a Main Street, and a hub leading to each area of interest.

Walt revisited *Tivoli* Gardens several times, fascinated by its mood and atmosphere. That park's ambiance embodied what Walt hoped to capture for *Disneyland*™.

Television

With Disney handling its own distribution, Walt placed a new stipulation. It stated that gaining the right to air a Disney TV program would require an investment in *Disneyland*™ Park.

By the end of 1953, Disney Studios were once again struggling to remain solvent. Walt racked his brain over where the money would come from, saying...

"We need another windfall like 'Snow White and the Seven Dwarfs™*' or 'Steamboat Willie*™*.' What are we going to do?"*

Walt was convinced that their best hope for saving the studio was his park. However, no one, including Roy, believed in his vision. Yet Roy always did his best to support his little brother even when he disagreed. So, he contacted all his usual money sources, only to be turned down by every potential lender.

He then applied to more than 300 different banks with the same results. Though Bank of America also shunned the project, they did connect him with a smaller bank that offered help but nothing close to what was needed.

Disney believed television was the only way to build the park and save the company. Yet the major Hollywood studios pressured him not to support television productions. They thought that television would ruin the movie business and saw it as a threat to steal away their audiences and profits.

Since Disney's products had always been short and feature films, it seemed odd to Hollywood that they would even consider embracing that new medium. Although, where others saw danger, Walt saw an opportunity. So, he convinced Roy to go to New York City and seek a contract with one of the television networks. Neither CBS nor NBC was interested, but ABC was a different story.

The American Broadcasting Company was a fledgling new network that desperately needed quality programming and TV shows that would make them competitive. So on March 29, 1954, Roy struck a deal with Leonard Goldman of ABC.

The network agreed to invest $500,000.00 in *Disneyland*™ and guaranteed additional Disney loans for up to $4.5 million. ABC would own 34.4% of the theme park and receive all the profits from its concessions for the next decade. In exchange, Disney agreed to provide ABC with programming that would allow them to compete with the more established networks.

With his newfound money, Walt purchased a 235-acre site near Anaheim. On April 2, 1954, he announced plans for a theme park called *Disneyland*™ and a TV series of the same name.

Disneyland™

"Here you leave today and enter the world of yesterday, tomorrow and fantasy" —Walt Disney

Construction of the park began on July 16th, 1954, and continued at breakneck speed. In October, the Disneyland™ TV series aired, reaching an audience of 10's of millions. Each program presented a different section of the park. It showed viewers tantalizing previews of what *Disneyland*™ would offer. Every show was introduced by Walt. Just one year and a day after construction began, the park held its Grand Opening.

On June 22nd, 1955, Disney released the first cartoon feature filmed in Cinemascope™ and Technicolor™, The Lady and the Tramp. Later that year, *Disneyland*™ television opened its second season with Dumbo™. The Mickey Mouse™ Club debuted as the first-ever TV show designed especially for children.

With the release of Davy Crockett, everything started to look up at the studio. Not only was the movie a hit, but The Ballad of Davy Crockett soared to #1 and remained there for 13 weeks. It sold more than 10 million copies and netted over $2.5 million. Crockett's Coonskin Hats also sold in similar numbers.

In December, Walt used WED Enterprises to employ and manage a hand-picked creative team that he assembled from internal and outside talent. WED owned and operated several of the park's attractions, including *The Santa Fe* and *Disneyland*™ *Railway* and *The Monorail System*.

"WED Enterprises" is the precursor to today's Walt Disney Imagineering.

20,000 Leagues Under the Sea won Academy Awards for Best Art Direction and Best Special Effects.

As mentioned earlier, Walt had seriously considered building a small *Mickey Mouse*™ Park near the Burbank studios. But WWII got in the way. However, Disney's idea for a place where the whole family could enjoy their time together was about to come to fruition. Only one year and 17 million dollars after construction began, *Disneyland*™ was ready to open its doors for a preview by invited guests.

And though it was ultimately never built, Mickey Mouse™ *Park significantly influenced Disneyland*™'*s design and the many theme parks that have tried to emulate its success.*

Disneyland™'s First Actual Guests

Before the park opened, Walt hosted a few preview events for close friends and dignitaries but no real guests. However, four days before the event, *The Santa Fe* and *Disneyland*™ *Railway* made the news for its first trip around the park.

That's when Walt learned of a young boy dying of leukemia.

The child's only wish was, "*I want to ride on Mr. Disney's train.*" So, Walt invited him and his family to visit *Disneyland*™ before it opened to the public. Walt sent a taxi to bring him and his family for a train ride and a personally guided tour of *Disneyland*™ by the park's namesake. The little boy got to ride the train and blow its whistle. It was the high point of his short life.

On July 17th, 1955, ABC aired *Disneyland*™'s opening on a live broadcast hosted by Art Linkletter. Viewers at home got to glimpse the culmination of Walt's dream. Although TV's depiction of the park's first day successfully portrayed it as a magical kingdom, the day was actually a nightmare for Walt and his guests.

Black Sunday

Opening day ticket holders included celebrities, the press, friends, family, Disney VIPs, officials, and sponsors. Expected attendance shouldn't have exceeded 11,000. And when *Disneyland*™ opened its gates for the first time on July 17, 1955, it featured 18 rides and attractions. There were five lands, including *Adventureland, Frontierland, Fantasyland, Tomorrowland, and Main Street, USA.*

Over 70 million people watched it on TV, the largest audience in history. 52% of all US TV sets were tuned to ABC, and all American eyes were on Disney's dream.

The day started out with a short speech from Walt,

"To all who come to this happy place: Welcome! Disneyland™ is your land. Here age relives fond memories of the past, and here youth may

savor the challenge and promise of the future. Disneyland™ is dedicated to the ideals, the dreams, and the hard facts that have created America, with the hope that it will be a source of joy and inspiration to all the world."

Unfortunately, everything from that point went downhill, so much so that the day would become known as "Black Sunday." So, what went wrong at the "Happiest Place on Earth?" Well, everything...

- Traffic around the park backed up for 7 miles.
- Celebrities were delayed getting to their scheduled appearances
- Counterfeit tickets resulted in extreme overcrowding
- The California sun caused the freshly poured asphalt- tar walks to melt
- Women's high heel shoes stuck to the tar on the paths
- Due to a plumber strike, water fountains did not work
- Guests assumed the fountains were off because of the sponsorship of Pepsi
- Gas leaks caused 3 of the 5 "Lands" to close
- Concession stands ran out of food & drink
- Many of the rides were not yet completed, and others just stopped working
- Fewer than 18 attractions couldn't service the almost 30,000 guests
- Some boat rides started to sink due to overloading

For Walt Disney, the day was a nightmare. But in true Disney fashion, the next day, he went on TV and assured the nation that all of the kinks would be ironed out and that everything would be fixed and working smoothly in no time. And he was right; within two months, over one million people had walked through the gates of the first magic kingdom. And in just one year, more than 5 million guests had been welcomed to "The Happiest Place on Earth."

After Black Sunday

Even with the glitches of "Black Sunday," Walt's tenacity and perseverance turned what could have spelled doom for his park into a colossal personal and financial success. Disneyland™ became an integral part of Americana, and by 1958, over 10 million guests visited the park in a year.

"All the adversity I've had in my life, all the troubles and obstacles, have strengthened me. You may not realize it when it happens, but a kick in the teeth may be the best thing in the world for you."
—Walt Disney

Disneyland™ pushed the boundaries of technology and creativity. In the years that followed, it influenced the design of theme parks, roller coasters, and other attractions worldwide. To this day, it's still the most popular theme park in the world.

The New Mickey Mouse™ Club

On October 3, 1955, The Mickey Mouse™ Club TV show aired. It was Disney's second television series, the first being Disneyland™. Walt used both shows to finance and promote his new theme park.

The club was a variety show specifically designed for children that featured a newsreel, a cartoon, and a serial, as well as music, talent, and comedy segments. The series was a massive success!

In 1956, *Sleeping Beauty* was put into production. Yet with Walt's attention still focused on Disneyland™, the project took three years and cost more than $6 million. The following year the studio introduced Zorro on TV and the live-action feature, *Old Yeller*.

In 1958, 10 million people visited Disneyland™. *The Shaggy Dog* experienced a surprising success, earning more than $9.5 million in North America alone. Conversely, *Sleeping Beauty* was another financial disappointment in 1959. And 1960 saw *Swiss Family Robinson* and *Pollyanna* win Academy Awards.

The Disneyland™ TV Series was an unconventional idea to promote an unconventional park dreamed up by an unconventional man. Today we don't think of it much, but television helped make Disneyland™ possible.

Over time the partnership with ABC deteriorated. Walt wasn't pleased with the terms of their deal and didn't like being held back by ABC's inability to provide color. Conversely, the network felt that Disney focused too much on *Disneyland™* and that the deal wasn't good for them in the long run.

Walt asked the courts for nullification, but an out-of-court settlement was reached instead. ABC sold its 34.4% back to Disney for $7.5 million.

Halfway through 1961, Bank of America was repaid, and Walt Disney Productions took full ownership of the park. The TV shows moved to NBC, and *Walt Disney Presents* became *Walt Disney's Wonderful World of Color*. Also that year, Disney purchased the film and merchandising rights to Winnie-the- Pooh™ books and released *One Hundred and One Dalmatians*.

Winnie-the-Pooh™ books are still a leading source of revenue for "Disney."

The debut of Walt Disney's Wonderful World of Color happened in September. On November 14, 1961, Diane's 5th child was born and named Walter Elias Disney Miller after Walt.

In addition to the success of *Disneyland™*, Walt Disney Productions released a series of animated masterpieces from the mid-'50s into the mid-'60s.

Those included...
- Cinderella - 1950
- Alice in Wonderland - 1951
- Peter Pan - 1953
- Lady and the Tramp- 1955
- Sleeping Beauty - 1959
- 101 Dalmatians - 1961
- The Sword in the Stone - 1963
- Mary Poppins - 1964

Mary Poppins

Almost twenty years earlier (1944), as Walt tucked Diane into bed, she showed him her favorite book, "Daddy, you should read it; it would make a good movie." After reviewing the book, Walt promised his daughter that one day he would make it into a movie just for her. The book was Mary Poppins by Pamela (P.L). Travers.

However, when he approached Travers about purchasing the movie rights to her story, she promptly turned him down...

"Oh no, Mary Poppins is not for sale!"

Travers had seen movies made from books and wasn't impressed. And she especially didn't care for cartoons.

However, Walt didn't like being told *"no"* and wasn't one to let go of a good idea. So, for the next two decades, he personally appealed to Travers, only to find her more steadfast than before against selling her screen rights.

Then in 1944, he tried sending Roy to talk to her, but the results were no better. So for another ten years, Walt continued to make offers, but Travers always turned him down. Nevertheless, Disney persisted.

Anytime he traveled to England, a visit to see Pamela was scheduled.

He charmed her with his pleasant personality and shared his inspiring ideas for the film at those meetings. Then he always ended with a father's promise to his little girl (not mentioning that Diane was then in her 20s).

In 1959, Walt traveled to London to oversee a film and once more visited Travers. He was finally granted the provisional rights to produce "*Mary Poppins*" with strings attached. Yet Travers's change of heart was less motivated by Disney's friendly persistence and more by his money.

By then, her royalties from the *Mary Poppins* series had dwindled. So when Walt offered her $100,000.00 (almost one million dollars in today's money) and 5% of the movie's gross earnings, some of her resistance melted away. The final straw came when Walt agreed to make her a consultant and granted her final script approval.

Travers said, "Talking to Walt was like talking to a friendly, charming uncle who took from his pocket a gold pocket watch and dangled it enticingly before your eyes."

After her first few weeks at the Disney Studios in Burbank, PL became known for her *"No! No! No!"* refrains to the creative team. For 2 ½ years, Disney's artists and composers poured over both scripts and scores. Yet, when Pamela read or listened to their work, she always disapproved. Eventually, after numerous revisions, Travers grudgingly agreed that, with certain conditions, the film could be made.

Mary Poppins not only incorporated everything that Disney had learned over his illustrious career but also introduced revolutionary technology that changed the movie industry. The "Sodium Process," a precursor to today's green screen, "Matte Painting" for background scenes, and "Animatronics," for robotics.

Disney wasted no time completing the production, and once the movie was completed, Travers attended a screening. Her immediate question to Walt was, *"When do we start cutting?"* But Walt had his film and refused to make any changes.

You see, though Disney had granted Mrs. Travers the final script approval, he hadn't given her the editing rights.

The author was furious and vowed never to work with him again. But the result of their collaborations became a beloved (1964) film classic.

Mary Poppins was nominated for best picture, received 12 other Academy nominations, and won five Oscars. Yet, despite the film's critical acclaim, and commercial success, Travers wasn't a fan. She literally wept at the movie's premiere, exclaiming, *"Oh God, what have they done?"* Although, as far as I can tell, she did accept all of those 5% commission checks.

The financial success of Mary Poppins was a significant contributor to the building of Walt Disney World™.

A Bigger Park

Disneyland™ showed the world the potential of a theme park. Though soon after the gates to *The Magic Kingdom*™ opened, the orange groves outside were quickly replaced with a collection of seedy hotels, souvenir shops, and liquor stores.

Due to funding restrictions, Walt only acquired enough land to build his kingdom, a parking lot, and one small hotel. So, other businesses purchased the adjoining properties and fed off Disney's success. Walt truly regretted this, stating...

"One of the things I've learned from Disneyland™ is to control the environment. Without that, we get blamed for the things everyone else does."

Still, there was something about the park that he really did appreciate.

Unlike a movie, he could still make changes when it was completed. Anxious to fix problems and infuse the park with more and new ideas, he found that its small size restricted his efforts. And though ten million guests visited in its first 3 years, Walt noticed that 60% were from California, and only a small percentage came from the east coast.

Though Disney turned down numerous requests by city fathers willing to fund one of his parks in their community, he did want another theme park. But he wanted this new one to have room to expand and grow. So, he started planning a new venture.

Disney World™ started with a covert mission team headed by a past agent and founder of the CIA. Their assignment was to find an ideal location for a bigger and better *Disneyland*™.

Walt didn't want to compete with beaches, stating, *"We'll make our own lakes and waterways where we want them."*

In 1959 the team reported that their research found Florida to be the prime location. Continued efforts narrowed their target to the Central Florida area. Still, Walt wasn't convinced that an east coast audience would embrace a Disney Park. But then, he was presented with the perfect place to economically test market his concepts to an audience from the East Coast.

The 1964 *New York World's Fair* welcomed four of Disney's attractions, all paid for by corporate sponsors. This allowed Walt to gauge an East Coast audience's response to a Disney- style park. Attendance at the fair reached 51.5 million, and 47 million sought out Disney attractions.

While preparing for the fair, Walt continued searching for his next location. And in November of 1963, he and his team boarded a plane to explore Central Florida. After a week of fruitless searching, the team was headed home when Walt instructed the pilot to fly low so he could view the land.

"That's it!" Walt exclaimed as he spotted the intersection of Interstate 4 and the Sunshine State Parkway. *"A park at that location will have easy access from anywhere on the East Coast!"*

The Florida Project

The brothers called their most trusted executives to a top- secret meeting a few days later. Walt laid out the criteria for this highly classified mission. He instructed the team to acquire 5,000 and 10,000 acres of swampland and orange groves in a specified area near Orlando.

But the most crucial part of this mission was that it must be done in secrecy. If the media or the general public learned that Disney was looking to buy parcels of land in Florida, those land values would skyrocket. Walt even re-routed his California calls to appear to come from New York.

After scouring through US geological surveys and tax assessor maps, the team located 16 properties that would satisfy their directive. Unfortunately, many of those parcels were profitable orange groves and would be difficult to purchase. Team leader Bob Foster flew to Orlando to locate the owners and obtain options to acquire the land.

Disney engaged the prestigious legal firm *Donovan, Ledger, Mutin, and Irvine,* whose founder, William J Donovan, was also the founder of the CIA. In addition, he brought on board Paul Helliwell, a fellow agent on the original CIA team. Disney's land-seeking efforts would certainly be safe with a man whose life involved keeping national secrets.

Although Foster and Helliwell whittled down the 16 potential properties to just a few, those few were the most difficult to acquire. A large portion of them was owned by a single family. But the remaining parcels were swamp land, sold in 5-acre sections over fifty years earlier. Most of the properties were inaccessible, and their owners had never seen them.

Reaching out to land owners over 50 years after their purchase was incredibly challenging and time-consuming. Still, Walt got his way; and after a 12-hour back and forth with the largest landowner, the team finally secured an option for $25,000.00. The option gave them 6 months of exclusivity to purchase the land for $145.00 an acre. The owners had no idea they were dealing with Walt Disney.

The 6-month option also gave Disney's team time to attempt to purchase the property's mineral rights. Florida had previously separated subsurface rights from its properties due to its lucrative phosphorous content.

Without the ownership of the land and mineral rights, a third party could create havoc for a theme park. The team finally convinced the remaining owners to sell; once, they provided a geographical survey showing no oil or phosphorous on the property.

Even with the land and mineral rights in hand, Walt was still concerned that he would have another *Disneyland*™ situation without more land.

So, the team continued buying properties. They purchased *Bay Lake*, a 1,250-acre property, and *The Hemrick Tract*, with 2,700 acres.

Their next challenge was to obtain the small parcels spread throughout the *Demitree Estate*. It wasn't easy, but each owner was located by phone, mail, or showing up at their last known residence. Slowly the team found and purchased all the parcels but one. The final owner held out until Disney officially announced it was his project. Only then did she begrudgingly agree, after receiving a lifetime pass to *Disneyland*™ and *Disney World*™.

Donovan and Helliwell used their CIA experience to remain "under the radar" by cleverly naming several shell companies for Disney to hide behind. Some of those names included *"Latin-American Development and Management Corp.," "Tomahawk Properties," "Bay Lake Properties," "Reedy Creek Properties,"* and my favorite, *"M.T. Lott Co."*

Ultimately, Walt's dream of 5,000 to 10,000 acres was more than realized.

He purchased over 27,000 acres in the heart of Central Florida (42 square miles), and each transaction was handled in cash to avoid being traced. A total of $5,000,000 was spent on property, equaling an average of less than $200 per acre.

On September 14, 1964, Walt received the Medal of Freedom, the nation's highest civilian honor.

And though Walt was pleased that no other business could back up to his park, he still had no roads, no power lines, and no utilities. But, he could construct everything exactly as he wanted with this blank slate.

Rumors began to spread about a mysterious organization scooping up all of Central Florida. Speculation ranged from it being the government to an automobile manufacturer or possibly an airline. Walt just fanned those flames every chance he got.

And he would have continued purchasing property had he not been asked, during a TV interview, if he was behind the land grab.

Although he denied it, his facial expression gave him away. The cat was out of the bag, and the following week (November 15, 1965), Walt, Roy, and Florida's Governor officially announced that Disney was coming to Florida. Walt declined to give out specifics, time frames, or expected expenditures, but it was official; Orlando was about to welcome a Disney Park.

The 27,000 acres gave Walt more space than he needed for his park, so he decided to tackle a new project. He planned to create the *Experimental Prototype Community of Tomorrow - EPCOT™*.

Team Meeting

In June of 1965, Disney's Florida Project group met and drafted a proposal to form a Special District allowing Disney to govern itself. The plan asked Florida for the right to create, manage, and maintain all the systems needed to run the cities inside the district. Funding for the systems would be raised from levying taxes and issuing bonds.

They decided to form two new cities, *Bay Lake* for the theme park and *Reedy Creek* for the Airport and entrance complex. These cities could then grant Disney the right to:

• Issue business licenses
• Establish a police force
• Setup a civil court
• Build health care facilities
• Manage communication
• And operate a cemetery

Should a problem arise, it wouldn't affect the theme park, airport, or industrial park by locating EPCOT™ between the two cities. The Disney proposals pointed out that a Special District would relieve the state and its counties of the responsibilities of:

• Roads, Water
• Waste management
• Utilities
• Building codes
• Mosquito management
• Etc.

The Reedy Creek Improvement District would be unique to Florida and, most importantly, allow Disney to control everything.

A Full Plate

By 1966, Walt Disney Productions was at the top of its game, and Walt was involved in a myriad of projects. He guided the production of *The Jungle Book* and *The Happiest Millionaire,* each to be released the following year. He oversaw the transition of the *Disney World's Fair* attractions, from their temporary stage in New York to their permanent residence at *Disneyland*™.

Walt was also supervising the development of the *Mineral King,* a ski resort in *Sequoia National Park.* Once completed, the *Mineral King* would be a grand attraction for skiers worldwide. It was projected that the resort would host a million visitors per year. And it was to feature shops, restaurants, movie theaters, ice rinks, a convention center, a five-story hotel, and a high-capacity ski lift.

And, with Walt in charge, the project was swiftly coming together.

But that's not all; for years, Walt had contributed to The California Institute of the Arts (CalArts). Its purpose was to foster students pursuing careers in visual and performing arts. Walt hoped to provide a campus to develop future talent that could house and champion creative learning.

And though he had a lot going, nothing was more important to him than shaping a better future for the world's cities. The driving force behind his *"Florida Project"* was EPCOT™ (*Experimental Prototype Community of Tomorrow*), Walt's living blueprint of the future. It was to become a functioning city that would revolutionize industry, transportation, recreation, and even education.

He wanted EPCOT™ to solve the mounting problems in cities and provide lasting solutions for them. When completed, it would have a bearing on the future of the nation and the world.

Disney's plate was overflowing, but no one doubted he was up to the task. His life had been filled with incredible missions, and he'd overcome many hurdles.

Nevertheless, having dealt with those challenges only made him stronger.

Also, in 1966, Winnie the Pooh™ and The Honey Tree were released.

Family Time

In July, Walt took his two daughters, their husbands, and seven grandchildren on a 140-foot yacht for a 13-day voyage off the coast of British Columbia. During the trip, he worked on the *"Florida Project"* and his vision for EPCOT™.

EPCOT™

Although excited about the *Disney World*™ project, *EPCOT*™ was Walt's priority. His future vision involved delegating everything else to his staff and concentrating on two things, *EPCOT*™ and *CalArts*. He believed he could make them a reality by giving them his total concentration for the next 15 years.

EPCOT™ was to be a precisely planned community, housing around 20,000 living experiments to improve organization, technology, and control. His goal was to provide answers to the problems facing American cities.

Walt believed that *Disneyland*™'s success could be attributed to its carefully controlled layout and design. And he planned to exercise that same control to create his prototype city.

Now it's Time to Say Goodbye

In the fall, Walt hosted a TV event to showcase what would be the pinnacle of his storied career, *EPCOTT*™, his city of the future. After that, he checked into a hospital for minor back surgery to relieve his pain from an old polo injury.

But in preparation for that operation, a tumor the size of a walnut was discovered in his left lung. Emergency surgery was performed to remove the lump. A subsequent biopsy revealed that his cancer was malignant and spreading fast. Disney was informed that he only had a few months to live.

Although the hospital released him to spend Thanksgiving with his family, his condition deteriorated quickly. By his birthday (December 5th), he had returned to the hospital.

As his situation worsened, only his immediate family was allowed to see him. He didn't want anyone to remember him in that condition. Consequently, no one at the studio was informed that Walt was ill.

Roy stayed by his side and made sure he remained as comfortable as possible. The hospital was located across the street from the Disney campus. Roy arranged to have all the studio's lights stay on throughout the night so Walt could see them through his window.

In his final conversation with Roy, he vividly described the "*Florida Project*" layout as he envisioned it on the ceiling above his bed. Walt had so much he still wanted to do, but his heart quietly stopped at 9:30 a.m. on December 15th. He was only 65.

When the TV and radio stations announced the sad news, many broadcasts played the closing theme from the Mickey Mouse™ Club.

"Now it's time to say goodbye... to all our company,

M-I-C; See you real soon.

K-E-Y; Why? Because we like you,

M--O--U--S--E."

The nation and much of the world were in mourning; they collectively wept over the loss of one of their most creative geniuses.

A small service was held the next day for his immediate family. According to his wishes, the ceremony was private. One would be hard-pressed to find themselves unaffected by the man and his influences.

Even though most of Disney's wishes had come to pass, near the end of his life, his fondest desire was to continue living. He even offered to trade his vast fortune for more time on earth. Some say that that belies *"Anything your heart desires will come to you."* However, in his short time on Earth, Walt experienced more and accomplished more than any ten other 65-year-olds.

And though his body is no longer with us, his spirit indeed remains. It is evident in the joy and laughter of the children. As long as the name Disney represents entertainment, Walt Disney will remain alive in the hearts and minds of his many fans.

The Lamp

The following morning, *Disneyland*™ opened as usual, but there was a notable difference. As the park was being built, Walt wanted a place for him and his family to watch the activity.

So he had an apartment constructed on the second floor over the *Main Street Firehouse.*

Private and hidden from the rest of the park, it was the perfect place to observe, work, or be with his family. A single lamp glowed from the apartment's window, alerting the park's employees of his presence.

So when *Disneyland*™ opened on December 16, 1966, the employees found the lamp in the Firehouse glowing. And that same lamp continues to shine even these many years later. It remains a source of inspiration to the park's cast and its guests, and some say, *"If you look closely from Main Street, you can sometimes see Walt smiling down on the kids as they mingle with his characters."*

Walt Disney World™

Walt's unexpected death put the plans for *Disney World*™ on hold. Without him in charge, everyone wondered, what would happen to his projects? Yet, as quickly as this question arose, Roy set aside his retirement plans and took the reins.

His first order of business was to let everyone know that *Disneyland*™ would continue and that the company would move forward with *Disney World*™

He then renamed *Disney World*™ *Walt Disney World*™ and pledged to see that his little brother's dream would come to pass.

In a meeting with his project managers, he instructed them to continue phase one of the *Walt Disney World*™ project. Roy was the park's savior and saw that the *"Reedy Creek Improvement District"* was presented to Florida and signed into law. Considering what that state had to gain from Disney Park, it was no surprise they passed Disney's requests with little resistance.

However, the months after Walt's death saw a massive change in the company. Without his leadership and unique vision, *EPCOT*™ was tabled.

And, when problems arose with the Mineral King ski resort, that project was dropped. Still, Roy kept his promise, and the construction of *Walt Disney World*™ began in 1967.

Five years later (October 1, 1971), when *Walt Disney World*™ opened, Walt's dream of *EPCOT*™ still held promise. However, when Roy passed away two months later (December 20), all hope for a city of the future died with him. For the first time since its beginnings fifty years earlier, *Walt Disney Productions* no longer had a Disney at its helm.

As time passed, plans for the city of Lake Buena Vista also faded. Eventually, a section of the park was named *EPCOT*™. Still, without a Disney in charge, no one was left to champion Walt's dream city.

Legacy

During his lifetime, Walt's companies struggled through: bankruptcy due to a customer defaulting on a contract, two attempted takeovers, a debilitating strike, a catastrophic war, several box-office failures, and pushback from its own board of directors.

It took home runs like *Steamboat Willie*™, *Snow White and the Seven Dwarfs*™, and *Disneyland*™ to keep the company afloat and erase its massive debts.

None of that could have happened without Walt's relentless work and unwavering belief in his dreams. He withstood the many obstacles life placed before him and used them as stepping stones. From each setback, Disney learned a valuable lesson. And, after each success, he took on even more significant risks, which, combined with the wisdom he gained from his failures, led to extraordinary personal and financial rewards.

Walt Disney's number one goal was to bring joy to everyone by engaging in the things he loved most. His boyish enthusiasm was infectious, as was his desire to create a world that existed to make people happy.

It was never easy for him, but he was a man of passion; he refused to allow any situation to keep him down. Walt was unique, and there will never be another like him. He was a dreamer willing to risk everything he had to achieve his goals.

His last wish was to live on, and even that dream has been realized. Disney's memory lives on in the smiles of the children and the fun that individuals and families experience from his movies, theme parks, cruise ships, toys, cartoon characters, and TV programs. He brought, and still brings, great joy to countless people, and his spirit still lives as long as people remember the name "Disney"; which will probably be for quite a long time.

Little Known Disney "Facts"

- Mickey™'s full name is Michael Theodor Mouse (the first M™)
- Mickey™'s ears are always circles regardless of his position
- Off-screen, Mickey™ and Minnie™ are secretly married (according to Walt)
- Mickey™ and Minnie™ were born the same day
- Minnie™ is a nickname. Her actual name is Minerva
- Walt did not like "Goofy™."
- His favorite meal was canned chili. (He carried some with him and asked the restaurants to warm it up.)
- "Donald Duck™'s" middle name is Fauntleroy.
- Donald Duck™ has a twin sister, Della Duck.
- Original Tickets to *Disneyland*™ were $1.00.
- Mickey Mouse™ was the first cartoon character ever to speak.
- Walt's favorite song later in life was *Feed the Birds* from *Mary Poppins*

"When you wish upon a star, it makes no difference who you are. Anything your heart desires will come to you!"
~ Ned Washington

Some Disney Accomplishments

- Co-founded the first cartoon studio in Hollywood
- Created and developed Oswald the Rabbit™
- Created Mickey Mouse™ and a large cast of characters
- Revolutionized the animation industry through innovation
- Created a new Cinematic Art
- First animated film with Synchronized Sound
- Steamboat Willie™, 1928
- An international celebrity by age 30
- First animated film in three-strip Technicolor™
- Flowers and Trees 1932
- The first feature-length animated film, Snow White and the 7 Dwarfs, 1937
- Invented the Multi-plane Camera, first used on The Old Mill, 1937
- Introduced stereophonic sound (Fantasound™)
- Fantasia™, 1940
- Introduced the first full episode TV programs in 1954
- First TV program made exclusively for Children, The Mickey Mouse™ Club
- Invented a New Vacation Destination
- Revolutionized the Amusement Park Industry
- Built Disneyland™, 1955
- Produced 111 feature films and more than 500 cartoon shorts
- More than 4,000 briefings and other films for the WWII effort
295
- Envisioned Walt Disney World™ and planned EPCOT™
- Built a Media & Entertainment Company that Dwarfed his Competition
- Received 59 Academy Award nominations - Most in history
- Won 26 Oscars - Most in history
- Received 4 Emmy Award nominations, winning one
- Awarded The Presidential Medal of Freedom, 1963
- Awarded Honorary degrees at Harvard & Yale
- Received more than 950 honors
- Founded The California Institute of the Arts (CalArts)

- Snow White was awarded AMI's Greatest American Film of All Time
- Mary Poppins received 13 nominations and won 5 Academy Awards
- Produced the two Highest Grossing Films of their time
- Planned and purchased the property for Disney World™

"See you real soon!"
~ Jimmie Dodd

"*Whatsoever a man soweth,
that shall he also reap.*"

Galatians 6:7 KJV

PUTTIN' ON THE RITZ

Fred Astaire is considered the greatest male dancer of the 20th Century. Appearing in 43 movies, he earned the industry's respect by taking home Emmy's, Grammy's, and Oscars. Yet, his start in show business was less than spectacular. The first twenty years were spent in Vaudeville and Broadway musicals. Yet Fred's dream was to be recognized as a famous movie star and dancer.

At the age of 30, he attended his first movie audition. But the director was not impressed and noted on his scorecard, "Can't act, cant's sing is balding. Can dance a little ."

However, Fred's desire was strong enough that he wasn't deterred by a failed audition; he persevered, and his reputation grew.

Then, he was dealt a severe blow when his sister and dance partner married and moved to England. Though things seemed grim, he focused on his dream and pressed on, eventually landing a small role in Dancing Lady with Joan Crawford. That led to better parts, and his big break came when he was cast for the starring role in Flying Down to Rio with Ginger Rogers.

Astaire did not want to be paired with Rogers or anyone. But it was already too late. The public demand for the two was so great that the studio offered Fred 10% of the profits from any picture where they appeared together. From that point, he had no problem with being paired with Rogers.

Fred and Ginger almost single-handedly saved RKO Studios from bankruptcy in the early 1930s as they danced their way into Hollywood history. Fred's tenacity and focus on his dream paid off; today, his name is synonymous with the ultimate dancer.

"If it doesn't look easy, it is that we
have not tried hard enough yet."
~ Fred Astaire

WINDOW SHOPPING

When **Roland H. Macy** started his career, few people would have guessed he would become one of the world's largest retail operators. Macy's success can be attributed to his inventive spirit, perseverance, and willingness to learn from his mistakes. Though his endeavors eventually laid the groundwork for the modern-day department store, his first business attempts were dismal failures.

At 15, Roland left home to become a sailor on a whaling ship. Then, after four years at sea, he returned and opened a needle-and-thread store. That shop failed, along with a dry goods store he opened two years later.

In 1849 Macy became a 49er (not a football player). The California Gold Rush was in full swing, so RH decided to go west and seek his fortune. Like most other prospectors, Roland didn't find much gold, so he returned to Massachusetts to start a dry goods store. The store only experienced modest success, prompting another move. Then York City became the home of *RH Macy & Co.*

First-day sales were $11.06. Yet as more people discovered his location, his business began to grow. By the end of the second year, his total sales were almost $85,000. Roland worked hard to expand operations, and Macy's continued to advance. Ever-increasing sales allowed the purchase and expansion of his store into eleven adjacent buildings.

In addition to the size increase, Macy added to the store's merchandise categories and created a section for each. Those unique changes subsequently grew into what we know today as a department store.

Roland developed many other innovations and made changes that transformed the retail industry. Customers flocked to Macy's for an unrivaled shopping experience.

His store was the first in New York City to feature Santa Claus at Christmas. In 1864, he installed lighted window displays that attracted passers-by, giving birth to the now- common tradition of *window shopping.*

RH Macy's tenacity and brilliant innovations led to the giant chain we know today as "Macy's Department Stores ."

"The people who are crazy enough to think they can change the world are the ones who do."
~ Steve Jobs

Famous Failures

THE EMPEROR'S SEEDS

Author Unknown

An aged emperor of a kingdom in the Far East realized it was time to pick his successor. Passing on his generals and children, he chose a different path and gathered all the young men in his kingdom. *"It is time for me to step down and choose my successor, and I've decided to choose one of you."*

As an air of excitement swept over the gathering, the Emperor continued, *"Today, I will give each of you a special seed. You are to plant, tend and water it, and bring it back one year from today. At that time, I will judge your plants, and the bearer of the plant I choose will become the Emperor!"*

One young boy, Liang, received a seed and rushed home to tell his mother the exciting news. Eagerly she helped him find a pot and fill it with planting soil. Liang carefully planted the seed and placed it on a sunny window ledge.

Each day he cared for and watered his treasure. After a few weeks, he overheard some other boys boasting about the growth and progress of their plants. But Liang's seed showed no sign of change. Three weeks passed, then four and five, but Liang's seed had not yet sprouted.

As the other boys touted their plant's success, Liang remained silent. Six months passed, and still no sign of life. Liang became concerned, *"Have I done something to harm my plant?"*

Then, some boys began to display their beautiful flowers and trees. But Liang's pot contained only dirt.

Keeping to himself, the youngster could only continue to tend his seed. Every morning he would check for any sign of growth, but there was none. Finally, the day arrived when every young man in the kingdom was ordered to return to face the Emperor.

"Oh, Mother, I'm so frightened! I do not want to show the Emperor an empty pot."

"Liang, you simply must be honest about what has happened."

And though he was embarrassed and feared the consequences, he bravely took his mother's advice and set out to face his fate.

Upon arriving at the palace, Liang was stunned to see the wide variety of flowers and plants. There were brilliant colors and flora of all shapes and sizes. Then, Liang placed his barren pot on the floor. When the boys saw that empty vessel, some laughed, and a few patted his back.

Then the Emperor entered the grand hall, and suddenly there was silence. Every eye turned to him as he surveyed the room. Attempting to be inconspicuous, Liang bowed his head and stood behind others.

"My, what beautiful plants, trees, and flowers you have grown. Today, one of you will become the Emperor of my Kingdom!" Then, the Monarch spotted Liang's pot and saw him hiding. *"Guards, bring that pot and that young man to me!"*

Everyone watched in stunned silence as Liang was ushered to the throne. Liang's knees buckled as he tried to walk, and he was helped by the guards. Terrified, Liang assumed, *"The Emperor knows I have failed him, and I will probably be executed!"* Once he reached the throne, Liang kneeled at the Emperor's feet and bowed his head.

"Is that your pot, young man?" *"It is, Your Eminence!"*

A few boys snickered as others shook their heads. *"Silence!"* snapped the Emperor. *"What is your name, son?"* *"My name is Liang."*

Placing his scepter on Liang's shoulder, the Sovereign announced, *"Behold, I present to you, Emperor Liang!"* And, when the old man knelt before him, everyone else followed suit.

As Liang was wrapped in a purple velvet robe, handed the jeweled scepter, and crowned with a golden crown, he uttered, *"How can this be? I couldn't even grow a seed."*

Then the elder statesman explained, *"One year ago, I gave each boy a seed and instructed them to plant it, care for it and bring it back. But those seeds were boiled; none of them could grow. Thus, everyone except Liang brought back living plants and flowers. I knew only Emperor Liang possessed the integrity and courage to stand and tell the truth in the face of grave danger. Only he demonstrated the strength and character necessary to rule this great kingdom."*

"Whatsoever a man soweth, that shall he also reap."
~ Galatians 6:7 KJV

Whatever You Sow, That Shall You Also Reap!

Author Unknown

If you plant honesty, you will reap trust.
If you plant goodness, you will reap friends.
If you plant humility, you will reap greatness.
If you plant perseverance, you will reap victory.
If you plant consideration, you will reap harmony.
If you plant hard work, you will reap success.
If you plant forgiveness, you will reap reconciliation.
If you plant openness, you will reap intimacy.
If you plant patience, you will reap improvements.
If you plant faith, you will reap miracles.
But:
If you plant dishonesty, you will reap distrust.
If you plant selfishness, you will reap loneliness.
If you plant pride, you will reap destruction.
If you plant envy, you will reap trouble.
If you plant laziness, you will reap stagnation.
If you plant bitterness, you will reap isolation.
If you plant greed, you will reap loss.
If you plant gossip, you will reap enemies.
If you plant worries, you will reap wrinkles.
If you plant sin, you will reap guilt.

Be careful what you plant today, for that will determine what you reap tomorrow. The seeds you scatter now will either make the future better or worse. You can either enjoy the fruits of your harvest or deal with the bitter weeds of your poor choices.

"Do things today that will have a positive impact on tomorrow."
~ Dennis J. Henson

"KNOCK, AND IT SHALL BE OPENED!"

Jack Canfield, the author of *Chicken Soup for the Soul*, tells the story of his friend, **Dr. Ignatius Piazza**. After Dr. Piazza graduated from chiropractic school, he planned to open an office in Monterey, California. Then he visited the Monterey Chiropractic Association and applied for membership. But the association's management told him,

"We already have more than enough chiropractors in this city, one for every eight people. Your prospects for success here are not good!"

Unwilling to let their *"facts"* dictate his reality, Dr. Piazza didn't abandon his dream. Instead, he became more determined than ever to succeed and to do so in Monterey.

The good doctor pondered how to set himself apart from the other chiropractors. Using a visualization board, he placed a pin on a map where he wanted to open his office and drew concentric circles around the pin. Then he printed a map of the streets in those circles and planned to visit every neighborhood inside those rings.

Over the next six months, Dr. Piazza knocked on every door on his map, introduced himself, and asked each resident…

- What hours do you think I should open?
- Where do you think I should advertise?
- What is a good name for my practice?
- Would you like an invitation to my Open House?

Then, he left his business card and thanked them for helping him. Piazza knocked on over 12,500 doors and talked to 6,500 people. He gathered more than 4,000 names of people who wanted to be invited to his Open House.

When the good doctor opened his practice, the police were forced to close the street because of the traffic. Within a month, the business netted $72,000.00, and its first year's gross was over a million dollars.

Imagine what would happen if you took your dream and knocked on 12,500 doors.

Information acquired from speeches by Jack Canfield on YouTube.

"Everything you want is out there waiting for you to ask."
~ Jack Canfield

Poems

Building the Bridge
By Will Allen Dromgoole

An old man traveling a lone highway,
Came at the evening cold and gray,
To a chasm vast, deep and wide,
Through which was flowing a sullen tide.

The old man crossed in the twilight dim;
The sullen stream held no fears for him;
But he turned when safe on the other side,
And builded a bridge to span the tide.

"Old man," cried a fellow pilgrim near,
"You're wasting your time in building here.
Your journey will end with the closing day;
You never again will pass this way.

You have crossed the chasm deep and wide.
Why build you this bridge at eventide?"
The Builder lifted his old gray head:
"Good friend, in the path I have come," he said,

"There followeth after me today,
A youth whose feet must pass this way.
This stream, which has been as naught to me,
To the fair-haired youth, may a pitfall be:

He, too, must cross in the twilight dim.
Good friend, I am building this bridge for him."

Don't Quit
By John Greenleaf Whittier

When things go wrong, as they sometimes will,
When the road you're trudging seems all uphill,

When the funds are low and the debts are high
And you want to smile, but you have to sigh,

When care is pressing you down a bit,
Rest if you must, but don't you quit.

Life is queer with its twists and turns,
As every one of us sometimes learns

And many a failure comes about,
When he might have won had he stuck it out;

Don't give up though the pace seems slow—
You may succeed with another blow.

Success is failure turned inside out—
The silver tint of the clouds of doubt,

And you never can tell just how close you are,
It may be near when it seems so far;

So stick to the fight when you're hardest hit—
It's when things seem worst that you must not quit.

It Couldn't Be Done
By Edgar Guest

Somebody said that it couldn't be done
But he with a chuckle replied
That "maybe it couldn't," but he would be one
Who wouldn't say so till he'd tried.
So he buckled right in with the trace of a grin
On his face. If he worried he hid it.
He started to sing as he tackled the thing
That couldn't be done, and he did it!

Somebody scoffed: "Oh, you'll never do that;
At least no one ever has done it;"
But he took off his coat and he took off his hat
And the first thing we knew he'd begun it.
With a lift of his chin and a bit of a grin,
Without any doubting or quiddit,
He started to sing as he tackled the thing
That couldn't be done, and he did it.

There are thousands to tell you it cannot be done,
There are thousands to prophesy failure,
There are thousands to point out to you one by one,
The dangers that wait to assail you.
But just buckle in with a bit of a grin,
Just take off your coat and go to it;
Just start in to sing as you tackle the thing
That "cannot be done," and you'll do it.

"A New Day"
By Heartsill Wilson

"This is the beginning of a new day. God has given me this day to use as I will. I can waste it or use it for good. What I do today is very important because I am exchanging a day of my life for it. When tomorrow comes, this day will be gone forever, leaving something in its place I have traded for it. I want it to be gain, not loss — good, not evil. Success, not failure, in order that I shall not forget the price I paid for it."

I ain't never been nothing but a winner! ~ Paul Bear Bryant

My Wage
By Jessie B. Rittenhouse

I bargained with Life for a penny,
And Life would pay no more,
However I begged at evening
when I counted my scanty store;

For Life is a just employer,
He gives you what you ask,
But once you have set the wages,
why, you must bear the task.

I worked for a menial's hire,
only to learn, dismayed,
That any wage I had asked of Life,
Life would have willingly paid

It's Allin the State of Mind
By Walter D.Wintle

If you think you are beaten, you are.
If you think that you dare not, you don't,
If you'd like to win, but don't think you can,
it's almost a cinch you won't.

If you think you'll lose, you've lost,
for out in the world you'll find
Success begins with a fellow's will—
it's all in the state of mind.

Full many a race is lost ere even a step is run,
And many a coward fails ere even his work is begun,

Think big, and your deeds will grow;
Think small, and you'll fall behind;
Think that you can, and you will!
It's all in the state of mind.

If you think you are out-classed, you are;
you've got to think high to rise;
You've got to be sure of yourself before
you ever can win a prize,

Life's battles don't always go,
to the stronger or faster man;
But sooner or later, the man who wins
is the fellow who thinks he can.

If
By Rudyard Kipling

If you can keep your head when all about you,
Are losing theirs and blaming it on you,

If you can trust yourself when all men doubt you,
But make allowance for their doubting too;

If you can wait and not be tired by waiting,
Or being lied about, don't deal in lies,

Or being hated, don't give way to hating,
And yet don't look too good, nor talk too wise:

If you can dream-and not make dreams your master;
If you can think-and not make thoughts your aim;

If you can meet with Triumph and Disaster,
And treat those two impostors just the same;

If you can bear to hear the truth you've spoken
Twisted by knaves to make a trap for fools,

Or watch the things you gave your life to, broken,
And stoop and build'em up with worn-out tools:

If you can make one heap of all your winnings
And risk it on one turn of pitch-and-toss,

And lose, and start again at your beginnings
And never breathe a word about your loss;

If you can force your heart and nerve and sinew,
To serve your turn long after they are gone,

And so hold on when there is nothing in you,
Except the Will which says to them: "Hold on!"

If you can talk with crowds and keep your virtue,
Or walk with Kings-nor lose the common touch,

If neither foes nor loving friends can hurt you,
If all men count with you, but none too much;

If you can fill the unforgiving minute,
With sixty seconds' worth of distance run,

Yours is the Earth and everything that's in it,
And-which is more-you'll be a Man, my son!

I Keep Six Honest Serving Men
By Rudyard Kipling

I keep six honest serving-men (They taught me all I knew);
their names are What and Why and When and How and
Where and Who.

I send them over land and sea, I send them east and west;
But after they have worked for me, I give them all a rest.

Opportunity
By Walter Malone

They do me wrong who say I come no more,
when once I knock and fail to find you in;
For every day I stand outside your door,
and bid you wake, and rise to fight and win.

Wail not for precious chances passed away!
Weep not for golden ages on the wane!
Each night I burn the records of the day—
At sunrise every soul is born again!

Dost thou behold thy lost youth all aghast?
Dost reel from righteous Retribution's blow?
Then turn from blotted archives of the past,
and find the future's pages white as snow.

Art thou a mourner? Rouse thee from thy spell;
Art thou a sinner? Sins may be forgiven;
Each morning gives thee wings to flee from hell,
each night a star to guide thy feet to heaven.

Laugh like a boy at splendors that have sped,
to vanished joys be blind and deaf and dumb;
My judgments seal the dead past with its dead,
but never bind a moment yet to come.

Though deep in mire, wring not your hands and weep;
I lend my arm to all who say "I can!"
No shame-faced outcast ever sank so deep,
but yet might rise and be again a man!

The Touch of the Master's Hand
By Myra Brooks Welch

T'was battered and scarred,
and the auctioneer thought it scarcely worth his while
To waste much time on the old violin,
but he held it up with a smile.

"What am I bidden, good folk?" he cried.
"Who'll start the bidding for me?
A dollar, a dollar...then two...only two...
Two dollars, and who'll make it three?"

"Three dollars once, three dollars twice, Going for three"

...but no!
From the room far back, a gray-haired man came forward
and picked up the bow.

Then wiping the dust from the old violin,
and tightening the loosened strings,
He played a melody pure and sweet
as a caroling angel sings.

The music ceased, and the auctioneer,
with a voice that was quiet and low,
Said, "Now, what am I bid for the old violin?"
And he held it up with the bow.

"A thousand dollars...who'll make it two?
Two thousand, and who'll make it three?
Three thousand once, three thousand twice...
And, going and gone!" said he.

The people cheered, but some of them cried,
"We don't quite understand...
What changed its worth?" Swift came the reply:
"T'was the touch of the master's hand."

And many a man with his life out of tune,
and battered and scarred with sin,
Is auctioned cheap by the thoughtless crowd,
much like the old violin.

A "mess of pottage," a glass of wine;
a game - and he travels on.
"He's going" once, and "going twice,
He's going and almost gone.

But the Master comes, and the foolish crowd
never can quite understand,
The worth of a soul and the change that is wrought

by the touch of the Master's hand.

The Face in the Glass
By Dale Wimbrow

When you get what you want in your struggle for self,
and the world makes you king for a day,
Just go to a mirror and look at yourself,
and see what that face has to say,

For it isn't your father or mother or wife,
whose judgment upon you must pass,
The person whose verdict counts most in your life,
is the one staring back from the glass?

Some people might think you're a straight-shootin' chum,
and call you a great gal or guy,
But the face in the glass says you're only a bum,
if you can't look it straight in the eye.

That's the one you must please, never mind all the rest,
that's the one with you clear to the end,
And you know you have passed your most dangerous test,
if the face in the glass is your friend.

You may fool the whole world down the pathway of years,
and get pats on the back as you pass,
But your final reward will be heartache and tears,
if you've cheated the face in the glass.

God Forgive Me When I Whine
Author Unknown

Today, upon a bus, I saw a lovely girl with golden hair,
I envied her; she seemed so gay and wished I was so fair.

When suddenly she rose to leave, she hobbled down the aisle.
She had one leg and wore a crutch, but as she paused, a smile.

Oh God forgive me when I whine; I have two legs; the world is mine.

I stopped to buy some candy, the lad who sold it had such charm,
I talked with him, he seemed so glad, if I am late, it'll do no harm.

And as I left, he said to me, "I thank you. You have been so kind.
It's nice to talk with folks like you, you see," he said, "I'm blind."

Oh God, forgive me when I whine; I have two eyes, the world is mine.

Later, while walking down the street, I saw a child with eyes of blue.
He stood and watched the others play; he didn't know what to do.

I stopped a moment, and then I said, "Why don't you join the others,
dear?"
He looked ahead without a word, and then I knew he couldn't hear.

Oh God, forgive me when I whine; I have two ears, the world is mine.

With feet to take me where I go, with eyes to see the sunset glow
With ears to hear what I would know

Oh God, forgive me when I whine; I'm blessed indeed; the world is
mine.

Victory
By Herbert Kauffman

You are the Man who used to boast that you'd achieve the uttermost,
some day.
You merely wished to show, to demonstrate how much you know and
prove the distance you can go..
Another year we've just passed through.
What new ideas came to you? How many big things did you do?
Time left twelve fresh months in your care how many of them did
you share with opportunity and dare again where you so often
missed?
We do not find you on the list of makers good. explain the fact!
Ah No, 'Twas not the chance you lacked!
As usual - you failed to act!

Invictus
By William Ernest Henley

Out of the night that covers me, black as the pit from pole to pole,
I thank whatever gods may be, for my unconquerable soul.

In the fell clutch of circumstance, I have not winced nor cried aloud.
Under the bludgeonings of chance, my head is bloody, but unbowed.

Beyond this place of wrath and tears, looms but the Horror of the
shade,
And yet the menace of the years, finds and shall find me unafraid.

It matters not how strait the gate, how charged with punishments the
scroll,
I am the master of my fate, I am the captain of my soul.

Persistence
By Calvin Coolidge

Nothing in the world can take the place of persistence.
Talent will not; nothing is more common than unsuccessful men with
talent.

Genius will not; unrewarded genius is almost a proverb.
Education will not; the world is full of educated derelicts.

Persistence and determination alone are omnipotent.
The slogan "press on" has solved and always will solve the problems
of the human race.

The Road Not Taken
By Robert Frost

Two roads diverged in a yellow wood,
and sorry I could not travel both
And be one traveler, long I stood,
and looked down one as far as I could
To where it bent in the undergrowth;

Then took the other, as just as fair,
and having perhaps the better claim,
Because it was grassy and wanted wear;
though as for that, the passing there
Had worn them really about the same,

And both that morning equally lay,
in leaves, no step had trodden black.
Oh, I kept the first for another day!
Yet knowing how way leads on to way,
I doubted if I should ever come back.

I shall be telling this with a sigh,

somewhere ages and ages hence:
Two roads diverged in a wood,
and I—I took the one less traveled by,
And that has made all the difference.

I've Dreamed Many Dreams
By Ron DeMarco

I've dreamed many dreams that never came true.
I've seen them vanish at dawn.
But I've realized enough of my dreams,
thank the Lord, to make me want to dream on.

I've prayed many prayers when no answer came,
though I've waited patient and long,
But answers have come to enough of my prayers,
to make me keep praying on.

I've trusted many a friend that failed,
and left me to weep alone,
But I've found enough of my friends that are really true,
that will make me keep trusting on.

I've sown many seeds that have fallen by the way,
for the birds to feed upon,
But I've held enough golden sheaves in my hand,
to make me keep sowing on.

I've drunk from the cup of disappointment and pain,
I've gone many days without song,
But I've sipped enough nectar from the Roses of Life,
to make me keep living on!

Plain Old Oyster
Author Unknown

*There once was an oyster, whose story I'll tell
Who found that some sand, got into his shell*

*It was only a grain, but gave him great pain.
For oysters have feelings, although they are plain.*

*But, did he berate the harsh workings of fate.
That had brought him to such a deplorable state?*

*"No," he said; "Since...I cannot remove it,"
I'll lie in my shell, and think how to improve it,"*

*The years rolled around, as the years always do,
And he came to his ultimate destiny... stew.*

*Now the small grain of sand that had bothered him so,
Was a beautiful pearl all richly aglow,*

*This tale has a morale, for isn't it grand,
What an oyster can do with a morsel of sand?*

*Think...what could we do, if we'd only begin,
With some of the things, that get under our skin.*

Slow Me Down, Lord
By Wilfred A. Peterson

*Slow me down, Lord. Ease the pounding of my heart, by the quieting of my mind.
Steady my hurried pace, with a vision of the eternal march of time.
Give me amid the confusion of the day, the calmness of the eternal hills.
Break the tension of my nerves and muscles,*

With the soothing music of the singing streams
That live in my memory.
Help me to know the magical restoring power of sleep.
Teach me the art of taking minute vacations, of slowing down to look
at a flower,
To chat with a friend, to pat a dog, to read a few lines of a good book.

Slow me down, Lord. And inspire me to send my roots
Deep into the soil of life's enduring values,
That I may grow toward the stars of my greater destiny.

Stopping by Woodsona Snowy Evening
By Robert Frost

Whose woods these are, I think I know.
His house is in the village though;
He will not see me stopping here,
to watch his woods fill up with snow.

My little horse must think it queer,
to stop without a farmhouse near
Between the woods and frozen lake,
the darkest evening of the year.

He gives his harness bells a shake,
to ask if there is some mistake.
The only other sound's the sweep,
of easy wind and downy flake.

The woods are lovely, dark and deep,
but I have promises to keep,
And miles to go before I sleep,
and miles to go before I sleep.

Casey at the Bat
By Earnest Lawrence Thayer

It looked extremely rocky for the
Mudville nine that day;
The score stood two to four, with but one
inning left to play.

So, when Cooney died at first, and
Burrows did the same,
A pallor wreathed the features of the
patrons of the game.

A straggling few got up to go, leaving
there the rest,
With that hope which springs eternal
within the human breast;

For they thought if only Casey could get
a whack at that,
They'd put even money now with Casey
at the bat.

But Flynn preceded Casey, and likewise
so did Blake,
The former was a pudding, and the
latter was a flake;

So on that stricken multitude, a
deathlike silence sat,
For there seemed but little chance of
Casey, at the bat.

But Flynn let drive a single to the
wonderment of all,
And the much-despised Blakey tore the
cover off the ball,

And when the dust had lifted, they saw
what had occurred,
There was Blakey safe on second, and
Flynn a-hugging third.

Then from the gladdened multitude
went up a joyous yell,
It bounded from the mountain-top and
rattled in the dell,

It struck upon the hillside, and
rebounded on the flat,
For Casey, mighty Casey, was advancing
to the bat.

There was ease in Casey's manner as he
stepped into his place;
There was pride in Casey's bearing, and
a smile on Casey's face;

And when responding to the cheers, he
lightly doffed his hat,
No stranger in the crowd could doubt'
twas Casey at the bat.

Ten thousand eyes were on him as he
rubbed his hands with dirt,
Five thousand tongues applauded as he
wiped them on his shirt;

And while the writhing pitcher ground
the ball into his hip,
Defiance gleamed from Casey's eye, a
sneer curled Casey's lip.

And now the leather-covered sphere
came hurtling through the air,

And Casey stood a-watching it in
haughty grandeur there;

Close by the sturdy batsman, the ball
unheeded sped--
"That hain't my style," said Casey.
"Strike one," the umpire said.

From the bleachers black with people,
there rose a sullen roar,
Like the beating of the storm-waves on a
stern and distant shore;

"Kill him! Kill the umpire!" shouted
someone from the stand--
And it's likely they'd have done it, had
not Casey raised his hand.

With a smile of Christian charity great
Casey's visage shone;
He stilled the rising tumult, he bade the
game go on;

He signaled to the pitcher, and again
the spheroid flew,
But Casey still ignored it, and the
umpire said, "Strike two."

"Fraud!" cried the maddened
thousands, and the echo answered
"Fraud,"
But one scornful look from Casey, and
the audience was awed;

They saw his face grow stern and cold;
they saw his muscles strain,
And they knew that Mighty

Casey wouldn't let the ball go by again.

The sneer is gone from Casey's lips; his
teeth are clenched with hate,
He pounds with cruel violence his bat
upon the plate;

And now the pitcher holds the ball, and
now he lets it go,
And now the air is shattered by the force
of Casey's blow.

Oh! Somewhere in this favored land the
sun is shining bright,
The band is playing somewhere, and
somewhere hearts are light,

And somewhere men are laughing, and
somewhere children shout,
But there is no joy in Mudville--mighty
Casey has "Struck Out."

Author's Note:
Take heart, no one bats a thousand. There will be other games!

Equipment
By Edgar Guest

Figure it out for yourself, my lad,
you've all that the greatest of men have had,

Two arms, two hands, two legs, two eyes,
and a brain to use if you would be wise.

With this equipment they all began,
so start for the top and say "I can."

Look them over, the wise and great,
they take their food from a common plate

And similar knives and forks they use,
with similar laces they tie their shoes,

The world considers them brave and smart.
But you've all they had when they made their start.

You can triumph and come to skill,
thou can be great if only you will,

You're well equipped for what fight you choose,
you have legs and arms and a brain to use,

And the man who has risen, great deeds to do,
began his life with no more than you.
You are the handicap you must face,

you are the one who must choose your place,
You must say where you want to go.
How much you will study the truth to know,

God has equipped you for life, But He
--lets you decide what you want to be.
Courage must come from the soul within,

the man must furnish the will to win,

So figure it out for yourself, my lad,
You were born with all that the great have had,

With your equipment they all began.
Get hold of yourself, and say: "I can."

The Rainy Day
By Henry Wadsworth Longfellow

The day is cold, and dark, and dreary;
It rains, and the wind is never weary;
The vine still clings to the mouldering wall,
But at every gust the dead leaves fall,
And the day is dark and dreary.

My life is cold, and dark, and dreary;
It rains, and the wind is never weary;
My thoughts still cling to the mouldering Past, But the hopes
of youth fall thick in the blast,
And the days are dark and dreary.
Be still, sad heart and cease repining;
Behind the clouds is the sun still shining;
Thy fate is the common fate of all,
Into each life some rain must fall,
Some days must be dark and dreary.

A 50-Year Collection of
Powerful Quotes

"The things I want to know are in books;
my best friend is the man who'll get me a book I ain't read."
— Abraham Lincoln

"The happiest people don't have the best of everything;
they just make the best of everything."
— Anonymous

"Winning is not a sometimes thing; it's an all-the-time thing. You
don't win once in a while; you don't do things right once in a while;
you do them right all the time. Winning is a habit.
Unfortunately, so is losing ."
— Vince Lombardi

"When you wish upon a star, it makes no difference who you are.
Anything your heart desires will come to you!"
— Ned Washington

"To desire is to obtain, to aspire is to achieve"
—James Allen

"You are what you think."
— Confucius

"Any man who considers everything from the standpoint of the most
good to the most people will never want for anything."
— Henry Ford

"What the mind of man can conceive and believe, it can achieve.
— *Napoleon Hill*

"Achieving business success is similar to fighting a battle. To have a chance to win, take setbacks in stride and continue to move forward."
— *Dennis J. Henson*

If you read for just 20 minutes a day, at the end of the year, you'll have read twenty 200-page books. That's 19 more books than the average person reads each year!
Imagine how much that could change your life.
— *Zig Ziglar*

"I probably read five to six hours a day."
—*Warren Buffet (at one time the richest man in the world!)*

"More gold has been mined from the thoughts of men than has been taken from the earth."
— *Napoleon Hill*

"Live today. If there will be problems tomorrow, wait until tomorrow to experience them. You can't know if you'll be alive or if you will win the lottery tomorrow. Just take care of today and let tomorrow take care of itself."
— *Dennis J. Henson*

"A man who suffers before it is necessary, suffers more than is necessary."
— *Lucius Seneca*

"One idea can be worth a fortune."
— *Earl Nightingale*

"Everything you will ever want or need to know can be found in books."
— *Dennis J. Henson*

"It is easy to hate, and it is difficult to love. This is how the whole scheme of things works. All good things are difficult to achieve, and bad things are very easy to get."
— Confucius

"Ask God to bless your work. Don't ask Him to do it for you."
— Paul "Bear" Bryant

"Someone's opinion of you does not have to become your reality."
— Les Brown

"There is more treasure in books than in all the pirates loot on Treasure Island and at the bottom of the Spanish Main – and best of all, you can enjoy these riches every day of your life."
— Walt Disney

"Failure is the opportunity to begin again more intelligently."
— Henry Ford

"Create courageous thoughts, and fearful thoughts will be crowded out of your life."
— Dr. Forrest C. Shaklee

"It is not that we have so little time but that we lose so much. The life we receive is not short, but we make it so; we are not ill provided but use what we have wastefully."
— Lucius Seneca

"Imagination is more important than knowledge. Knowledge is limited. Imagination encircles the world."
— Albert Einstein

"If your ship doesn't come in, swim out to meet it!"
— Jonathan Winters.

"Nothing great is created suddenly, any more than a bunch of grapes or a fig. If you tell me that you desire a fig. I answer you that there must be time. Let it first blossom, then bear fruit, then ripen."
— Epictetus

"Life is ten percent what happens to you and ninety percent how you respond to it. "
— Lou Holtz

"We should not look back unless it is to derive useful lessons from past errors, and for the purpose of profiting by dearly bought experience."
— George Washington

"Wisdom begins in wonder."
— Socrates

"If you want to increase your success rate, double your failure rate!" — Thomas J. Watson

"You can't connect the dots looking forward; you can only connect them looking backward. So you have to trust that the dots will some-how connect in your future. You have to trust in something-your gut, destiny, life, karma, whatever."
— Steve Jobs

"The man who moves a mountain begins by carrying away small stones."
— Confucius

"It is better to be alone than in bad company."
— George Washington

"A man who dares to waste one hour of time has not discovered the value of life."
— Charles Darwin

*"If you're not making what you want to make,
there is something you don't know!"*
— *Stefanie Hartman*

"Change your thoughts, and you change your world."
—*Norman Vincent Peale*

*"The more man meditates upon good thoughts,
the better will be his world and the world at large."*
— *Confucius*

"You are either on the way or in the way."
— *Les Brown*

*"True happiness is to enjoy the present, without anxious dependence
upon the future, not to amuse ourselves with either hopes or fears but
to rest satisfied with what we have, which is sufficient,
for he that is so wants nothing."*
— *Lucius Annaeus Seneca*

*"Never worry. Worry only stands in the way
of finding solutions."*
— *Dennis J. Henson*

*"Knowledge is everything; and everything you want to know has
been written down by someone, somewhere."*
— *Earl Nightingale's Mother*

*"When it is obvious that the goals cannot be reached,
don't adjust the goals, adjust the action steps."*
— *Confucius*

"Associate with people who are likely to improve you."
— *Lucius Annaeus Seneca*

"Every adversity brings with it the seed of an equivalent advantage."
— *Napoleon Hill*

"People get moving through motivation or desperation."
— Jack Gregory

"Everything is risky. Life is risky. Let me tell you how risky life is:
You won't come out of it alive"
— Jim Rohn

"If you are the smartest person in the room,
then you are in the wrong room."
— Confucius

"Consider the lilies of the field, how they grow; they toil not, neither
do they spin: yet I say unto you, that even Solomon in all his glory
was not arrayed like one of these. But if God doth so clothe the grass
of the field, which today is, and tomorrow is cast into the oven, shall
he not much more clothe you"
— Jesus of Nazareth, Matthew 6:28-30 KJV

"Luck is what happens when preparation meets opportunity."
— Lucius Annaeus Seneca

"Success consists of going from failure
to failure without loss of enthusiasm."
— Winston Churchill

"If you really want to escape the things that harass you, what you're
needing is not to be in a different place but to be a different person."
— Lucius Annaeus Seneca

"Change your self-talk and change your life!"
— Mitch Stephen

"Don't complain about the snow on your neighbor's
roof when your own doorstep is unclean."
— Confucius

"The greatest pollution problem we face is negativity."
— Mary Kay Ash

"Cherish your visions. Cherish your ideals. Cherish the music that stirs in your heart, the beauty that forms in your mind, the loveliness that drapes your purest thoughts. For out of them will grow all delightful conditions, all heavenly environment."
— James Allen

"Choose a job you love, and you will never have to work a day in your life."
—Confucius

"No matter how low funds are or how high debt, you are always just one idea away from massive riches."
— Dennis J. Henson

"Don't stop when you are tired, stop when you are done"
— Norma Jean Baker

"My favorite things in life don't cost any money. It's really clear that the most precious resource we all have is time."
— Steve Jobs

"First say to yourself what you would be, and then do what you have to do."
— Epictetus

"By failing to prepare, you are preparing to fail."
— Benjamin Franklin

"No matter how busy you make think you are, you must find time for reading, or surrender yourself to self-chosen ignorance." — Confucius
"If a man neglects education, he walks lame to the end of his life."
— Plato

"*Everything built by man was once a desire in someone's mind.*"
— *Dennis J. Henson*

"*Begin at once to live, and count each separate day as a separate life.*"
— *Lucius Seneca*

"*Hate is poison for the soul, and love is the antidote.*"
— *Dennis J. Henson*

"*True wisdom comes to each of us when we realize how little we understand about life, ourselves, and the world around us.*"
— *Socrates*

"*A smooth sea never made a skilled sailor.*"
— *Franklin D. Roosevelt*

"*Most of the important things in the world have been accomplished by people who have kept on trying when there seemed to be no hope at all.*"
— *Dale Carnegie*

"*Education is an ornament in prosperity and a refuge in adversity.*"
— *Aristotle*

"*Money won't make you happy, but it's right up there with oxygen.*"
— *Les Brown*

"*Think of tomorrow. The past can't be mended.*"
— *Confucius*

"*Success is the progressive realization of a worthy goal or ideal.*"
— *Earl Nightingale*

"*A man's friendships are one of the best measures of his worth.*"
— *Charles Darwin*

"The man who asks a question is a fool for a minute,
the man who does not ask is a fool for life."
— Confucius

"You will become as great as your dominant aspiration."
— James Allen

"Just before you go to sleep, ask for a solution
to your most important problem."
— Dennis J. Henson

"Play like you are two touchdowns behind."
— Paul Bear Bryant

"Respect yourself, and others will respect you."
— Confucius

"You have power over your mind - not outside events.
Realize this, and you will find strength."
— Marcus Aurelius

"Give me a stock clerk with a goal, and I will give you a man who
will make history. Give me a man without a goal,
and I will give you a stock clerk."
— JC Penny

"Motivation without Instruction and Education is
Ultimately Frustrating."
— Zig Ziglar

"Your work is going to fill a large part of your life, and the only way
to be truly satisfied is to do what you believe is great work. And
the only way to do great work is to love what you do. If you haven't
found it yet, keep looking. Don't settle. As with all matters of the
heart, you'll know when you find it."
— Steve Jobs

"Throw me to the wolves, and I will return leading the pack."
— Lucius Annaeus Seneca

"You may delay, but time will not." — Benjamin Franklin
"Faith is the substance of things hoped for, the evidence of things not seen."
— Hebrews 11:1

"Without promotion, something terrible happens
– NOTHING!"
— P.T. Barnum

"Your life is what your thoughts make it."
— Confucius

"Our thoughts make us what we are."
— Dale Carnegie

"You don't have to be great to start, but you have to start to be great."
— Joe Sabah

"Your blessings will always outweigh your sorrows,
but you have to give them a chance."
— Dennis J. Henson

"By three methods we may learn wisdom: First, by reflection,
which is noblest; second, by imitation, which is easiest; and third by
experience, which is the bitterest."
— Confucius

"Imagination is the true magic carpet ."
— Norman Vincent Peale

"Wise men speak because they have something to say; Fools because
they have to say something."
— Plato

"Weeds do not need encouragement to grow."
— Les Brown

"As is a tale, so is life: not how long it is,
but how good it is, is what matters."
— Lucius Seneca

"A man is literally what he thinks, his character being the complete
sum of all his thoughts. Circumstances do not make the man;
they reveal him."
— James Allen

"Life is like riding a bicycle.
To keep your balance, you must keep moving."
— Albert Einstein

"Study the past, if you would divine the future."
— Confucius

"Every success story is a tale of constant adaptation,
revision, and change."
— Richard Branson

"The steady stroke of a sharpened axe can fell the largest tree!"
— Dennis J. Henson

"The past cannot be changed. The future is yet in your power."
— Unknown

"In the long history of humankind (and animal kind, too), those who
learned to collaborate and improvise most effectively have prevailed."
— Charles Darwin

"Success without happiness is worthless"
— Og Mandino

"If you're going through hell, keep going."
— Winston Churchill

"The more you are grateful for what you have,
the more you will have to be grateful for."
— Zig Ziglar

"Have the courage to follow your heart and intuition. They somehow
know what you truly want to become."
— Steve Jobs

"Make a list of the things for which you are grateful
and add something every day."
— Dennis J. Henson

"Advertising is like learning – a little is a dangerous thing."
— P.T. Barnum

"To be wronged is nothing unless you continue to remember it."
— Confucius

"List the 10 people you love most, and tell them you love them!"
— Dennis J. Henson

"The person who sends out positive thoughts activates the world
around him positively and draws back to himself positive results."
— Norman Vincent Peale

"It takes guts to get out of the ruts."
— Robert H. Schuller

"They lose the day in expectation of the night,
and the night in fear of the dawn."
— Lucius Seneca

"All that a man achieves and all that he fails to achieve is the direct result of his own thoughts."
— James Allen

"All people are the same; only their habits differ."
— Confucius

"Do not be anxious about anything, but in every situation, by prayer and petition, with thanksgiving, present your requests to God.
— Philippians 4:6 KJV

"The important thing is not to stop questioning. Curiosity has its own reason for existence."
— Albert Einstein

"Man's mind may be likened to a garden, which may be intelligently cultivated or allowed to run wild."
— James Allen

"I hear, and I forget. I see, and I remember. I do, and I understand."
— Confucius

"Never let the future disturb you. You will meet it, if you have to, with the same weapons of reason which today arm you against the present."
— Marcus Aurelius

"Motivation gets you going, and habit gets you there."
— Zig Ziglar

"Quality is more important than quantity. One home run is much better than two doubles."
— Steve Jobs

"How you get there is by realizing you are already there."
— Buddha

"I'm drinking from a saucer because my cup has overflowed."
— Jimmy Dean

"The man who says he can, and the man
who says he cannot are both correct."
— Confucius

"Difficulties strengthen the mind, as labor does the body."
— Lucius Annaeus Seneca

"The dreamers are the saviors of the world. As the visible world is
sustained by the invisible, so men, through all their trials and sins
and sordid vocations, are nourished by the beautiful
visions of their solitary dreamers."
— James Allen

"Give me six hours to chop down a tree, and I will spend
the first four sharpening the axe ."
— Abraham Lincoln

"Rejoice in your success, and from your failure."
— Dennis J. Henson

"Learn as if you were not reaching your goal and as
though you were scared of missing it."
— Confucius

"Happiness is a warm puppy."
— Charles Schultz

"Don't worry about losing, just focus on winning."
— Dennis J. Henson

"Try not to become a man of success, but rather
try to become a man of value."
— Albert Einstein

"I will act now." The scroll marked IX,
"The Greatest Salesman in the World" — Og Mandino

"Act with kindness but do not expect gratitude."
— Confucius

"Success is not final, failure is not fatal: it is the
courage to continue that counts."
— Winston Churchill

"To live longer, drink water, eat vegetables, and walk daily."
— Dennis J. Henson

"The roots of education are bitter, but the fruit is sweet."
— Aristotle

"Nobody cares how much you know until they know
how much you care."
— Theodore Roosevelt

"Reading the ideas of great people is like planting seeds of success.
Seeds that will grow your bank account, your car, your home, and in
the person you will become."
— Dennis J. Henson

"Tell me, and I forget, teach me,
and I may remember, involve me, and I learn."
— Benjamin Franklin

"The difference between a successful person and others is not a lack
of strength, nor a lack of knowledge, but rather a lack of will."
— Vince Lombardi

"If you do not expect the unexpected, you will not find it."
— Heraclitus

*"Write down the 20 things you want most, prioritize them, and concentrate on the top 1 until you
have it or until your desire something else more!"*

— Dennis J. Henson

"Never underestimate your problem or your ability to deal with it."
— Robert H. Schuller

"The happiness of your life depends upon the quality of your thoughts: therefore, guard, and take care that you entertain no notions unsuitable to virtue and reasonable nature."
— Marcus Aurelius

*"If you don't design your own life plan, chances are you'll fall into someone else's plan. And guess what they
may have planned for you? Not much!"*
— Jim Rohn

"If you put off everything till you're sure of it, you'll get nothing done."
— Norman Vincent Peale

"The people who are crazy enough to think they can change the world are the ones who do."
— Steve Jobs

*"Time is the most valuable coin in your life. You and you alone will determine how that coin will be spent.
Be careful that you do not let other people spend it for you."*
— Carl Sandburg

*"To attract attractive people, you must be attractive. To attract powerful people, you must be powerful. T
o attract committed people, you must be committed."*
— Jim Rohn

"It is not because things are difficult that we do not dare; it is because
we do not dare that things are difficult."
— Lucius Annaeus Seneca

"Nothing is particularly hard if you divide it into small jobs."
— Henry Ford

"What you receive is a result of what you become."
— Dennis J. Henson

"A person is limited only by the thoughts that he chooses."
— James Allen

"It is the power of the mind to be unconquerable."
— Lucius Annaeus Seneca

"Success depends upon previous preparation, and without such
preparation, there is sure to be failure."
— Confucius

"Learning "specific knowledge" is like a voyage, where the first port of
call is wisdom, and the final destination is success."
— Dennis J. Henson

"Our greatest glory is not in never falling,
but in rising every time we fall."
— Confucius

"Once you become a master at planning, you
will never have to work again."
— Dennis J. Henson

"In all human affairs, there are efforts, and there are results, and the
strength of the effort is the measure of the result."
— James Allen

"Focus on the most important thing!!
— *Dennis J. Henson*

"Man is affected not by events but by the view he takes of them."
— *Lucius Annaeus Seneca*

"All our dreams can come true if
we have the courage to pursue them."
— *Walt Disney*

"You can never make progress in your life until you
appreciate the assets you already have."
— *Og Mandino*

"Not what he wishes and prays for does a man get but what he justly
earns. His wishes and prayers are only gratified and answered when
they harmonize with his thoughts and actions."
— *James Allen*

"Problems are not stop signs, they are guidelines."
— *Robert H. Schuller*

"It is not the man who has too little, but the man
who craves more, that is poor."
—*Lucius Seneca*

"Profits are better than wages.
Wages make you a living; profits make you a fortune!"
— *Jim Rohn*

"Ask, and it shall be given you; seek, and ye shall find; knock, and it
shall be opened unto you."
— *Matthew 7:7 KJV*

"If you really want to help the homeless,
give to the Salvation Army regularly."
— *Dennis J. Henson*

"A Penny Saved is a Penny Earned"
— Benjamin Franklin

"To accomplish great things, we must not only act but dream."
— Anatole France

"If you can dream it, you can do it."
— Walt Disney

"An ounce of practice is worth a thousand words."
— Mahatma Gandhi

"Two men looked out from prison bars, one saw the mud,
the other saw stars."
— Dale Carnegie

"Take care of your body. It's your Earthly home."
— Dennis J. Henson

"We suffer more often in imagination than in reality."
— Lucius Annaeus Seneca

"Men are anxious to improve their circumstances but are unwilling
to improve themselves; they, therefore, remain bound."
— James Allen

"Therefore I say unto you, whatsoever you desire, when you pray,
believe that you will receive them, and you shall have them."
— Jesus of Nazareth, Mark 11:24 KJV

"When anger rises, think of the consequences."
— Confucius

"Time and money spent in helping men to do more for
themselves is far better than mere giving."
— Henry Ford

"Most people who succeed in the face of seemingly impossible conditions are people who simply don't know how to quit."
— Robert H. Schuller

"The way to get started is to quit talking and begin doing."
— Walt Disney

"Life is very short! Savor every moment."
— Dennis J. Henson

"Those who cannot forgive others break the bridge over which they themselves must pass."
— Confucius

"For as a man thinks in his heart, so is he."
— Proverbs 23:7 KJV

"If you can believe, all things are possible to you."
— Jesus of Nazareth, Mark 9:23

"I will form good habits and become their slave."
The scroll marked I, The Greatest Salesman in the World by Og Mandino.

"According to your faith, it will be done to you."
— Jesus of Nazareth, Matthew 9:29

"When you want something bad enough, you will find a way to get it."
— Dennis J. Henson

"Time heals what reason cannot."
— Lucius Annaeus Seneca

"There is no secret to success, there is a system to success, and it works if you will work it."
— Les Brown

"If you think in terms of a year, plant a seed; if in terms of ten years, plant trees; if in terms of 100 years, teach the people."
— *Confucius*

"Make a habit of counting your blessings daily and be grateful."
— *Dennis J. Henson*

"Calmness is power."
— *James Allen*

"The future depends on what you do today."
— *Mahatma Gandhi*

"Make failure your teacher, not your undertaker."
— *Zig Ziglar*

"Hang on to your youthful enthusiasms
— you'll be able to use them better when you're older."
— *Lucius Annaeus Seneca*

"Courage isn't having the strength to go on;
it's going on when you haven't the strength."
— *Napoleon Bonaparte*

"Anyone who stops learning is old, whether at twenty or eighty. Anyone who keeps learning stays young."
— *Henry Ford*

"Successful people look for the opportunities in every change ."
— *Dennis J. Henson*

"A man is literally what he thinks." — *James Allen*

"It does not matter how slowly you go as long as you do not stop."
— *Confucius*

"If you don't know where you're going, any road will take you there."
The Cheshire Cat-Alice in Wonderland by Lewis Carroll

"It doesn't matter which side of the fence you get off on sometimes.
You cannot make progress without making decisions."
— Jim Rohn

"Always look at what you have left. Never look at what you have lost."
— Robert H. Schuller

"All you have to do is know where you're going. The answers will
come to you of their own accord."
— Earl Nightingale

"Ninety-nine percent of the failures come from
people who have the habit of making excuses."
— George Washington Carver

"A journey of a thousand miles begins with a single step."
— Confucius

"Reaffirming your goals daily is like installing a rudder on a ship."
— Dennis J. Henson

"As you think, you travel, and as you love, you attract."
— James Allen

"If you listen to your fears, you will die never knowing what a great
person you might have been."
— Robert H. Schuller

"If you can't read, it's going to be hard to realize dreams."
— Booker T. Washington

"Obstacles are the frightful things you see
when you take your eyes off the goal."
— Henry Ford

"Everything manmade started with a single thought!"
— Dennis J. Henson

"True desire is always accompanied by a sense of urgency."
— Dennis J. Henson

"If a man knows not to which port he sails, no wind is favorable."
— Lucius Annaeus Seneca

"Better a diamond with a flaw than a pebble without."
— Confucius

"I didn't fail the test. I just found 100 ways to do it wrong."
— Benjamin Franklin

"Stop being ashamed of how many times you've fallen, and start being proud of how many times you got up!"
— Dennis J. Henson

"Man is made or unmade by himself. By the right choice, he ascends. As a being of power, intelligence, and love, and the commander of his own thoughts, he holds the key to every situation."
— James Allen

"Thinking will not overcome fear, but action will."
— W. Clement Stone

"We are always complaining that our days are few, and acting as though there would be no end of them."
— Lucius Annaeus Seneca

"He who knows all the answers has not been asked all the questions."
— Confucius

"Avoid situations, acquaintances, and associates who tend to hold you back."
— W. Clement Stone

"Things will only change for you after you've changed"
— *Dennis J. Henson*

"As iron sharpens iron, so a friend sharpens a friend."
— *King Solomon*

"Many people die at twenty-five and aren't buried until they are seventy-five."
—*Benjamin Franklin*

"The will to win, the desire to succeed, the urge to reach your full potential, these are the keys that will unlock the door to personal excellence."
— *Confucius*

"The true value of a self-help book is not what the writer puts into the book, but what you, the reader, take out of the book and put into your life."
—*W. Clement Stone*

"Time is priceless; what you have is all you have, and you can not buy more."
—*Dennis J. Henson*

"You will become as small as your controlling desire, as great as your dominant aspiration."
— *James Allen*

"Peace of mind is a habit; regrettably, so is apprehension!"
— *Dennis J. Henson*

"When you do something, put your heart into it. Give it everything you've got – then relax!"
— *W. Clement Stone*

"Do not be anxious about tomorrow, for tomorrow will be anxious for itself. Let the day's own trouble be sufficient for the day."
— Jesus of Nazareth, Matthew 6:34

"People succeed because they start for a specific destination and keep going until they reach it."
— W. Clement Stone

"Never ruin an apology with an excuse."
— Benjamin Franklin

"Constantly strive to make the world a better place for yourself and others."
— W. Clement Stone

"It is the food with which you nourish your mind that determines the whole character of your life."
— Emmet Fox

"Books are not expensive, but not reading them can cost you a fortune."
— Dennis J. Henson

"You cannot open a book without learning something."
— Confucius

"Either write something worth reading or do something worth writing."
— Benjamin Franklin

"The man who does not shrink from self-crucifixion can never fail to accomplish the object upon which the heart is set."
— James Allen

"A fool is wise in his own eyes."
— King Solomon

"Run if you can, walk if you have to, crawl if you must!"
— Dean Karnazes

"Self-control is strength." — James Allen

"Again and again, the impossible problem is solved when we see that the problem is only a tough decision waiting to be made."
— Robert H. Schuller

"Some time ago, I stopped having problems and started having projects."
— Dennis J. Henson

"Take delight in the Lord, and He will give you the desires of your heart." — King David, Psalm 37:4 KJV

"Wherever you go, go with all your heart."
— Confucius

"It's the attention you pay to the small things that make you great."
— Dennis J. Henson

"The only place where your dream becomes impossible is in your own thinking."
— Robert H. Schuller

"What you see (dream) IS what you get."
— Dennis J. Henson

"Ask, and it shall be given you; seek, and ye shall find; knock, and it shall be opened unto you" Jesus of Nazareth, Matthew 7:7 KJV
"We are all born ignorant, but one must work hard to remain stupid." — Benjamin Franklin

"What is important is seldom urgent, and what is urgent is seldom important."
— Dwight D. Eisenhower

"Happiness is a state of mind.
If you believe you are happy, you are happy."
— Dennis J. Henson

"Whether you think you can or you can't, you're right."
— Henry Ford

"If you want to see a miracle – just look in a mirror."
—Dennis J. Henson

"A man has to learn that he cannot command things but that he can
command himself; that he cannot coerce the wills of others but that
he can mold and master his own will; and things serve him who
serves Truth; people seek guidance of him who is master of himself."
— James Allen

"He that can have patience can have what he will."
— Benjamin Franklin

"Give a bowl of rice to a man, and you will feed him for a day. Teach
him how to grow his own rice, and you will save his life."
— Confucius

"Never go to sleep without a request to your subconscious mind."
— Thomas Edison

"A lack of resources may slow you down, but don't let it make you
throw away a big idea. Give God all the time He needs t
o bring the resources to you!"
— Robert H. Schuller

"I will persist until I succeed." The scroll marked III, "The Greatest
Salesman in the World" by Og Mandino.

"If you want to lift yourself up, lift up someone else."
— Booker T. Washington

"We must all suffer from one of two pains: the pain of discipline or the pain of regret. The difference is discipline weighs ounces while regret weighs tons."
— Jim Rohn
"No duty is more urgent than that of returning thanks."
— James Allen

"Finally, brethren, whatsoever things are true, whatsoever things are honest, whatsoever things are just, whatsoever things are pure, whatsoever things are lovely, whatsoever things are of good report; if there be any virtue, and if there be any praise, think on these things."
Paul the Apostle, Philippians 4:8 KJV

"Study the past if you would divine the future."
— Confucius

"If a man is called to be a street sweeper, he should sweep streets even as a Michelangelo painted, or Beethoven composed music, or Shakespeare wrote poetry. He should sweep streets so well that all the hosts of heaven and earth will pause to say, 'Here lived a great street sweeper who did his job well.'"
— Martin Luther King, Jr.

"Happiness starts with you, not with your relationships, not with your job, not with your money, but with you." — Dennis J. Henson
"The bravest sight in the world is to see a great man struggling against adversity."
— Seneca

"If you fail to prepare, you prepare to fail."
— Ben Franklin

"If failure is not an option, then neither is success."
— Seth Godin

"To accomplish great things, we must not only act but also dream; not only plan but also believe."
— Anatole France

"Never let worry enter into your mind; it cannot help but will always hurt!!"
— Dennis J. Henson

"Run when you can, walk if you have to, crawl if you must; just never give up."
— Dean Karnazes

"Life is like a dogsled team. If you ain't the lead dog, the scenery never changes."
— Lewis Grizzard

"The price of apathy towards public affairs is to be ruled by evil men."
— Plato

"If you always think positive thoughts, your results will always be more positive. The converse is also true!!"
— Dennis J. Henson

"There comes a special moment in everyone's life, a moment for which that person was born. When he seizes it it is his finest hour."
— Winston Churchill

"The only way to have a lot more is to give a lot more."
— Dennis J. Henson

"For what shall it profit a man if he shall gain t he whole world and lose his own soul?"
— Jesus of Nazareth

*"Folks are usually about as happy as they
make their minds up to be."*
— *Abraham Lincoln*

*"If you spend an extra hour each day of study in your chosen field,
you will be a national expert in that field in five years or less."*
— *Earl Nightingale*

"Embrace failure. She is a master teacher!"
— *Dennis J. Henson*

*"When you experience obstacles to you goal, ignore them, and con-
centrate on where you are going."*
— *Dennis J. Henson*

"If you find yourself in a hole, the first thing to do is stop digging."
— *Will Rogers"*

"If you don't make many offers, you won't get many deals."
— *Dennis J. Henson*

"Get'er done!"
— *Arthur L. Williams Jr.*

*"Visualize this thing that you want, see it, feel it, believe in it. Make
your mental blueprint, and begin to build."*
— *Robert Collier*

"People with goals succeed because they know where they're going."
— *Earl Nightingale*

"Never put off until tomorrow what you can avoid altogether."
— *Mark Twain*

"It's not that I'm so smart; it's just that I stay with problems longer."
— *Albert Einstein*

*"Business opportunities are like buses;
there's always another one coming."*
— Richard Branson

"Success is a pile of failure that you are standing on."
— Dave Ramsey

"Losers are people who are afraid of losing."
— Robert Kiyosaki

"What we fear most is usually what we most need to do."
— Timothy Ferriss

*"When it is obvious that the goals cannot be reached, don't adjust the
goals; adjust the action steps."*
— Confucius

"Yesterday's home runs don't win today's games."
— Babe Ruth

*"If one doesn't know to which port one is sailing,
no wind is favorable."*
— Seneca

"Quit or be exceptional. Average is for losers."
— Seth Godin

*"The easiest thing to find on God's green earth is
someone to tell you all the things you cannot do."*
— Richard Devos

*"I am not a product of my circumstances.
I am a product of my decisions."*
— Stephen Covey

"Don't waste a good mistake. Learn from it"
— Robert Kiyosaki

"I'm not leaving until you say yes."
— *Wayne Huizenga*

*"An intelligent person hires people who are
more intelligent than he is."*
— *Robert Kiyosaki*

*"The two most important days in your life are the day you are born,
and the day you find out why."*
— *Mark Twain*

*"Success is the result of detailed planning, hard work,
and learning from failures."*
— *Dennis J. Henson*

*"You get to decide where your time goes. You can either spend it moving forward, or you can spend it putting out fires. And if you don't
decide, others will decide for you."*
— *Tony Morgan*

*"If you keep on doing what you've always done, you'll keep on getting
what you've always got."*
— *W. L. Bateman*

*"The successful person has the habit of
doing the things failures don't like to do."*
— *Thomas Edison*

*"Vision without action is daydream.
Action without vision is nightmare."*
— *Japanese Proverb*

"If your ship doesn't come in, swim out to meet it!"
— *Jonathan Winters*

"I've always said that education without execution is just entertainment."
— Tim Sanders

"There are four ways, and only four ways, in which we have contact with the world. We are evaluated and classified by these four contacts: what we do, how we look, what we say, and how we say it."
— Dale Carnegie

"People become really quite remarkable when they start thinking that they can do things. When they believe in themselves, they have the first secret of success."
— Norman Vincent Peale

"Move out of your comfort zone. You can only grow if you are willing to feel awkward and uncomfortable when you try something new."
— Brian Tracy

"Accept responsibility for your life. Know that it is you who will get you where you want to go, no one else."
— Les Brown

"Every day, you may make progress."
— Winston Churchill

"If you want to change your life – You have to change your life."
— Larry Goins

"Entrepreneurs are simply those who understand that there is little difference between obstacle and opportunity and are able to turn both to their advantage."
— Niccolo Machiavelli

"People who point out problems are common. Valuable people point out solutions."
— Dennis J. Henson

"An investment in knowledge always pays the best interest."
— Benjamin Franklin

"A goal properly set is halfway reached."
— Zig Ziglar

"Thomas Edison dreamed of a lamp that could be operated by electricity, began where he stood to put his dream into action, and despite more than ten thousand failures, he stood by that dream until he made it a physical reality. Practical dreamers do not quit."
— Napoleon Hill

"Real Estate is at the core of almost every business, and it's at the core of most people's wealth.
In order to build your wealth, you need to know real estate."
— Donald Trump

"Don't worry about failures. Worry about the chances you miss when you don't even try."
— Jack Canfield

"I like thinking big. If you're going to be thinking anything, you might as well think big." — Donald Trump

"Experience is a hard teacher because she gives the test first, the lesson afterwards."
— From the Movie "Red Tails"

"There are no limits. There are only plateaus, and you must not stay there. You must go beyond them."
— Bruce Lee

"What you become from striving to achieve great things is more valuable than achieving those things"
— Dennis J. Henson

"Desire is the starting point of all achievement, not a hope, not a wish, but a keen pulsating desire which transcends everything."
—Napoleon Hill

"Everything in the world we want to do or get done, we must do with and through people"
— Earl Nightingale

"There are no limitations except those you acknowledge. Whatever you can conceive and believe, you can achieve."
— Napoleon Hill

"Those who embrace change understand it and recognize the opportunities it brings will profit from it."
— John Schaub

"You can never earn in the outside world more than you earn in your own mind."
— Brian Tracy

"Murphy's law of cash flow says it's always going to cost more to hold a property than you project!"
— John Schaub

"Your destination will be determined, not by the bearing of the winds, but by the set of your sails."
— Dennis J. Henson

"The foundation for success in any business is a rock solid education."
— Dennis J. Henson

"Commit yourself to lifelong learning. The most valuable asset you'll ever have is your mind and what you put into it."
— Brian Tracy

"I would rather earn 1% off 100 people's efforts than 100% of my own efforts."
— *John D. Rockefeller*

"Successful people are simply those with successful habits."
— *Brian Tracy*

"There isn't a person anywhere who isn't capable of doing more than he thinks he can." — *Henry Ford*

"If you just hold on long enough, everyone looks smart after a while."
— *John Schaub*

"Successful people invest in themselves first."
— *Dennis J. Henson*

"Where there is no vision, the people perish."
— *King Solomon*

"Picture yourself in your mind's eye as having already achieved your goal. See yourself doing the things you will be doing when you've reached your goal."
— *Earl Nightingale*

"Do you understand residual income? If you did, you'd walk through a brick wall to get it."
— *Art Jonak*

"The future you see is the future you get."
— *Robert G. Allen*

"Create a definite plan for carrying out your desire and begin at once, whether you ready or not, to put this plan into action."
— *Napoleon Hill*

"I am the greatest. I said that even before I knew I was."
— *Muhammad Ali*

"It is not the strongest of the species that survives, neither the most intelligent that survives. It is the one that is t he most adaptable to change."
— Charles Darwin

"The relationship between making excuses and making money is adverse."
— Dennis J. Henson

"You can have everything in life you want if you will just help enough other people get what they want."
— Zig Ziglar

"Fear melts when you take action toward a goal you really want."
— Robert G. Allen

"It is not the critic who counts; not the man who points out how the strong man stumbles or where the doer of deeds could have done them better. The credit belongs to the man who is actually in the arena, whose face is marred by dust and sweat and blood; who strives valiantly; who errs, who comes short again and again because there is no effort without error and shortcoming; but who does actually strive to do the deeds; who knows great enthusiasms, the great devotions; who spends himself in a worthy cause; who at the best knows, in the end, the triumph of high achievement, and who at the worst, if he fails, at least fails while daring greatly, so that his place shall never be with those cold and timid souls who neither know victory nor defeat."
— Theodore Roosevelt

"If you think a $95 seminar is expensive, you should try learning from experience."
— John Schaub

"Your profit is in direct proportion to the number of good offers you are willing to make to get a deal."
— Dennis J. Henson

"Many an optimist has become rich by buying out a pessimist."
— Robert G. Allen

"Don't wait. The time will never be just right."
— Napoleon Hill

"Losing doesn't make me want to quit. It makes
me want to fight that much harder."
— Paul "Bear" Bryant

"How many millionaires do you know who have become
wealthy by investing in savings accounts? I rest my case."
— Robert G. Allen

"For successful people, school is never out."
— Dennis J. Henson

"It isn't what you have or who you are or where you are or what you
are doing that makes you happy or unhappy.
It is what you think about it."
— Dale Carnegie

"It's not the will to win that matters – everyone has that. It's the will
to prepare to win that matters."
— Paul "Bear" Bryant

"It all comes down to this: if your subconscious "financial blueprint"
is not "set" for success, nothing you learn, nothing you know, and
nothing you do will make much of a difference."
— T. Harv Eker

"Never quit. It is the easiest cop-out in the world. Set a goal, and
don't quit until you attain it. When you do attain it, set another goal,
and don't quit until you reach it. Never quit."
— Paul "Bear" Bryant

"Unlike any other investment, when you buy Real Estate, something amazing happens--your net worth increases!"
— Dennis J. Henson

"There's a lot of blood, sweat, and guts between dreams and success."
— Paul "Bear" Bryant

"Never, never, never, never give up" Winston Churchill
"If you want to change the fruits, you will first have to change the roots."
— T. Harv Eker

"If you believe in yourself and have dedication and pride – and never quit – you'll be a winner. The price of victory is high, but so are the rewards."
— Paul "Bear" Bryant

"A good coach will ask more of you than you ask of yourself."
— Dennis J. Henson

"Destiny is not a matter of chance; it's a matter of choice."
— Unknown

"Things may come to those who wait, but only things left by those who hustle."
— Abraham Lincoln

"In life, you'll have your back up against the wall many times. You might as well get used to it."
— Paul "Bear" Bryant

"People are always blaming their circumstances for what they are. I don't believe in circumstances. The people who get on in this world are the people who get up and look for the circumstances they want, and if they can't find them, make them."
— George Bernard Shaw

"When there is a strong enough why, the how will take care of itself."
— Dennis J. Henson

"It had long since come to my attention that people of accomplishment rarely sat back and let things happen to them. They went out and happened to things."
— Elinor Smith

"When you make a mistake, there are only three things you should ever do about it: 1. Admit it. 2. Learn from it, and 3. Don't repeat it."
— Paul "Bear" Bryant

"Don't worry if you lose that big deal. The deal of the century comes along about once a week."
— Dr. Dolf De Roos

"Your mind is for having ideas, not holding them."
— David Allen

"What are you doing here? Tell me why you are here. If you are not here to win a National Championship, you're in the wrong place. You, boys, are special. I don't want my players to be like other students. I want special people. You can learn a lot on the football field that isn't taught in the home, the church, or the classroom. There are going to be days when you think you've got no more to give, and then you're going to give plenty more! You are going to have pride and class. You are going to be very special. You are going to win the National Championship for Alabama."
Paul "Bear" Bryant (And they won six of them!! Roll Tide!)

"A man is but the product of his thoughts what he thinks, he becomes"
— Mahatma Gandhi

"Overcoming fear is an important part of success."
— Dennis J. Henson

"If you want to walk the heavenly streets of gold, you gotta know the password, "Roll, Tide, Roll!"
— Paul "Bear" Bryant

"Rich people focus on opportunities. Poor people focus on obstacles."
— T. Harv Eker

"Never let a deal die on your side of the table. Always leave them with an offer you can live with."
— Mitch Stephen

"All you need is the plan, the road map, and t he courage to press on to your destination."
— Earl Nightingale

"People, who are always complaining and finding things wrong, are like magnets attracting bad things to themselves. Look for the good in life, and you will be pleasantly surprised at how much you can find."
— Dennis J. Henson

"If you are not making the progress that you would like to make and are capable of making, it is simply because your goals are not clearly defined." — Paul J. Meyer

"If you are willing to do only what's easy, life will be hard. But if you are willing to do what's hard, life will be easy." — T. Harv Eker
"To solve any problem, ask yourself, How can I do this? Where can I go to find this answer? And, who do I know that can do this better than me?"
— Dennis J. Henson

"If you think training is expensive, try ignorance!" — Peter Drucker
"Whatever you vividly imagine, ardently desire, sincerely believe, and enthusiastically act upon must inevitably come to pass"
— Paul J. Meyer

*"The mind moves in the direction of our
currently dominating thought."*
— *Earl Nightingale*

*"Joy is what happens to us when we allow ourselves to recognize how
good things really are."*
— *Marianne Williamson*

"Just work through the fear"
— *Dennis J. Henson*

"If you don't know where you are going, any road will get you there."
— *Lewis Carroll*

*"Take the first step in faith. You don't have to see the whole staircase.
Just take the first step."*
— *Dr. Martin Luther King Jr.*

*"Smart business people adapt. No matter what the state of the econo-
my, the basic principles still apply."*
— *Dennis J. Henson*

"Don't ask for money; ask for advice."
— *Robert Shemin*

"Repetition is the master of any skill."
— *Dennis J. Henson*

"Work on what is closest to money."
— *Hank Harenberg*

"If you learn from defeat, you haven't really lost."
— *Zig Ziglar*

*"People create their own success by learning what they need to learn
and then by practicing it until they become proficient at it."*
— *Brian Tracy*

"Ask yourself–what else could I be doing with my money?"
— Wade Cook

"It doesn't matter where you are coming from. All that matters is where you are going."
— Brian Tracy

"Change, "I can't do that!" To, "How can I make that happen?"
— Dennis J. Henson

"A goal is a dream with a deadline."
— Napoleon Hill

"If there is any one secret of success, it lies in the ability to get to other person's point of view and see things from that person's angle as well as from your own."
— Henry Ford

"When faced with a problem, ask yourself: How can I ? Who can I get to ? Where can I find help to ?"
— Dennis J. Henson

"Wisdom is not a product of schooling but of the lifelong attempt to acquire it."
— Albert Einstein

"Dwelling on past problems and indiscretions will get you nowhere. Making a plan and getting busy can take you anywhere!
— Dennis J. Henson

"When everything seems to be going against you, remember that the airplane takes off against the wind, not with it!"
— Henry Ford

"We are what we repeatedly do. Excellence, therefore, is not an act, but a habit."
— Aristotle

"Discipline is the stairway from desire to achievement."
— *Dennis J. Henson*

"The ultimate measure of a man is not where he stands in moments of comfort and convenience, but where he stands at times of challenge and controversy."
— *Dr. Martin Luther King Jr.*

"Obstacles are those frightful things you see when you take your eyes off your goals."
— *Henry Ford*

"We do not want to gain at someone else's loss; we want to gain while helping the other person to also gain."
— *Jose Silva*

"Unnecessary fear of a bad decision is a major stumbling block to good decisions."
— *Jim Camp*

"One of the greatest discoveries a person makes, one of their great surprises, is to find they can do what they were afraid they couldn't do."
— *Henry Ford*

"Nothing can add more power to your life than concentrating all your energies on a limited set of targets."
— *Nido Qubein*

"We can let circumstances rule us, or we can take charge and rule our lives from within."
— *Earl Nightingale*

"You never know how far a bullfrog can jump when it's sitting on the creek bank."
— *Charles Bowden*

"When asked why he robbed banks, the famous criminal Willie Sutton said, "Because that's where the money is!" Willie had one thing right—you have to go where the money is to find it."
— *Dennis J. Henson*

"Most people spend more time and energy going around problems than in trying to solve them."
— *Henry Ford*

"A resourceful person can see opportunity when others only see obstacles."
— *Garrett Gunderson*

"Most of the stress people experience comes from inappropriately managed commitments they make or accept."
— *David Allen*

"You become what you think about."
— *Earl Nightingale*

"If you are not embarrassed by the offer you are making, you are probably paying too much."
— *Carleton Sheets*

"Success is not for the timid. It is for those who seek guidance, make decisions, and take decisive action."
— *Jose Silva*

"Failure is simply an opportunity to begin again, this time more intelligently."
— *Henry Ford*

"Anyone can find problems; valuable people find solutions."
— *Dennis J. Henson*

"Logic will get you from A to B.
Imagination will take you everywhere."
— Albert Einstein

"Successful people value time more than money."
— Dennis J. Henson

"Don't judge the day by the harvest
you reap but by the seeds you plant."
— Robert Louis Stephenson

"It's not the will to win but the will to prepare
to win that makes the difference."
— Coach Bear Bryant

"No man will make a great leader who wants to do it all himself or
get all the credit for doing it."
— Andrew Carnegie

"Accept discord; it is inevitable, but strive for harmony."
— Dennis J. Henson

"No one can become rich without enriching others. Anyone who adds
to prosperity must prosper in turn."
— G. Alexander Orndorff

"When you get in bed with the devil, you
are going to have bad dreams."
— Dennis J. Henson

"The whole secret of a successful life is to find out what is
one's destiny to do, and then do it."
— Henry Ford

"A specific goal + a burning desire + specialized knowledge + a good
plan + Action + Action + Action = Success, most every time."
— Dennis J. Henson

"If you care enough for a result, you will most certainly attain it."
— *William James*

"One hour per day of study will put you at the top of your field within three years. Within five years, you'll be a national authority. In seven years, you can be one of the best people in the world at what you do."
— *Earl Nightingale*

"Look at what rich people do and do that."
— *Jim Rohn*

"Everything comes to him who hustles while he waits."
— *Henry Ford*

"If you are not a little bit embarrassed by what you are asking, you probably are not asking for enough."
— *Carleton Sheets*

"No man, apart from the insane, takes any sort of action without a motive." The 9 basic Motives are Emotion of Love, Emotion of Sex, Desire for Material Gain, Desire for Self- Preservation, Desire for freedom of body and mind, Desire for self-expression and recognition, Desire for life after death, Desire for revenge, and Emotion of Fear."
— *Napoleon Hill*

"If money is your hope for independence, you will never have it. The only real security that a man can have in this world is a reserve of knowledge, experience, and ability."
— *Henry Ford*

"It's okay! This is not supposed to be easy!"
—*Gregg Popovich*
(Talking to the San Antonio Spurs after a last-second shot led to a 2nd overtime in the NBA playoffs. The Spurs went on to win the Championship.)

*"The secret of success in life is for a man to be ready
for his opportunity when it comes."*
— Benjamin Disraeli

*"Don't think of all the reasons a thing will not work.
Ask yourself, "How can I do this?"*
— Dennis J. Henson

"And what are you prepared to do?"
— Sean Connery as Malone in "The Untouchables"

"Readers are leaders!"
— Charles "Tremendous" Jones

*"A fisherman might have the nicest boat and the most expensive
tackle. But fish only bite the lure that they see as attractive."*
— Dennis J. Henson

"Success is 99% failure"
— Henry Ford

"Inch by inch, anything is a cinch."
— Robert Schuller

*"We are at our very best, and we are happiest when we are fully engaged in work we enjoy on the journey toward the goal we've
established for ourselves. It gives meaning to our time off and
comfort to our sleep. It makes everything
else in life so wonderful, so worthwhile."*
— Earl Nightingale

*"When people are greedy, be fearful.
When people are fearful, be greedy."*
— Warren Buffet

*"There is no man living who isn't capable of doing
more than he thinks he can do."*
— Henry Ford

*"Though my soul may set in darkness, it will rise in perfect light; I
have loved the stars too fondly to be fearful of the night."*
— Sarah Williams

*"If you're not in a hurry, you're probably not
going anywhere very important!"*
— Dennis J. Henson

*"You'll be motivated to change only when you clearly understand the
reason why you want to change your life - and your reason is more
important to you than any excuses you have for not changing."*
— Jason Frenn

*"The critical ingredient is getting off your butt and doing something.
Not tomorrow. Not next week. But today."*
— Nolan Bushnell

*"Don't wish it was easier. Wish you were better. Don't wish for less
problems; wish for more skills. Don't wish for fewer
challenges; wish for more wisdom."*
— Jim Rohn

*"No plan is worth the paper it is printed on
unless it starts you doing something."*
—William Danforth

"Remember that credit is money."
— Benjamin Franklin

*"Act now! There is never any time but now,
and there never will be any time but now."*
— Wallace Wattles

"You affect your subconscious mind by verbal repetition."
— W. Clement Stone

"To do more for the world than the world does for you –
that is success."
— Henry Ford

"Genuine wealth comes not from having money,
but is a state of mind."
— Dennis J. Henson

"Whatever we plant in our subconscious mind and nourish with
repetition and emotion will one day become a reality."
— Earl Nightingale

"First comes the thought; then organization of that thought, into
ideas and plans; then transformation of those plans into reality. The
beginning, as you will observe, is in your imagination."
— Napoleon Hill

"You can't build a reputation on what you are going to do."
— Henry Ford

"The difference between the impossible and the possible
lies in a person's determination."
— Tommy Lasorda

"Ask yourself what is the most valuable use of my time right now!"
— Bryan Tracy

"Don't find fault; find a remedy; anybody can complain."
— Henry Ford

"Failure is not an option!"
— Gene Kranz from the Apollo 13 Movie

"He who believes is strong; he who doubts is weak.
Strong convictions precede great actions."
— Louisa May Alcott

"Now remember, when things look bad, and it looks like you're not
gonna make it. Then you gotta get mean. I mean plumb, mad-dog
mean! 'Cause if you lose your head and you give up, then you
neither live nor win. That's just the way it is."
— Josey Wales in "The Outlaw Josey Wales"

"In all labor and strong effort, there is profit,
but talk leads only to poverty."
— King Solomon

"Thinking is the hardest work there is,
which is probably the reason, so few engage in it."
— Henry Ford

"Adversity either makes you bitter or better." — Steven Scott
"The greater danger for most of us lies not in setting our aim too high
and falling short, but in setting our
aim too low and achieving our mark."
— Michelangelo

"Action is the real measure of intelligence."
— Napoleon Hill

"I am a creative problem solver."
— Carleton Sheets

"If you don't have enough time, you haven't
spent enough time planning."
— Dennis J. Henson

"The only real mistake is the one from which we learn nothing."
— Henry Ford

"Whatsoever thy hand findeth to do, do it with thy might."
— *King Solomon*

*"Notice the good things in the people in your
life more than the bad things."*
— *Dr. Daniel Amen*

*"Create a definite plan for carrying out your desire, and begin at
once, whether you're ready or not, put it into action."*
— *Napoleon Hill*

*"Excellence is an art won by training and habituation. We do not act
rightly because we have virtue or excellence, but we rather have those
because we have acted rightly."*
— *Aristotle*

*"It has been my observation that most people
get ahead during the time that others waste."*
— *Henry Ford*

*"Successful people, because they are trying to
achieve, are constantly experiencing problems."*
— *Carleton Sheets*

"The very best time to get up and get moving is right now!!
— *Dennis J. Henson*

*"The human mind once stretched by a new
idea never goes back to its original dimensions."*
— *Oliver Wendell Holmes*

"Risk comes from not knowing what you're doing."
— *Warren Buffet*

*"Show me someone who has done something worthwhile, and I'll
show you someone who has overcome adversity."*
— *Lou Holtz*

"Nothing is particularly hard if you divide it into small jobs."
— Henry Ford

"It's not whether you get knocked down; it's whether you get up."
— Vince Lombardi

"Worry is nothing more than the misuse of your mind. Choosing to focus on what you don't want to have happen vs. what you do want to have happen."
— Ed Forman

"You can get anything you want if you help enough people get what they want!"
— Zig Ziglar

"Take massive action."
— Dennis J. Henson

"Ability is what you're capable of doing. Motivation determines what you do. Attitude determines how well you do it."
— Lou Holtz

"Carpe diem - Seize the Day."
— Horace

"If you are not making what you want to make, there is something you do not know."
— Stephany Hartman

"All the money you will ever need is available to you."
— Dennis J. Henson

"The mind is everything. What you think, you become."
— Buddha

"Find out where the people are going a
nd buy the land before they get there."
— Will Rogers

"Seeking riches is futile-seek wisdom, wisdom leads to riches."
— Dennis J. Henson

"The cave you fear holds the treasure you seek."
— Joseph Campbell

"It's not who you know. It's what you know and who you know."
— Dennis J. Henson

"Your Imagination is your preview of life's coming attractions."
— Albert Einstein

"Become the tortoise and the hare!"
— Dennis J. Henson

"One of the most difficult things everyone has to learn is that for your
entire life, you must keep fighting and adjusting if you hope to sur-
vive. No matter who you are or what your position is, you must keep
fighting for whatever it is you desire to achieve."
— George Allen

"It is what you are doing that counts, not what you are going to do."
— Dennis J. Henson

"Give a man a fish, and you feed him for a day. Teach a man to fish,
and you feed him for a lifetime."
— Chinese Proverb

"What you do speaks so loud I cannot hear what you say."
— Ralph W. Emmerson

"Work joyfully and peacefully, knowing that right thoughts and right efforts will inevitably bring about right results."
— James Allen

"Every problem has in it the seeds of its own solution. If you don't have any problems, you don't get any seeds."
— Norman Vincent Peale

"Obstacles are the scary things you see when you take your eyes off your goals."
— Russ Whitney

"Courage is moving from failure to failure without losing enthusiasm!"
— Winston Churchill

"You don't choose your passions; your passions choose you!"
— Jeff Bezos

"Be grateful for what you have while you strive for the things you want."
— Dennis J. Henson

"Life is but a dream."
— From Row Row Row Your Boat

"Yesterday is history. Tomorrow is a mystery. Today is a gift from god. Which is why we call it the present."
— Bill Keane

"There is only one thing that makes a dream impossible to achieve: the fear of failure."
— Paulo Coelho

"Wealth flows from energy and ideas!"
— William Feather

"Attitude is a little thing that makes a big difference."
— Winston Churchill

"The difference between try and triumph is just a little umph!"
— Marvin Phillips

"We are stubborn on vision and flexible on details."
— Jeff Bezos

"Bravery is being the only one who knows you're afraid."
— Franklin P. Jones

*"Every success story is a tale of constant adaption,
revision, and change."*
— Richard Branson

*"Challenges are what make life interesting; overcoming
them is what makes life meaningful."*
— Joshua J. Marine

*"With self-discipline, most anything is possible." Theodore Roosevelt
"If you can imagine it, you can achieve it. If you can
dream it, you can become it."*
—William Arthur Ward

*"Whether you're looking for problems or solutions,
you will surely find them."*
— Dennis J. Henson

*"If your actions inspire others to dream more, learn more, do more,
and become more, you are a leader."*
— John Quincy Adams

"Perseverance, secret of all triumphs."
— Victor Hugo

"Imagine where you want to be, and it will be so."
— *Gladiator*

"When the going gets tough, the tough get going."
— *Joan W. Donaldson*

"There's no telling how many miles you will have to run while chasing a dream."
— *Author Unknown*

"If we are facing in the right direction, all we have to do is keep on walking."
— *Budda*

"The U. S. Constitution doesn't guarantee happiness, only the pursuit of it. You have to catch up with it yourself." — Benjamin Franklin
"Life has no remote! You have to get up and change it yourself!"
— *Mark A. Cooper*

"Financial Freedom happens when your wants and your needs are surpassed by passive income." — Author Unknown
"The chains of habit are too weak to be felt until they are too strong to be broken."
— *Samuel Johnson*

"Find a way!"
— *Diana Nyad, Marathon Swimmer*

"Catch on fire with enthusiasm, and people will come for miles to watch you burn."
— *John Wesley*

"Imagination is everything. It is the preview of life's coming attractions."
— *Albert Einstein*

"The act of taking the first step is what separates the winners from the losers."
— *Brian Tracy*

"Successful people embrace and adapt to change."
— *Dennis J. Henson*

"There is no elevator to success. You have to take the stairs!"
— *Zig Ziglar*

"You must form a clear and definite mental picture of what you want; you cannot transmit an idea unless you have it yourself"
— *Wallace Wattles*

"Winners make a habit of doing the things losers don't want to do."
— *Lucas Remmerswaal*

"If a man empty his purse into his head, no man can take it away from him. An investment in knowledge always pays the best dividends."
— *Benjamin Franklin*

"All the world loves a winner and has no time for a loser."
— *Knute Rockne*

"Your thoughts will determine your fate."
— *Dennis J. Henson*

"I can't tell you how many people have asked me if those seminars and courses really work. To which I say, most of them work if you work. And none of them work if you don't work."
— *Mitch Stephen*

"Take up one idea. Make that one idea your life – think of it, dream of it, and live on that idea. Let the brain, muscles, nerves, every part of your body, be full of that idea, and just leave every other idea alone. This is the way to success." — *Swami Vivekananda*

"Continuous effort – not strength or intelligence –
is the key to unlocking our potential."
— Winston Churchill

"The successful warrior is the average man, with laser-like focus."
— Bruce Lee

"I will tell you how to become rich. Close the doors. Be fearful when
others are greedy. Be greedy when others are fearful."
— Warren Buffett

"In investing, what is comfortable is rarely profitable."
— Robert Arnott

"When you have collected all the facts and fears and made your deci-
sions, turn off your fears and go ahead."
— General George S. Patton

"Motivation gets you out of bed while
good habits get you to the bank."
— Dennis J. Henson

"Yesterday is but a dream; tomorrow is only a vision. But today, well
lived makes every yesterday a dream of happiness, and every tomor-
row a vision of hope."
— Kālidāsa

"When faced with a mountain, I will not quit! I will keep striving
until I climb over, find a pass through, tunnel underneath, or simply
stay and turn the mountain into a gold mine."
— Dr. Robert Schuller

"It's simple arithmetic. Your income can grow
only to the extent that you do."
— T. Harv Eker

"Some people think that the only way you can move up in business is by stepping on people to get there. The truth is the opposite. A business is successful because it provides value for people. The more you give, the more you receive. Go the extra mile every single day."
— Robert Shemin

"Both poverty and riches are the offsprings of thought."
— Napoleon Hill

"Do you want to know how to become a champion? It's easy! Turn your dream into your goal, Place it deep into your heart, and for the next ten years, eat, sleep, breathe, laugh and cry without ever taking your eye off your goal. Not even for one second."
— Gabby Douglas, U.S. Olympic Champion

"He who refuses to embrace a unique opportunity loses the prize as surely as if he had failed."
— William James

"If you want to reach a goal, you must see the reaching in your own mind before you actually arrive at your goal."
— Zig Ziglar

"Innovation distinguishes between a leader and a follower."
—Steve Jobs

"Find someone in your life that has the results in the area where you are not happy with the results."
— Orrin Woodward

Lloyd Christmas: Just give it to me straight! I came a long way just to see you, Mary. The least you can do is level with me. What are my chances?" Mary Swanson: "Not good."
Lloyd Christmas: "You mean, not good like one out of a hundred?"
Mary Swanson: "I'd say more like one out of a million." Lloyd Christmas: "So you're telling me there's a chance?!" From "Dumb and Dumber" (These two actors actually did marry.)

"Leaders make tough calls, both personally and professionally."
— *Orrin Woodward*

"He that is down needs fear no fall…"
— *John Bunyan*

"Energy and persistence conquer all things."
— *Benjamin Franklin*

"A man is about as happy as he makes his mind up to be."
— *Abraham Lincoln*

"You can, you should, and if you're brave enough to start, you will."
— *Stephen King*

"Some of the world's greatest feats were accomplished by people not smart enough to know they were impossible."
— *Doug Larson*

"The only way to eliminate problems in business is to close the business."
— *Dennis J. Henson*

"Waste no more time arguing about what a good man should be. Be one."
— *Marcus Aurelius*

"You are today where your thoughts have brought you; you will be tomorrow where your thoughts take you."
— *James Allen*

"The only time you fail is when you fall down and stay down."
— *Stephen Richards*

"The brain is wider than the sky."
— *Emily Dickinson*

"The starting point of all achievement is desire. Keep this constantly in mind. Weak desire brings weak results, just as a small fire makes a small amount of heat."
— *Napoleon Hill*

"A pessimist sees the difficulty in every opportunity; an optimist sees the opportunity in every difficulty."
— *Winston S. Churchill*

"Look for the silver lining."
— *B. G. DeSylva*

"In life, lots of people know what to do, but few people actually do what they know. Knowing is not enough! You must take action."
— *Anthony Robbins*

"Riches without wisdom will eventually disappear."
— *King Solomon*

"The most difficult thing is the decision to act; the rest is merely tenacity"
— *Amelia Earhart*

"Believe you can, and you're halfway there."
— *Theodore Roosevelt*

"Don't let anyone tell you there are no good deals in this economy."
— *Dennis J. Henson*

"The strongest single factor in prosperity consciousness is self-esteem: believing you can do it, believing you deserve it, believing you will get it."
— *Jerry Gilles*

"Sometimes it's better to make a quick nickel than a slow dime."
— *Joe McCall*

"Success isn't a result of spontaneous combustion.
You must set yourself on fire."
— Arnold H. Glasow

"It is always the start that requires the greatest effort."
— James Cash (J.C.) Penney

"For whatsoever a man soweth, that shall he also reap."
— Paul the Apostle

"Inaction breeds doubt and fear. Action breeds confidence and cour-
age. If you want to conquer fear, do not sit home and think about it.
Go out and get busy."
— Dale Carnegie

"The fastest way to complete a project is to get someone better and
less expensive than you to do it!"
— Dennis J. Henson

"I keep six honest serving men; they taught me all I knew;
their names are What, and Why, and When, and
How, and Where, and Who."
— Rudyard Kipling

"The happiness of your life depends upon
the quality of your thoughts."
— Marcus Aurelius

"If you don't see yourself as a winner, then
you cannot perform as a winner."
— Zig Ziglar

"Stop worrying about running out of money and
focus on how to make more."
— Steve Siebold

*"As long as you believe it is impossible, you will actually never find
out if it is possible or not."*
— John Seymour

*"Brains aren't designed to get results; they go in directions.
If you know how the brain works, you can set your own direction. If
you don't, then someone else will."*
— Richard Bandler

"How can you catch a fish if you don't have your bait in the water?"
— Robert Allen

*"Most banks will be willing to loan you money as long as you can
prove to them that you really don't need it!"*
— Dennis J. Henson

*"An old Cherokee told his grandson, "My son, there is a battle be-
tween two wolves inside us all. One is Evil. It is anger, jealousy,
greed, resentment, inferiority, lies, and ego. The other is good. It is
joy, peace, love, hope, humility, kindness, empathy, & truth." The boy
thought about it and asked, "Grandfather, which wolf wins?" The old
man quietly replied, "The one you feed."*
— Author unknown

*"It doesn't matter what the economy does!
All that matters is what you do!"*
— Dennis J. Henson

*"A happy person is not a person in a certain set of circumstances, but
rather a person with a certain set of attitudes."*
— Hugh Downs

*"The greatest battle you wage against failure occurs on the inside, not
on the outside. Your thought life, not your circumstances, determines
your success. If you think you can do it, you can! But if you doubt
yourself, well, no amount of encouragement will get you there."*
— John C. Maxwell

*"The very best thing you can do for the whole world
is to make the most of yourself."*
— *Wallace Wattles*

*"Nothing can stop the man with the right
mental attitude from achieving his goal."*
— *Thomas Jefferson*

*"Once you're a good enough planner, you
will never have to work again!"*
— *Dennis J. Henson*

"I haven't failed. I've just found 10,000 ways that won't work."
— *Thomas Edison*

"You can't act like a skunk without someone getting wind of it."
— *Lorene Workman*

*"With the willingness to learn—you will acquire
both the tools and the knowledge over time."*
— *Robert Woodruff*

*"Very little is needed to make a happy life;
it is all within yourself in your way of thinking."*
— *Marcus Aurelius*

*"By thought, the thing you want is brought to you.
By action, you receive it."*
— *Wallace Wattles*

*"Investing in yourself is the best investment you will ever make. It
will not only improve your life, it will improve the
lives of all those around you."*
— *Robin S. Sharma*

"An investment in knowledge pays the best interest."
— *Benjamin Franklin*

"Wealth is more easily attracted than pursued."
— Dennis J. Henson

"Sales are contingent upon the attitude of the salesman,
not the attitude of the prospect."
—W. Clement Stone

"Success is not the key to happiness.
Happiness is the key to success. If you love what you are doing,
you will be successful."
—Albert Schweitzer

"You have to learn the rules of the game.
And then you have to play better than anyone else."
— Albert Einstein

"The greatest ability in business is to get along
with others and to influence their actions."
— John Hancock

"Believe it can be done. When you believe something can be done,
really believe, your mind will find the ways to do it. Believing a solu-
tion paves the way to a solution."
— David J. Schwartz

"Buy what appreciates, lease what depreciates."
— J. Paul Getty

"O wad some Pow'r the giftie gie us, to see oursels as ithers see us!"
— Scots language poem Robert Burns

"If you want a thing done well, find someone who
can do it better than you!"
— Dennis J. Henson

"Winners are those people who make a habit of d oing the things losers are uncomfortable doing."
— Ed Foreman

"Financial freedom is available to those who learn about it and work for it." —Robert Kiyosaki

"The best time to plant a tree was 20 years ago. The second best time is now."
— Chinese Proverb

"Achievement seems to be connected with action. Successful men and women keep moving. They make mistakes, but they don't quit."
— Conrad Hilton

"Even if you are on the right track, you will get run over if you just sit there!"
— Will Rogers

"It doesn't matter what your why is! It only matters that your why is stronger than your reason to quit."
— Chris McClatchey

"Thought + Education + Energy = Income."
— Dennis J. Henson

"The only person you are destined to become is the person you decide to be."
— Ralph Waldo Emerson

"Your business is never really good or bad "out there" your business is either good or bad right between your own two ears."
— Zig Ziglar

"When there are no more problems, there will be no more good deals. Until then, business will be good!"
— Dennis J. Henson

"When you pick the payment, every deal can cash flow."
— Chris McClatchey

"Money is just a tool to spend your time the way you want to."
— Larry Goins

"Every successful investor I know, including myself, was just a new investor that didn't quit."
— Brant Phillips

"Sometimes the cheapest is the most expensive."
— Dennis J. Henson

"A mind is like a parachute. It doesn't work if it's not open"
— Frank Zappa

"When your desires are strong enough, you will appear to possess superhuman powers to achieve."
— Napoleon Hill

"Success takes one of two things inspiration or desperation!"
— Jack Gregory

"Achieve success in any area of life by identifying the optimum strategies and repeating them until they become habits."
— Charles J. Givens

"If you're almost out of time, spend what time you have planning."
— Dennis J. Henson

"Your attitude, not you aptitude, will determine your altitude!"
— Zig Ziglar

"Your brain is for having ideas, not for holding them."
— David Allen

"Never give up on a dream just because of the time it will take to accomplish it. The time will pass anyway."
— Earl Nightingale

"You miss 100% of the shots you don't take."
—Wayne Gretzky

"If you want to be happy… Be happy!!!"
— Dennis J. Henson

*"Real Estate Investing is like fishing.
Don't quit if you don't get a strike on the first cast."*
— Dennis J. Henson

"I'm from Alabama, and my Mama taught me that, in polite company, you don't discuss politics, religion, sex, or Auburn Football!'"
— Dennis J. Henson (Roll Tide!)

"Success is the sum of small efforts – repeated day in and day out."
— Robert Collier

"Leveraging time, money, and people is the way to freedom."
— Paul Finck

*"Your beliefs become your thoughts, your thoughts become your words, your words become your actions, your actions become your habits, your habits become your values, and your
values become your destiny."*
— Mahatma Gandhi

*"The game of life is a lot like football. You have to tackle your problems, block your fears, and score your points when you
get the opportunity."*
— Lewis Grizzard

"Let great people shape your life."
— Napoleon Hill

"Marketing is not optional! Marketing is an essential tool for the success of all business and nonprofit activity.
What matters is not what you do; what matters is that you communicate what you do so that others will take interest in it, buy it, support it, join it, and tell friends about it."
— Peter Drucker

"There are only two things in a business that make money – innovation and marketing; everything else is cost."
— Peter Drucker

"It's not how far you fall but how high you bounce that counts."
— Zig Ziglar

"To connect with "Infinite Intelligence," just ask yourself...
"How can I ?"
— Dennis J. Henson

"Success comes to those who set goals and pursue them regardless of obstacles and disappointments."
— Napoleon Hill

"80% of life is just showing up!"
— Woodie Allen

"We change when the pain to change is more than t he pain to remain as we are."
— Ed Foreman

"You can lead a horse to water, but teaching him the backstroke can be a challenge!"
— Dennis J. Henson

"If there's a will, prosperity can't be far behind."
— W.C. Fields

*"Our rewards in life will always be in exact proportion
to our contributions."*
— *Earl Nightingale*

"If you don't go for your dreams, who will?"
— *Joe Vitale*

"We must view with profound respect the infinite capacity of the human mind to resist the introduction of useful knowledge."
— *Thomas R. Lounsbury*

"Success is a process of continually seeking answers to new questions."
— *Sir John Templeton*

"Your life, the way it looks today, is a result of your choices… What will you choose today for your tomorrow?"
— *Anonymous*

"Nothing draws a crowd quite like a crowd."
— *P T Barnum*

*"Success is no accident. It is hard work, perseverance, learning,
studying, sacrifice and most of all, love of
what you are doing or learning to do."*
— *Pele*

"Desire creates the power!"
— *Raymond Holliwell*

"I don't think you should just do what makes you happy. Do what makes you great. Do what's uncomfortable and scary and hard but pays off in the long run… Let yourself fail… And pick yourself up and fail again. Without that struggle, what is your success anyway?"
— *Charlie Day*

"People do what they make up their minds to do!"
— *Earl Nightingale*

"Just do it!"
— AL Williams

"The heartiest plants survive because they weather the storms and never stop reaching for the light"
— Robert Clancy

"Your thoughts determine your fate!"
— Dennis J. Henson

"Do not give up. It's amazing how things can turn themselves around!"
— Karen Salmansohn

"Our goals can only be reached through a vehicle of a plan, in which we must fervently believe and upon which we must vigorously act. There is no other route to success."
— Pablo Picasso

"The indispensable first step to getting the things you want out of life is this: decide what you want."
— Ben Stein

"Pain is a message asking for our help."
— Gerald Epstein

"If you don't inspect it, it doesn't get fixed."
— Dennis J. Henson

"What you imagine you create."
— Buddha

"You can't stop the waves, but you can learn to surf."
— Jon Kabat Zinn

"Little minds attain and are subdued by misfortunes:
but great minds rise above them."
— Washington Irving

"Successful people don't make excuses. If you want success, you need
to learn how to stop making excuses and start making progress."
— Brian Tracy

"Your net worth to the world is usually determined by what remains
after your bad habits are subtracted from your good ones."
— Benjamin Franklin

"Success comes from what you do, not from what
you say you are going to do."
— Larry Winget

"Intelligence without ambition is a bird without wings."
— Salvador Dali

"Little strokes fell great oaks."
— Benjamin Franklin

"Real estate provides the highest returns, the greatest values, and the
least risk. Buying real estate is not only the best way, the quickest way,
the safest way, but the only way to become wealthy."
— Marshall Field

"The dreams that you dare to dream really do come true!"
— Yip Harburg

"The most effective way to cope with change is to help create it."
— L.W. Lynett

"The time spent making quality plans will be
returned to you fourfold!"
— Dennis J. Henson

"Give me a lever long enough and a fulcrum on which to place it, and I shall move the world."
— *Archimedes*

"All achievements, all earned riches, have their beginning in an idea."
— *Napoleon Hill*

"A good coach will hold you accountable to the promises you've made to yourself."
— *Dennis J. Henson*

"Compound interest is the eighth wonder of the world. He who understands it earns it; he who doesn't pays it."
— *Albert Einstein*

"If we keep doing what we're doing, we're going to keep getting what we're getting."
— *Stephen Covey*

"Real estate cannot be lost or stolen, nor can it be carried away. Purchased with common sense, paid for in full, and managed with reasonable care, it is about the safest investment in the world."
— *Franklin D. Roosevelt*

"Ninety percent of all millionaires become so through owning real estate. More money has been made in real estate than in all industrial investments combined. The wise young man or wage earner of today invests his money in real estate."
— *Andrew Carnegie*

"If you think you are happy, you are!"
— *Dennis J. Henson*

"Money will not make you happy, but it is right up there with oxygen."
— *Les Brown*

"To live longer drink water, eat vegetables, walk every day."
— *Dennis J. Henson*

"Every crowd has a silver lining."
— *PT Barnum*

Life Changing Books

"If we encounter a man of rare intellect, we should ask
him what books he reads."
~ Ralph Waldo Emmerson

Read These First.

*Think and Grow Rich by
Napoleon Hill*

*The Greatest Salesman in the
World by OG Mandino*

*In Search of Excellence by
Thomas J. Peters and Robert H.
Waterman, Jr.*

Twelve Pillars by Jim Rohn

*The Richest Man in Babylon by
George S. Clason*

*Success the Glenn Bland Method
by Glenn Bland*

*Breakthroughs by P. Ranganath
Nayak Ph.D. and Ketteringham
PhD*

The Go Getter by Peter B. Kyne

*How to Win Friends and
Influence People by Dale
Carnegie*

*Winning Through Intimidation
by Robert Ringer*

*Rich Dad Poor Dad by Robert T.
Kiyosaki with Sharon L. Lechter*

*Laws of Leadership by John C.
Maxwell*

*Do What You Love, The Money
Will Follow by Marsh Sinetar*

*Success Through a Positive Mental
Attitude by Napoleon Hill & W.
Clement Stone*

*The Master Key to Riches by
Napoleon Hill*

*The Science of Getting Rich by
Wallace D. Wattles & Dr. Judith
Powell*

*Getting Things Done by David
Allen*

*How I Raised Myself from Failure
to Success through Selling by
Frank Bettger*

*How to Sell Anything to Anybody
by Joe Girard*

*Looking Out For Number One by
Robert Ringer Road to Wealth by
Robert Allen*

*See You at the Top by Zig
Ziglar Strangest Secret by Earl
Nightingale*

*7 Strategies for Wealth &
Happiness by Jim Rohn*

Traction by Gino Wickman

Who Moved My Cheese? by Spencer Johnson

Why We Act the Way We Do by Tim La Haye

Philosopher by Jim Rohn

Acres of Diamonds by James Allen

The Bible Inspired by God!

How to Read a Book by Mortimer Adler

As a Man Thinketh by James Allen

The Lessons of History by William James Durant

Seven Secrets of Success by Dennis J. Henson

I Dare You! by William H Danforth

The Magic of Believing by Claude M. Bristol

Life is Tremendous by Charlie Jones

How to Stop Worrying and Start Living by Dale Carnegie

Wake Up and Live! by Dorothea Brande

Never Eat Alone by Keith Ferrazzi

I Believe by Grant Teaff

It Works: The Famous Little Red

Book That Makes Your Dreams Come True by RHJ

Leaders Eat Last by Simon Sinek

Rocket Fuel by Gino Wickman

Seasons of Life by Jim Rohn

The E Myth by Michael E. Gerber

Never Split the Difference by Chris Voss

The Law of Success in 16 Lessons by Napoleon Hill

The Treasury of Quotes by Jim Rohn

Tools of Titans by Tim Ferriss

Tough Times Never Last, but Tough People Do by Robert H. Schuller

"Miss a meal if you have to,
but don't miss a book."
~ Jim Rohn

Suggested Biographies

Abraham Lincoln — American President

Albert Einstein — Scientist, Theoretical Physicist

Albert Schweitzer — Author, Philosopher, Physician.

Alexander Graham Bell — Entrepreneur, Inventor

Alexander Hamilton — American President

Alexander the Great — Greek King and Conqueror

Alvin Cullum York — American WWI American Hero

Amelia Earhart — American Aviation Pioneer

Andrew Carnegie — American Industrialist

Anne Frank — Victim, Author

Aristotle — Philosopher

Aristotle Onesies — Industrialist

Arthur Brisbane — Newspaper Editor

Arthur Nash — Businessman, Author, Speaker

Asa Candler — Coke Founder

Asa Griggs Candler — American Business Tycoon

Audie Murphy WWII — American WWII Hero

Benjamin Franklin — American Statesman, Patriot

Bill Gates — Entrepreneur, Inventor

Billy Graham — Speaker

Booker T. Washington — Author, Speaker, Teacher

Capt. Harvey McNelly — Texas Ranger

Catherine the Great — Empress of Russia

Charles Darwin — Explorer

Charles Lindbergh — American Aviation Pioneer

Charles M. Schwab — American Steel Magnate

Christopher Columbus — Italian Explorer

Clarence Darrow — American Lawyer

Col. Robert A. Dollar — Scots-American industrialist

Colonel Sanders — Restaurateur

Cyrus H. K. Curtis — Publisher

Daniel Willard — Railroad Executive

Dave Thomas — Restaurateur

Donald Trump — American Businessman and U.S. President

Douglas McArthur — WWII U.S. General

Dr. David Starr Jordan — American Ichthyologist

Dwight D. Eisenhower — WWII Supreme Commander

E. M. Statler — American Businessman

Earl Nightingale — American Author and Speaker

Earnest Hemingway — Journalist, Author

Eddie Rickenbacker — American WWI Metal of Honor, Fighter Ace

Edward A. Filene — American Businessman

Edward R. Murrow — Reporter

Edwin C. Barnes — Salesman

Elbert Hubbard — American Writer

Elon Musk — Entrepreneur, Inventor

Erwin Rommel — WWII German General

Estee Lauder — Cosmetics

F. Woolworth — American Entrepreneur

Frances Scott Key — Patriot, Lawyer, Writer of "The Star Spangled Banner"

Frank A. Munsey — American Author

Frank A. Vanderlip — American Journalist

Fritz Haber — Nobel Prize Recipient – Shaped the World we live in

Galileo Galilei — Astronomer

George Eastman — American Entrepreneur

George Fredrick Handel — Composer

George Gershwin — Composer

George Orwell — English Novelist

George S. Parker — American Game Designer

George S. Paton — WWII General

George Washington — First American President

George Washington Carver — Educator, Inventor

Golda Meir — Israeli Prime Minister

Harry Truman — American President

Henry Ford — American Industrialist, Inventor

Henry L. Doherty — American financier

Herb Kelleher — Southwest Airlines CEO

Howard Hughes — Businessman, Inventor, Aviation Pioneer

Indira Gandhi — Prime Minister of India

Ingvar Kamprad — Swedish Business Magnate

Isaac Newton — English Scientist, Author

J. G. Chappline — American Educator

J. Odgen Armour — American Magnate

J. S Bach — Composer

Jack Welch — General Electric

Jack Welch — General Electric President

Jacques Cousteau — Explorer

James Cash Penny — Department Store Owner

James H. Doolittle — Military General, Aviation Pioneer

James J. Hill — American-Canadian Executive

Jeff Bezos — Entrepreneur, Inventor

Jesse Owens — Olympic Champion

Jim Thorp — Olympic Medalist Indian Football Player

Jimmy Steward — Actor

Joan of Arc — French War Hero

John Adams — American President

John Boyd — U.S. Airforce Fighter, Military Theorist

John D. Rockefeller — American Industrialist

John F. Kennedy — American President

John H. Patterson — American Industrialist

John Wanamaker — American

merchant

John Wayne — Actor

Julius Caesar — Roman Statesman, Military General

King C. Gillette — American Entrepreneur

Lee Iacocca and the Mustang Sports Car — Automotive Executive

Leonardo Da Vinci — Inventor, Artist

Lewis and Clark — American Explorers

Ludwig Van Beethoven — Composer

Luther Burbank — Botanist

Mahatma Gandhi — Great Spiritual and Political Leader of India

Margaret Thatcher — English Prime Minister

Marie Antoinette — Queen of France

Marie Curie — Scientist, Physicists, Nobel Prize Winner

Mark Twain — Author, Humorist

Martin Luther — Catholic Priest, Seminal figure in the Protestant Reformation

Martin Luther King, Jr. — Christian Minister and Activist

Mary Kay Ash — Business Woman Milton S. Hershey — Chocolatier

Mother Theresa — Saint Teresa of Calcutta

Napoleon Bonaparte — French Statesman, Military Leader

Napoleon Hill — Author, Speaker Neil Armstrong — Astronaut Nikola Tesla — Inventor

Og Mandino — Author

Orson Welles — Actor, Director, Writer

Orville and Wilbur Wright — Aviation Pioneers

P. T. Barnum — World's Greatest Marketer

Paul Revere — American Patriot

Paul William (Bear) Bryant — Alabama Football Coach

Plato — Philosopher

Pyotr Ilyich Tchaikovsky — Composer

Queen Victoria — Queen of

England Ralph Lauren — Clothier

Ralph Waldo Emmerson — American Essayist

Ray Kroc — McDonalds

Richard Branson — Entrepreneur, Inventor

Ronald Ragan — American President

Ross Perot — Entrepreneur, Inventor

Rudy Ruettiger — Notre Dame Football Player

Rudyard Kipling — Author

S. B. Fuller — American Businessman

Sam Walton — Walmart Founder

Shaka Zulu — African Zulu Chief Socrates — Philosopher

Stephen Hawking — Scientist

Steve Jobs — Entrepreneur, Inventor

Sun Tzu — Chinese General

Sylvester Stallone — Actor

Theodore Roosevelt — War Hero, American President

Thomas Edison — Inventor

Thomas J. Watson — IBM President

Thomas Paine — American Patriot

Tony Blair — Prime Minister of England

Vincent van Gogh — Artist

W. Clement Stone — Businessman, Philanthropist, Author

Walt Disney — Entrepreneur, Inventor

Warren Buffett — American Investor and Philanthropist

William (Billy) Mitchell — Father of the U. S. Airforce

William F. Buckley, Jr. — Author and Commentator

William Shakespeare — English Playwright

William Sydney Porter — American Short Story Writer

William Wrigley Jr. — American industrialist

Winston Churchill — Prime Minister of England Wolfgang Amadeus Mozart — Composer

Woodrow Wilson — American President

"You can have everything in life you want if you will just help enough other people get what they want."
~Zig Ziglar

Dennis J. Henson

A successful Real Estate Investor with over fifty years of experience, Dennis J. Henson is a teacher, business owner, bestselling author, and international speaker. His students are some of the most successful business owners in Texas. His books on business, self-improvement, and Real Estate are changing lives. Dennis is the long-time President of Vanguard Marketing and Investments, Inc.

Drawing from his years of experience and his degrees in education, Dennis perfected a unique mentoring program to train new and experienced entrepreneurs. His program teaches that the ability to succeed lies in understanding and implementing seven unchangeable laws of nature (The Seven Secrets of Success). By following these ageless principles, as his mentor, Tom Hendrix, would say: "You can no more fail than water can run uphill."

Connect with Dennis Online

Website: www.dennisjhenson.com

Made in the USA
Las Vegas, NV
03 July 2024

91840146R00213